The Biblical Seminar
59

READING LAW

READING LAW

The Rhetorical Shaping of the Pentateuch

James W. Watts

Sheffield Academic Press

To my parents,
John D.W. Watts
and
W. Lee Watts
with love and gratitude

Published by Sheffield Academic Press Ltd
Mansion House
19 Kingfield Road
Sheffield S11 9AS
England

Printed on acid-free paper in Great Britain
by Antony Rowe Limited
Bumper's Farm, Chippenham,
Wiltshire

British Library Cataloguing in Publication Data

A catalogue record for this book is available
from the British Library

ISBN 1-85075-997-9

CONTENTS

ACKNOWLEDGMENTS

The researching and writing of this book has been influenced by many people over a number of years. I am grateful to the National Endowment for the Humanities for a grant to attend a summer seminar on 'Law and Narrative in the Bible' at Cornell University in 1992, and to my host, Calum Carmichael, whose conversation and ideas encouraged my pursuit of this topic. My colleague at Hastings College, David Lovekin, provided crucial suggestions and constant encouragement. The critical insights of Bernard Levinson, Corrine Patton, Mark Smith and Ken Craig were very helpful even if I did not always follow their suggestions. I am especially grateful to Dale Patrick, who has been generous with his time in reading my drafts, in conversations about rhetoric and biblical studies, and in sharing parts of his own work *The Rhetoric of Revelation* prior to its publication. The encouragement and comments of my father, John D.W. Watts, have spurred me on and his own research has been a constant model for me of creative biblical interpretation. Finally, I am most grateful to my wife, Maurine McTyre-Watts, whose support and encouragement made this project possible.

Parts of this book have been published previously as 'Rhetorical Strategy in the Composition of the Pentateuch', *JSOT* 68 (1995), pp. 3-22; 'Public Readings and Pentateuchal Law', *VT* 45.4 (1995), pp. 540-57; 'The Legal Characterization of God in the Pentateuch', *HUCA* 67 (1996), pp. 1-14; 'The Legal Characterization of Moses in the Rhetoric of the Pentateuch', *JBL* 117 (1998), pp. 415-26; 'Reader Identification and Alienation in the Legal Rhetoric of the Pentateuch', *BI* 7.1 (1999), pp. 101-12. I am grateful to the publishers of these journals for permission to reprint this material in slightly altered form here.

ABBREVIATIONS

AB	Anchor Bible
ABD	*Anchor Bible Dictionary*
ABRL	Anchor Bible Reference Library
AnBib	Analecta Biblica
ANET	J.B. Pritchard (ed.), *Ancient Near Eastern Texts Relating to the Old Testament* (3rd edn with supplement)
AOAT	Alter Orient und Altes Testament
BBR	*Bulletin for Biblical Research*
BI	*Biblical Interpretation*
Bib	*Biblica*
BJS	Brown Judaic Studies
BKAT	Biblischer Kommentar: Altes Testament
BWANT	Beiträge zur Wissenschaft vom Alten und Neuen Testament
BZ	*Biblische Zeitschrift*
BZAW	Beihefte zur *ZAW*
CahRB	Cahiers de la *Revue Biblique*
CBQ	*Catholic Biblical Quarterly*
ConBOT	Coniectanea biblica, Old Testament
CRINT	Compendia rerum iudaicarum ad Novum Testamentum
EvT	*Evangelische Theologie*
FRLANT	Forschungen zur Religion und Literatur des Alten und Neuen Testaments
HAT	Handbuch zum Alten Testament
HBT	*Horizons in Biblical Theology*
HSM	Harvard Semitic Monographs
HTR	*Harvard Theological Review*
HUCA	*Hebrew Union College Annual*
Int	*Interpretation*
JBL	*Journal of Biblical Literature*
JCS	*Journal of Cuneiform Studies*
JSOT	*Journal for the Study of the Old Testament*
JSOTSup	*Journal for the Study of the Old Testament*, Supplement Series
JSS	*Journal of Semitic Studies*
JTS	*Journal of Theological Studies*
LXX	Septuagint

MT	Masoretic Text
NCB	New Century Bible
NICOT	New International Commentary on the Old Testament
OBO	Orbis biblicus et orientalis
OBT	Overtures to Biblical Theology
Or	*Orientalia*
OTL	Old Testament Library
OTP	James Charlesworth (ed.), *Old Testament Pseudepigrapha*
OTS	*Oudtestamentische Studien*
RB	*Revue biblique*
RelSoc	Religion and Society
RIDA	*Revue internationale des droits de l'antiquité*
SANE	Sources from the Ancient Near East
SBLDS	Society of Biblical Literature Dissertation Series
SBLMS	Society of Biblical Literature Monograph Series
SBLSS	Society of Biblical Literature Semeia Studies
SBT	Studies in Biblical Theology
TDNT	*Theological Dictionary of the New Testament* (ed. G. Kittel and G. Friedrich; trans. G.W. Bromiley; 10 vols.; Grand Rapids: Eerdmans, 1964–74)
VT	*Vetus Testamentum*
VTSup	*Vetus Testamentum*, Supplements
WAW	Writings from the Ancient World
WBC	Word Biblical Commentary
WMANT	Wissenschaftliche Monographien zum Alten und Neuen Testament
ZA	*Zeitschrift für Assyriologie*
ZAR	*Zeitschrift für altorientalische und biblische Rechtsgeschichte*
ZAW	*Zeitschrift für die alttestamentliche Wissenschaft*

INTRODUCTION

Lawyers and judges do not usually read law books from beginning to end like novels. Instead, laws are collected, compared, harmonized, codified, and in general arranged systematically so as to preclude the necessity of ever having to read the whole code through from start to finish.

The laws of the Pentateuch have received similar treatment from interpreters, both ancient and modern. Scholars arrange the provisions of Torah to produce, for example, the traditional enumeration of 613 laws, codes of *halakhah* (legal interpretation),[1] and comparisons of the regulations with their biblical and extra-biblical parallels.[2] So in the religious and academic as well as the legal spheres, the legal genre seems to invite readers to pick and choose, rearrange and codify to suit their purposes.

The laws of the Pentateuch offer fertile ground for such efforts because as they stand they show remarkably few signs of codification. Of course, there are codes that pay attention to systematization and organization (e.g. Lev. 1–7 or Deut. 12–26). But taken as a whole, Pentateuchal law contains a bewildering array of codes and independent provisions, and is marked by repetition, variation and occasional contradiction. It seems fair to ask, then, how the writers of biblical law expected it to be read. What does the lack of systematic codification indicate about the law's intended use?

One major indication that sequential reading *was* intended lies in the narrative contexts of Pentateuchal law. The laws' placement within stories suggests reading the laws within the narrative plot sequence. Yet

1. E.g. the *Shulhan Arukh* by Rabbis Joseph Karo and Moses Isserles (sixteenth century).

2. For examples of the former, see C.F. Kent, *Israel's Laws and Legal Precedents* (London: Hodder & Stoughton, 1907); of the latter, S.M. Paul, *Studies in the Book of the Covenant in the Light of Cuneiform and Biblical Law* (Leiden: E.J. Brill, 1970).

twentieth-century research has tended to focus on the instructional and narrative texts separately, despite the fact that J. Wellhausen's classic *Prolegomena* (1878) used the ritual instructions to establish the chronology of the Pentateuch's narrative sources. This tendency was already well advanced by the time of Rudolph Smend's source-critical analysis of 'Hexateuchal' narratives in 1912.[3] It was exacerbated by the subsequent rise of form-critical study of the oral traditions underlying the written documents in the works of Herman Gunkel, Martin Noth and others.[4] The oral forms and transmission of legal and narrative material differ considerably and invite separate analysis. Despite a resurgence of interest in the written sources, this situation still obtains for the most part today: though radical revisions of the Documentary Hypothesis have been suggested (by J. Van Seters, H.H. Schmid, R.N. Whybray),[5] they are based primarily on studies of the narratives. Some critics of the Documentary Hypothesis (e.g. Y. Kaufmann, I. Engnell)[6] discuss the history of the combined narrative and legal materials, yet their suggestions have not received as much support as a newer compositional theory (of R. Rendtorff and E. Blum)[7] which derives its claims about the whole Pentateuch primarily from analysis of the narratives.[8]

3.   R. Smend, *Die Erzählung des Hexateuch auf ihre Quellen untersucht* (Berlin: G. Reimer, 1912).

4.   E.g. H. Gunkel, *Genesis* (Göttingen: Vandenhoeck & Ruprecht, 5th edn, 1922) (trans. M. Biddle; Macon, GA: Mercer University Press, 1997); M. Noth, *A History of Pentateuchal Traditions* (trans. B.W. Anderson; Chico, CA: Scholars Press, 1981 [1948]), especially pp. 8-10.

5.   J. Van Seters, *Abraham in History and Tradition* (New Haven: Yale University Press, 1975); *idem*, *The Life of Moses: The Yahwist as Historian in Exodus–Numbers* (Louisville, KY: Westminster/John Knox Press, 1994); H.H. Schmid, *Der sogennante Jahwist* (Zürich: Theologischer Verlag, 1976); R.N. Whybray, *The Making of the Pentateuch: A Methodological Study* (JSOTSup, 53; Sheffield: JSOT Press, 1987).

6.   Y. Kaufmann, *The Religion of Israel* (ed. and trans. M. Greenberg; Chicago: University of Chicago Press, 1960); I. Engnell, 'The Pentateuch', in J.T. Willis (ed. and trans.), *A Rigid Scrutiny* (Nashville: Vanderbilt, 1969), pp. 50-67.

7.   R. Rendtorff, *The Problem of the Process of Transmission in the Pentateuch* (trans. J.J. Scullion; JSOTSup, 89; Sheffield: JSOT Press, 1990 [1977]); E. Blum, *Die Komposition der Vätergeschichte* (WMANT, 57, Neukirchen–Vluyn: Neukirchener Verlag, 1984). Blum's later work, however, extended the analysis to include the major legal sections as well: *Studien zur Komposition des Pentateuch* (BZAW, 189; Berlin: W. de Gruyter, 1990).

8.   Note the similar complaint of B.M. Levinson, *Theory and Method in*

Meanwhile, the increasing popularity of literary methods of analysis, that were developed for modern fiction and poetry, have reinforced the tendency to focus primarily or even exclusively on Pentateuchal narratives.[9] The few interpreters who attempted to read the Pentateuch as a whole (D.J.A. Clines, T.W. Mann, J.H. Sailhamer) did so from a narratological perspective.[10]

The time seems ripe, therefore, for a new analysis of the Pentateuch that will respect the generic conventions of both the legal and liturgical materials and their narrative contexts. The question 'Why are law and narrative combined in the Pentateuch?' can be asked another way: 'How was the combination of Pentateuchal narratives and laws intended to be read?' Formulating the latter question draws attention to ancient Israel's reading practices (Chapter 1), which in turn suggest yet another form of the question: 'What rhetorical effects does the combi-nation of law and narrative have on the Pentateuch's intended readers?' The three central chapters of this book therefore analyze the rhetorical effects of law and narrative's interaction within parts of the Pentateuch as well as the whole. This study concludes with a discussion of the historical ramifications of its rhetorical analysis for Persian-period Judaism, the composition of the Pentateuch (especially in its final stages), and the development of the idea of Scripture.

Biblical and Cuneiform Law: Revision, Interpolation and Development (JSOTSup, 181; Sheffield: Sheffield Academic Press, 1994), pp. 9-10.

9. An exception: Joe M. Sprinkle, *'The Book of the Covenant': A Literary Approach* (JSOTSup, 174; Sheffield: JSOT Press, 1994). An even more unusual application of narrative theory to the mixture of story and law in Genesis and Exodus is N. Stahl's *Law and Liminality in the Bible* (JSOTSup, 202; Sheffield: Sheffield Academic Press, 1995).

10. E.g. D.J.A. Clines, *The Theme of the Pentateuch* (JSOTSup, 10; Sheffield: JSOT Press, 1978); T.W. Mann, *The Book of Torah: The Narrative Integrity of the Pentateuch* (Atlanta, GA: John Knox Press, 1988); J.H. Sailhamer, *The Pentateuch as Narrative: A Biblical-Theological Commentary* (Grand Rapids, MI: Zondervan, 1992).

Chapter 1

READING

References to reading are remarkably sparse in the Hebrew Bible. Though the variety of styles and genres in the biblical books attests to an ancient literary culture in Israel, there is little explicit mention of reading prophecy and virtually no references to reading hymns or history. Most references to reading portray the reading of law. The Hebrew Bible provides more information on the reading of law than on reading any other genre of its literature.

1. *Public Readings*

The majority of the Hebrew Bible's references to reading law describe a public reading of an entire legal document: Moses reads the Book of the Covenant to the people of Israel at Mt Sinai and orders that the law be read to all Israel every seven years, Joshua fulfills that command by reading the whole law of Moses to the people on Mt Ebal, Josiah reads a whole covenant book to the people in the Temple, and Ezra dedicates several days to such public readings of law. Other allusions to the uses of laws and legal collections do not describe the activities in as much detail as do accounts of public law readings. The latter seem to have been of great interest to the writers of several different biblical narratives.

The Book of the Covenant
In the story of events at Sinai in Exodus, Moses uses a law document in a ceremony ratifying the covenant. Exodus 24 describes Moses' actions: 'he recited' and then wrote down 'all the words of YHWH' (vv. 3-4) and finally took 'the book of the covenant and read it in the hearing of the people' (v. 7).

Most interpreters have understood the document in v. 4 to be the

same as the 'book of the covenant' in v. 7, and that both consist of the
laws in Exodus 21–23 (these chapters are therefore frequently called
'the Book of the Covenant'). On the other hand, the sequence of oral
recitation followed by inscription followed by public reading convinced
U. Cassuto that the book does not contain 'all the words' of Exodus 19
and 21–23, which he argued would be superfluous to repeat on successive days. He concluded that it is rather 'a short general document, a
kind of testimony and memorial to the making of the covenant'.[1]

The legal ritual of covenant-making might require some repetition,
however, as rituals are apt to do. The scene in Exod. 24.3-8 portrays the
people's initial commitment on the basis of Moses' oral report (v. 3)
being formalized in writing and ritual (vv. 4-8). This sequence of
events, which begins with a statement of intent and ends with formaliz-
ing the agreement in writing, is typical of modern legal agreements as
well. There seems little reason therefore to deny that v. 7's 'book of the
covenant' contains 'all the words of YHWH' referred to in vv. 3-4.

The close proximity of this episode to the collection of laws in
Exodus 21–23 supports the identity of the 'book of the covenant' with
that collection. The precise boundaries of the book are hard to pin
down, due to the complicated structure and history of Exodus 19–24.[2] It
may well be, as M. Noth suggested, that 24.3-8 formed the original
conclusion to the independent law book containing most of chs. 21–23.[3]
For our present purposes, it is enough to note that in the current form of
Exodus, the covenant at Sinai is ritually completed by, among other
things, the public reading of a law code.

Deuteronomic Law
In Deut. 31.9, Moses writes 'this law'. He then commands the Levites
to read it to 'all Israel' every seventh year during the festival of booths
(v. 11). The emphasis is clearly on instruction, 'that they may hear and

---

1. U. Cassuto, *A Commentary on the Book of Exodus* (trans. I. Abrahams;
Jerusalem: Magnes Press, 1967), p. 312.

2. The stipulations of Exod. 20.22–23.33 seem to form a self-contained unity,
though with signs of internal layers of composition. But 'all the words' of 24.3-4
may presuppose the Ten Commandments (20.1-17) and the covenant preparations
of ch. 19 as well (so Cassuto, *Exodus*, pp. 212-13), or perhaps even a retelling of
the exodus from Egypt (so G.A.F. Knight, *Theology As Narration: A Commentary
on the Book of Exodus* [Grand Rapids, MI: Eerdmans, 1976], p. 156).

3. M. Noth, *Exodus: A Commentary* (trans. J.S. Bowden; OTL; London: SCM
Press, 1962), p. 198.

learn to fear YHWH your God and to keep all the words of this law to do them' (v. 12).

'This law' probably refers to much of Deuteronomy, in which case the sequence is similar to the recitation–inscription–reading sequence in Exodus 24: Moses' speech takes up most of Deuteronomy and ends in 31.1;[4] he then writes it down and orders the Levites to read it publicly. The major difference is that the public reading is not immediate, but to take place regularly every seven years.

Deuteronomy 31.9-11 thus portrays a legal document written to serve as a script for oral presentation. In this regard, as well as in the provisions for preserving the document (vv. 24-26), the resemblance to some ancient Near Eastern treaties is striking. They call for the treaty text to be deposited in a temple and to be read publicly on regular occasions as a reminder of the treaty's provisions.[5] Similarly, in Deuteronomy 31, the law's storage in the ark of the covenant and its public reading every seven years aims to remind Israel of the covenant with God.

Joshua's Law Book

When Joshua reads the law to the people on Mt Ebal in Joshua 8, the text emphasizes the comprehensiveness of the reading: 'he read all the words of the law, the blessings and the curses, as it was all written in the book of the law. There was not a word of anything that Moses commanded that Joshua did not read' (Josh. 8.34-35).

An explicit citation in v. 31 from 'the book of the law of Moses' referring to Deut. 27.4-6 makes clear that the reading is from Deuteronomy, and the mention of blessings and curses indicates that the

---

4.   Following 1Q5.13 ויכל משה לדבר and LXX καὶ συνετέλεσεν Μωυσῆς λαλῶν to translate v. 1 'So Moses finished speaking' (the identical sentence appears also in MT 32.45 after the psalm), instead of MT וילך משה וידבר 'Moses went and spoke'. A.D.H. Mayes argued that this reading is better than MT's, because 'a deliberate change from the MT to the text presupposed by LXX and offered by the Dead Sea Scrolls is less credible than a deliberate change in the other direction (in view of the fact that the following chapters do contain further words of Moses)' (*Deuteronomy* [NCB; London: Oliphants, 1979], pp. 372-73; cf. P.C. Craigie, *The Book of Deuteronomy* [NICOT; Grand Rapids, MI: Eerdmans, 1976], p. 369).

5.   This suggests simply that Deut. 31 reflects a common practice, not, however, that it is shaped by a set treaty form. D.J. McCarthy noted that 'reference to the document in the treaties…is simply too rare and devoted to too many diverse functions to be accounted an essential formal element' (*Treaty and Covenant: A Study in Form in the Ancient Oriental Documents and in the Old Testament* [Rome: Biblical Institute Press, 2nd rev. edn, 1981], p. 65).

writer was thinking of the book in more or less its present form. The
fact that the whole law is written on the altar as well as read has suggested to many commentators that originally the story referred to a
much shorter law code.[6] In the canonical context of the book of Joshua,
however, 'everything that Moses commanded' suggests the entire
Mosaic law and 'the book of the law' therefore implies most of the
Pentateuch. The text's compositional history has thus left indications of
all three referents—short law code, Deuteronomy, Pentateuch—in Josh.
8.30-35.[7]

The emphasis in Exodus 24 and Deuteronomy 31 on the creation of a
written record of previous oral proclamation is reversed in Joshua 8,
which emphasizes the public reading and inscription of the written text.
Here the book of the law functions as a script for oral proclamation and
publication.

Josiah's Law Book
Josiah's law book was read before him (implicitly all of it; 2 Kgs
22.10//2 Chron. 34.18) and then Josiah gathered 'all the people' and
'read in their hearing all the words of the covenant book', after which
he made a covenant (2 Kgs 23.2-3//2 Chron. 34.30-31). The identity
and size of the book are not indicated by the text, though the nature of
Josiah's reform once again suggests Deuteronomy, in whole or in part.

The emphasis in 23.2 falls on the comprehensiveness of the reading
('all the words') and the inclusiveness of the audience ('every man of
Judah and all the inhabitants of Jerusalem, the priests, the prophets and

---

6.   The emphasis on writing the whole law, though not reading it, is also found
in the instructions contained in Deut. 27.3, 8, where the law is to be written on plas-
ter-covered memorial megaliths rather than on the altar stones.

7.   T.C. Butler suggested a possible development of this tradition: 'The original
context of Deut 27 referred only to a small number of blessings and cursings. The
context of Deut 4.13; 5.22 referred only to the Ten Commandments as being written down. Deuteronomy 31.24-26 expanded the writing to include all the book of
Deuteronomy. The canonical tradition then expanded this to include the entire
Pentateuch. Joshua 8 takes the process one step further. Not only is the entire material to be written down for Israel, it is to be read to them in an annual ceremony and
is to be written on the altar. Here is the extreme to which the biblical writer felt
impelled to go to enforce his teachings upon the community. The community must
know the entire law. They must be reminded of the entire law. They must be
brought to pledge themselves to observance of the entire law' (*Joshua* [WBC, 7;
Waco, TX: Word Books, 1983], p. 94).

all the people'). Interpreters have expressed doubts regarding the feasibility of reading a long document such as Deuteronomy twice in private (22.8, 10) and then publicly to such a large audience (23.2). They have suggested on the basis of evidence internal to Deuteronomy that Josiah's document contained only some original 'core' of the present book.[8] However, the mention of 'the book of the law' within the present context of the story, near the end of a continuous narrative stretching back to Genesis, suggests identifying it with Deuteronomy as a whole and even with the larger bulk of Pentateuchal law, which has gone virtually unmentioned in the narrative since Joshua. So like Joshua 8, 2 Kings 22–23 contains tensions between the document required by the plot of the immediate account and the document implied by its context in a wider-ranging narrative.

Josiah's law book, like Joshua's, serves as a script for oral proclamation within a covenant renewal ceremony. The story goes beyond previous accounts of law readings, however, in making the book serve as a prescription for religious reform as well.[9] Public reading and communal assent to law (23.2-3) are now the prelude to royal enforcement of law (23.4-25).

Ezra's Law Book
Like Josiah, Ezra reads the law to 'all the people' (Neh. 8.1, 3, 5; this inclusive assembly included men, women and children old enough to understand, according to 8.2, 3).[10] The accounts of Ezra's reading of the law emphasize the amount of time spent rather than the completeness of the reading: 'he read from it from dawn until noon' (8.3); the

---

8.   See, e.g., H. Schmidt, *Die grossen Propheten* (Die Schriften des Alten Testaments, 2.2; Göttingen: Vandenhoeck & Ruprecht, 1915), p. 180; J. Gray, *I & II Kings: A Commentary* (OTL; London: SCM Press, 1964), pp. 651-52.

9.   Since the parallel account in 2 Chron. 34 has the reform *precede* the discovery of the law book, the sequence in Kings may well be a theological construction of the deuteronomistic editors, intent on elevating the authority of Deuteronomy in this account. For full discussion and other literature, see G.H. Jones, *1 and 2 Kings* (2 vols.; NCB; Grand Rapids: Eerdmans, 1984), II, pp. 603-606.

10.   T.C. Ezkenazi noted the intense emphasis on inclusivity in vv. 1-12: כל־העם 'all the people' appears nine times and עם 'people' alone three more times. 'Such density of repetition has no parallels in Ezra–Nehemiah' (*In an Age of Prose: A Literary Approach to Ezra–Nehemiah* [SBLMS, 36; Atlanta: Scholars Press, 1988], p. 97).

next day the elders gathered 'to understand the words of the law' (8.13) which led to celebrating the feast of booths, during which Ezra 'read from the book of God's law' daily (8.18).[11] At another gathering, the people read from the law for a quarter of the day (9.3).

Ezra's 'book of the law of Moses' (8.3) is clearly a large document and may well have been the Pentateuch, more or less as it is today. Little is known with certainty, however, and interpreters have come to widely divergent conclusions regarding the nature of Ezra's law book and the historicity of this episode.[12]

Despite the document's size, Ezra's law book still serves as a script for oral proclamation and teaching. The depiction of its public reading obviously intends to evoke comparison with the pre-exilic law readings mentioned above.[13] In Nehemiah 8, Ezra acts within the tradition of covenant renewals centered on law readings, a tradition that Israel traced back through Josiah and Joshua to Moses.

11. H.G.M. Williamson understood the idiom קרא ב 'read in' (instead of the verb followed by the direct object) in vv. 3 and 8 to imply that only extracts of the law were read: 'it is evident that the Book of the Law was a substantial document... Continuous reading would have been exhausting for reader and audience alike. As it was, the text was broken down into sensible units. This gave opportunity for others to share the physical task of reading with Ezra and for him to select those portions of the Law that he deemed most appropriate' (*Ezra, Nehemiah* [WBC, 16; Waco, TX: Word Books, 1985], pp. 288, 291).

12. Crüsemann noted: 'The figure of Ezra is currently very controversial in every respect. There is no consensus about anything. Sources, dating, and the circumstances of the law's appearance, in fact all issues concerning his law, are assessed in very diverse ways' ('Der Pentateuch als Tora: Prolegomena zur Interpretation seiner Endgestalt', *EvT* 49 [1989], pp. 250-67 [255] my translation).

13. U. Kellermann argued that Neh. 8–10 exhibits the same pattern as law readings in Chronicles (2 Chron. 15.1-18; chs. 29–31; 34.29–35.19), and that they all depend for their structure on the form of the synagogue service in the Chronicler's own time (*Nehemia: Quellen, Überlieferung und Geschichte* [BZAW, 102; Berlin: Alfred Töpelmann, 1967], pp. 29-30, 90-92). D.J.A. Clines added Solomon's assembly (2 Chron. 5–7) to the list of comparisons (*Ezra, Nehemiah, Esther* [NCB; Grand Rapids: Eerdmans, 1984], p. 183). These comparisons have been strongly challenged by Ezkenazi, who argued that the elements in Neh. 8–10 common to the accounts in Chronicles are also common to law-reading accounts in Kings, from which they were most likely borrowed directly (*Age of Prose*, pp. 105-10). At stake in this debate is the larger issue of the literary relationship between Chronicles and Ezra–Nehemiah.

Other Uses of Law

The Hebrew Bible depicts other uses of law books as well. Two passages from the deuteronomic tradition describe continuous study of the law: in Deut. 17.19 and Josh. 1.8, the king and Joshua are instructed to study the law daily. Their positions as leaders (and judges?) of the people suggest that the kind of study intended here is juridical in nature.[14] Other texts emphasize teaching the law to the people: in Lev. 10.11 and Deut. 33.10, the teachers are priests;[15] in 2 Chron. 17.7-9, they are a royal commission composed of officials, Levites and priests.[16] But none of these texts indicate what form the teaching of the law took. Strikingly absent from the Hebrew Bible is any reference to judicial use of written laws. Even Hammurabi's law code, though primarily motivated by the desire to glorify the king, nevertheless depicts a plaintiff referring to the written code: 'Let any wronged man who has a lawsuit come before the statue of me, the king of justice, and let him have my inscribed stela read aloud to him, thus may he hear my precious pronouncements and let my stela reveal the lawsuit for him; may he examine his case, may he calm his (troubled) heart...'[17] The Hebrew

14. 2 Kgs 11.12 suggests that royal authority was represented by possession of העדות 'the testimonies' which in some texts refers to tablets of law. See G. Widengren, 'King and Covenant', *JSS* 2 (1957), pp. 1-32 (5-7).

15. The priests' role as teachers of law is reflected in a number of prophetic critiques (Jer. 18.18; Hos. 4.6; Mal. 2.4-9). Various texts (Deut. 17.8-13; 21.5; Ezek. 44.23-24) show them administering as well as teaching the law.

16. The nature and contents of Jehoshaphat's law remain matters of debate. H.G.M. Williamson argued that the Chronicler was thinking of the Pentateuch as a whole, but whatever historical traditions might lie behind this account probably stemmed from Jehoshaphat's attempts to promulgate royal law, as clearly in 2 Chron. 19.4-11 (*1 and 2 Chronicles* [NCB; Grand Rapids: Eerdmans, 1982], p. 282). R.B. Dillard noted that even if royal law was originally in view, 'this pericope does attest to the early existence of authoritative writings regulative of Israel's life, i.e. it speaks of the concept of canonical writings at a time far earlier than critical reconstructions have ordinarily allowed' (*2 Chronicles* [WBC, 15; Waco, TX: Word Books, 1987], p. 134). G.N. Knoppers, on the other hand, argued that Jehoshaphat's law scroll and judicial reforms are the invention of the Chronicler ('Jehoshaphat's Judiciary and "the Scroll of YHWH's Torah"', *JBL* 113 [1994], pp. 59-80).

17. M.T. Roth, *Law Collections from Mesopotamia and Asia Minor* (WAW, 6; Atlanta: Scholars Press, 1995), p. 134; cf. *ANET*, p. 178. For the argument that this text in Hammurabi's Code does not indicate the code's legislative authority, see

Bible, on the other hand, portrays plaintiffs bringing legal cases before
Moses, elders or priests, but never appealing directly to written laws.
Instead, the biblical emphasis on using legal collections falls on read-
ings to public assemblies.

2. *The Possibility of Law Readings*

My purpose in describing these texts is simply to point out that the tradition of public reading of law is widely attested in the Hebrew Bible.
In response to the question, How was law read in Israel?, the Hebrew
Bible gives a definite answer: the whole law, or at least large portions
of it, was read aloud in public.[18]

The idea of public recitals of laws strikes many modern readers as
highly implausible. The legal collections, much less the whole Pentateuch, seem too large and the material too dense to hold the attention of
a public gathering. Thus the initial presumption of interpreters has
weighed against the possibility that public law readings were common
occurrences in ancient Israel.[19]

An intuitively more plausible scenario for modern interpreters is the
theory that the law-reading tradition developed out of the transmission
of *oral* law. The recitation of legal traditions to a public assembly
seems more likely in pre-literate or semi-literate societies. The Hebrew
Bible, however, invariably depicts the proclamation of law as either
dependent on or resulting in written texts.[20] The readings of written
law in Joshua, 2 Kings and Nehemiah depict the public proclamation of

---

R. Westbrook, 'Cuneiform Law Codes and the Origins of Legislation', *ZA* 79
(1990), pp. 201-20 (202-203).

18. As M. Greenberg has emphasized: 'The law is embedded in a narrative
framework, which tells of God's command that every law be proclaimed to the
Israelites... Publication is manifestly of the essence of lawgiving' ('Three Conceptions of the Torah in Hebrew Scriptures', in *Studies in the Bible and Jewish
Thought* [Philadelphia: Jewish Publication Society, 1995], pp. 11-24 [15]).

19. Note, e.g., the comments of Cassuto on Exod. 24 discussed above.

20. Perhaps the constant mention of written law simply emphasizes the law's
authority (so Kent, *Israel's Laws*, p. 13). In ancient Greece, new laws were apparently placed on public inscriptions to give them authority within the larger context
of traditional, oral law (R. Thomas, *Literacy and Orality in Ancient Greece*
[Cambridge: Cambridge University Press, 1992], p. 68). Claims to authority clearly
play a role in Israel's law readings as well.

old texts, a situation opposite to the theorized textualization of oral tradition. Only in its Mosaic origins is biblical law depicted as the transcription of orally proclaimed law (Exod. 24.4; Deut. 31.9) and even then, its core is received in writing (Exod. 31.18; 34.1; Deut. 5.22; cf. Exod. 34.28). Thus modern intuitions of the implausibility of public law readings do not correspond with the ancient writers' notions of plausibility. Whatever the actual origins of Israel's laws, the Bible depicts their oral proclamation as based on written texts.[21]

References to text-based performance are not unusual in ancient literatures. Ancient categories of literary genre often describe the nature of the text's performance (e.g. 'song', 'sayings', 'lesson').[22] Epics may refer explicitly to their own performance in chant as well as their preservation in memory and text.[23] From ancient Greece, according to R. Thomas, 'there is some evidence for oral laws being sung and performed'.[24] Roman laws were read aloud at the time of their promulgation.[25] In medieval Iceland, 'law-speakers' recited one-third of the communities' code at annual assemblies.[26] In the latter case, the practice clearly originated in the oral transmission of the laws; the Icelandic laws were written down two centuries after the settlement of the

21. E.W. Conrad observed correctly: 'The Old Testament, then, represents the relationship of books to orality in a way that is markedly different from that suggested by the way biblical scholarship has portrayed the development of Old Testament books' ('Heard but not Seen: The Representation of "Books" in the Old Testament', *JSOT* 54 [1992], pp. 49-59 [49-50]).

22. D. Damrosch, *The Narrative Covenant: Transformations of Genre in the Growth of Biblical Literature* (San Francisco: Harper & Row, 1987), p. 38. For a survey of genre labels used in Hebrew narrative to mark inset poetry, see J.W. Watts, '"This Song": Conspicuous Poetry in Hebrew Prose', in J.C. de Moor and W.G.E. Watson (eds.), *Verse in Ancient Near Eastern Prose* (AOAT, 42; Neukirchen–Vluyn: Neukirchener Verlag, 1993), pp. 345-58 (345-48).

23. E.g. the *Erra Epic* 5.49-59 (L. Cagni, *The Poem of Erra* [SANE, 1.3; Malibu, CA: Undena, 1977]). For discussion of its references to performance, see Damrosch, *Narrative Covenant*, p. 84.

24. Thomas, *Literacy and Orality*, p. 68.

25. Thomas, *Literacy and Orality*, p. 165, citing W.V. Harris, *Ancient Literacy* (Cambridge, MA: Harvard University Press, 1989), p. 161.

26. A. Dennis, P. Foote and R. Perkins, *Laws of Early Iceland, Grágás* (Winnipeg: University of Manitoba Press, 1980), p. 12. A. Alt discussed the Icelandic parallel in 'The Origins of Israelite Law', *Essays on Old Testament History and Religion* (trans. R.A. Wilson; Oxford: Basil Blackwell, 1966), pp. 102-103.

island.[27] The example nevertheless demonstrates that the oral recitation or reading of legal collections to public assemblies is both possible and attested in some cultures.

Form-critical studies of the Pentateuch have found indications of oral transmission in some texts containing or concerning law. For example, Rendtorff argued that Leviticus 1, 3 and 4 were shaped by a 'ritual' genre intended for recitation to fix the ritual sequence of making a sacrifice.[28] G. von Rad suggested on the basis of Deuteronomy, Exodus 19 and Joshua 24 that the Sinai tradition originally took a set liturgical form, the major features of which were (1) historical overview, (2) reading of law, (3) sealing of covenant, and (4) blessings and curses.[29] One need not accept the form-critics' speculative reconstructions of the settings out of which these oral genres grew in order to appreciate the oral origins of the formulae and structures in these texts.[30]

Modern distaste for the idea of reading lists of laws aloud is no reason, then, to dismiss the Hebrew Bible's depiction of law readings. The emphasis placed on such readings by the Bible suggests that their relationship to Pentateuchal law deserves to be explored. What does Israel's tradition of public law readings say about the nature and purpose of the Pentateuch? This study will use literary and rhetorical observations to argue that Israel's tradition of reading law aloud shaped not only the laws, but the whole Pentateuch as well.

3. *The Probability of Law Readings*

There are, of course, a host of questions surrounding the biblical texts depicting public law readings. The nature and extent of the law books,

27. The rhetorical phrasing of Icelandic law is reminiscent of Deuteronomy: 'It is generally agreed that...[the laws'] form is substantially the form they had in the Lawspeaker's recital. We are often reminded of the time and the place: we are told what we should do "here" at Thingvöllr "today" and "tomorrow" and what "I"—the Lawspeaker—have just said or am about to enumerate' (Dennis, Foote and Perkins, *Laws of Early Iceland*, p. 13).

28. *Die Gesetze in der Priesterschrift* (Göttingen: Vandenhoeck & Ruprecht, 1954), p. 22.

29. G. von Rad, 'The Form-Critical Problem of the Hexateuch', in *idem, The Problem of the Hexateuch and Other Essays* (trans. E.W. Trueman Dicken; Edinburgh: Oliver & Boyd, 1966), pp. 1-78 (13-40).

30. Note Rendtorff's cautions regarding the reconstruction of original settings, in *Leviticus* (BKAT, 3.1; Neukirchen–Vluyn: Neukirchener Verlag, 1985), pp. 18-21.

the social and religious setting for public readings, the role of the king—these issues require (and have received) sustained attention. Some of these topics will be discussed in subsequent chapters of this study, and others that are not crucial to the argument can be safely passed over. Two interpretive problems, however, challenge the historical probability of the Bible's depiction of public law readings and so must be dealt with here before this inquiry can proceed further.

Tradition History
The first involves the question of which traditions lie behind these accounts of law readings. Answers to this question strongly influence evaluations of the stories' literary function and historical worth. The possibility that the authors of these narratives constructed them by reading the customs of their own times into accounts of the past suggests that law readings may have originated as late as the fourth or third centuries BCE.[31] If that is the case, the repeated emphasis in the Hebrew Bible on public readings of law contains no information about practices that may have shaped the law codes themselves, but only indicates the interests of editors in the mid-Second Temple period. Or perhaps Ezra's reading of the law became the model upon which accounts of earlier covenant renewal ceremonies were based. In that case, public readings would still have developed only after much of the law was already written and edited. Either way, public readings of law would have had little influence on the composition and redaction of the biblical law codes.

The law-reading tradition contains signs of earlier origins, however. The above descriptions of public law readings shows that the tradition takes two different forms in the Hebrew Bible. The 'deuteronomic' form (found in Exod. 24.3-7; Deut 31.9-11; Josh. 8.30-35; 2 Kgs 22–

---

31. These Second Temple practices include not only the custom of reading law in the synagogue services (Kellermann, *Nehemia*, pp. 29-30, 90-92) but also royal law readings in the Temple. Kings such as Agrippa were the readers of law at Tabernacles (according to *m. Soṭ.* 7.8; see Widengren, 'King and Covenant', pp. 20-21). The Qumran sectarians anticipated an eschatological public reading of law: 'they shall read in [their] h[earing] [al]l the statutes of the covenant, and instruct them in all [th]eir judgments' (1QSᵃ 1.5-6, the 'Rule of the Congregation', translated by J.H. Charlesworth and L.T. Stuckenbruck in Charlesworth [ed.], *The Dead Sea Scrolls: Hebrew, Aramaic, and Greek Texts with English Translations*. I. *Rule of the Community and Related Documents* [Tübingen: J.C.B. Mohr (Paul Siebeck), 1994], p. 111).

23//2 Chron. 34) emphasizes the completeness of the readings and the textual nature of the law (by its inscription by Moses, its reinscription on the altar by Joshua, and its rediscovery by Josiah's priests).[32] These deuteronomic accounts maintain these emphases despite their setting in a wider literary context that, on the one hand, contains virtually no references to textualized legal traditions in monarchic Israel and, on the other hand, presents in the Pentateuch a corpus of law too large to take its place easily within this tradition of public reading. This loose fit between the Pentateuchal codes and the deuteronomic stories of public law readings indicates that the stories, as originally written, did not presuppose the final form of Pentateuchal law but rather some earlier, smaller law codes. Therefore the deuteronomic tradition of law reading must have arisen prior to the unifying redactions of the Pentateuch and have its origins in the practices and traditions of the monarchic or, at the latest, exilic periods.

The Nehemiah account emphasizes the long duration of the public readings of law, rather than their completeness, and adds to the recital of law a concern for its interpretation and ongoing study. Though the story of Ezra's law reading clearly presupposes the older deuteronomic tradition, these new elements distinguish his 'book of the law' as a large and complicated document—a description that fits Pentateuchal law more closely than that given in the deuteronomic law-reading tradition. Thus Nehemiah 8 seems to contain a separate tradition that, though informed by older practices and traditions, reflects the literary and social conditions of the Second Temple period.

Therefore the stories of public law readings found in the deuteronomic (and earlier) literature should not be dismissed simply as back-projections of Second Temple traditions and practices. The tradition of public law readings found a place already in Israel's earlier literature and its origins must be sought in the history and traditions of Israel's monarchic and exilic periods, prior to and during the time when Israel's legal traditions were being combined into the collections now found in the Pentateuch.[33]

32. By labelling this tradition 'deuteronomic', I do not wish to exclude the possibility of pre-deuteronomic law-reading traditions nor to maintain that Exod. 24.3-7 is necessarily a deuteronomic composition, but only to suggest that the deuteronomic literature presents the most prominent formulation of this type-scene.

33. Though the tradition is older than the literature of Ezra–Nehemiah and the Chronicler, this does not eliminate the possibility that anachronism shapes the

Literary Fictions

A second problem concerns the rhetorical role played by books of the law in Deuteronomistic literature. E.W. Conrad argued that the stories of reading law in the literary complex of Genesis through Kings enhance the narrator's authority as the only source of information about the law. The law book is lost and found not only in the Josiah story, but also in the reading experience of Genesis–Kings: the book disappears after Joshua to reappear only in 2 Kings. Conrad concluded, 'The rhetorical strategies empower the text by coercing its implied readers to look for the lost book in the only place available, the narrative of Genesis–2 Kings'.[34] He therefore contended that historical reconstructions of Josiah's or any other book mentioned in the Hebrew Bible are anachronistic because they ignore the literary function of the motif.

Conrad's argument depended heavily on the concept of the 'implied reader', a phrase commonly used in contemporary literary theory to describe how a text itself suggests the character of its ideal audience. In Conrad's interpretation, it is the implied reader of Genesis–Kings for whom the law is lost and found again and who depends on the narrator for access to it. He did not explain how this implied reader compares to any real readers of these stories. For modern readers of the Hebrew Bible, it is in fact the case that only the Pentateuchal narrator provides access to Mosaic law. The earliest readers of the Josiah story, however, were unlikely to have found the story within this larger literary context. Assuming an exilic date for completion of the Deuteronomistic History (Joshua–Kings), such hearers and readers would have had no Pentateuch (as we know it) but they were likely aware of, if not in possession of, a variety of competing collections of law.[35] Thus it is not necessarily

deuteronomic accounts of law reading. The stories of Moses' and Joshua's readings may well be back-projections of later monarchic practices.

34. 'Heard But Not Seen', p. 53.

35. R.E. Friedman reconstructed the nature of the legal competition in public readings: 'The royal and prophetic support of the promulgation of the book of the Torah lent prestige and, more important, legitimacy to the faction which produced it. Public reading gave it authority and fame. At the same time, however, the book of the Torah was anathema to the Aaronid priesthood... Composition of their own Torah documents, portraying the Mosaic age from their perspective, lending to their position the legitimacy which their rivals were achieving, was natural, advantageous, and perhaps critical' (*The Exile and Biblical Narrative: The Formation of the Deuteronomistic and Priestly Works* [HSM, 22; Chico, CA: Scholars Press, 1981], pp. 70-71).

anachronistic to assume that the story of Josiah's law book intends to refer to a real legal collection; instead, it is anachronistic to adopt a late literary construct (Genesis–Kings) as the only meaningful context.[36]

My point is not to deny the interpretive value of identifying an implied reader. However, the implied reader's identity depends on the scope of the literary context invoked by real readers.[37] In different literary contexts and cultures, a story's implied reader will vary considerably. The above survey of the stories of law readings has already shown that the size and nature of Joshua and Josiah's law books (i.e. short code or Deuteronomy or Pentateuch) depends entirely on how large a literary context the real readers decide to employ. The fact that the lost-and-found law has no external referentiality for later readers does not preclude such referentiality for earlier generations or for the authors of the story.[38]

Thus the tradition of reading law publicly seems to reflect a historical practice in ancient Israel.[39] In Judah in the seventh to fifth centuries BCE, public law readings were considered plausible events. That does not preclude the possibility that the accounts of Moses' and Joshua's law readings may well be retrojections of Josiah's practices, and that the depictions of Josiah's and Ezra's readings may have been amplified due to the powerful religious implications that they exert. The differences between the latter two attest, however, to historical memories at their roots. On at least some occasions, law collections were read aloud in their entirety to public assemblies.

36. See Chapter 3 below for a discussion of the rhetorical influence of lists of law on the tendency to collect almost all of Israel's stories into a single narrative complex.

37. The relationship between implied and real readers has become a topic of considerable debate in rhetorical theory. For theoretical and empirical studies of the various positions, see the collection of essays edited by G. Kirsch and D.H. Roen, *A Sense of Audience in Written Communication* (Written Communication Annual, 5; Newbury Park, CA: Sage Publications, 1990).

38. Authors and speakers, of course, conceive of themselves as addressing readers or an audience. We may therefore speak of an author's 'intended readers' (which may be either a generalized ideal or real people, and which in edited texts may be have multiple identities) in addition to the 'implied reader' which the real readers find in the text. (See Chapter 4 below for my own description of the Pentateuch's intended reader.)

39. So Greenberg: 'This published character of the Torah in its narrative setting must reflect in some way its place in life' ('Three Conceptions', p. 17).

4. *Writing Law for Public Reading*

From this observation, it is reasonable to hypothesize that much of Pentateuchal law was written or at least edited with such public read-ings in mind. In other words, laws were intended to be *heard* in the context of other laws and the narratives surrounding them. The writing of law would in that case require attention to rhetoric, mnemonics and narrative context.

The hypothesis that much of Israel's law was written and edited for public reading is supported by two kinds of evidence. First, the narra-tive context of Pentateuchal law confirms that the Torah is intended to be read as a whole and in order. Unlike law, narrative invites, almost enforces, a strategy of sequential reading, of starting at the beginning and reading the text in order to the end. The placement of law within narrative conforms (at least in part) the reading of law to the conven-tions of narrative. Together with frequent references to public readings of the whole law, the narrative context of law becomes evidence of the reading conventions intended by the writers (see Chapter 2).[40] Second, many features of the Pentateuch that are inexplicable according to the familiar norms of legal literature make sense as rhetorical devices to aid aural reception of the law. Chapter 3 will explore some of these features.

Several scholars have recently argued that the Pentateuch was designed for piecemeal public readings. E.S. Gerstenberger suggested that the regulations of Leviticus were compiled to be read aloud in syn-agogue services.[41] E.T. Mullen, Jr, also argued that the Tetrateuch is 'a repository of accounts that presented numerous options for selected

---

40. B.S. Jackson noted that 'both law and narrative concern goal-oriented human action, and that both have relatively non-reversible temporal dimensions. The literary structure of the Pentateuch is itself a mixture of these two forms of dis-course'; and concluded 'we should not exclude the possibility that the legal form can be used to transmit a narrative message' ('The Ceremonial and the Judicial: Biblical Law as Sign and Symbol', *JSOT* 30 [1984], pp. 25-50) (repr. in J.W. Rogerson [ed.], *The Pentateuch: A Sheffield Reader* [Sheffield: Sheffield Academic Press, 1996], pp. 102-27 [115-16]).

41. *Leviticus: A Commentary* (trans. D.W. Stott; OTL; Louisville, KY: West-minster Press, 1996), pp. 8-15, 26.

usage for particular didactic religious and ethnic, communal purposes'.[42] The Pentateuch did come to be used piecemeal for liturgical and
didactic purposes.[43] The text, however, shows relatively few signs of
having been shaped for shorter readings: some stories are episodic and
self-contained (e.g. in Gen. 12–25), but others span large blocks with
tightly woven plots (the Joseph and Exodus narratives); some instructions fall in topically organized blocks, but the larger codes of especially civil laws contain little legal codification or lectionary arrangement. Considering the dominance of piecemeal methods of reading
and interpretation in Jewish and Christian tradition, the Pentateuch
(and the rest of the Bible) is remarkably free of such organizational
concerns. Most of its structures seem designed for public reading of the
whole.

Before proceeding, however, I want to emphasize that not every
writer who had a hand in the Pentateuch's composition intended it for
public reading as a whole. There are passages that show the results of
systematic codification (Lev. 18) and others that emphasize instructions
for specialists (e.g. Lev. 6–7 apart from its context). Furthermore, it is
open to serious question whether the Law of Moses in its final Pentateuchal form was really intended to be read in public at one sitting.
More likely is that it simply follows the rhetorical strategies and
generic conventions laid down by earlier and smaller codes which it
incorporates. The decreased emphasis on completeness in the later
public readings (Neh. 8–9) suggests that in the Second Temple period,
the convention of a comprehensive public reading was old and no
longer practical.

Genres and their conventions, however, frequently outlive the conditions that create them. The conventions of public reading still governed
how most law was written and edited in the early Second Temple

---

42. *Ethnic Myths and Pentateuchal Foundations: A New Approach to the Formation of the Pentateuch* (SBLSS; Atlanta: Scholars Press, 1997), p. 11; also 55,
165, 183, 325, 328.

43. The liturgical calendar of the synagogue arranges the Torah passages
sequentially to read all of it in one year. B.P. Robinson posited liturgical recitation
as the Pentateuch's intended setting and thus as an interpretive key to its intended
effect on readers ('Moses at the Burning Bush', *JSOT* 75 [1997], pp. 107-22 [108-
10 and n. 6]).

period. It is my thesis that public reading established the literary forms of Israel's law in the monarchic period, and those forms remained unchanged long after public reading had become a rarity and perhaps an anachronism.

Chapter 2

RHETORIC

The tradition of public law readings points out the rhetorical function of law in ancient Israel. The accounts of readings depict these texts as influencing the audience's thoughts and persuading them to alter their behavior. Persuasion was thus a principal reason for reading law aloud in public.[1]

It is therefore legitimate to describe ancient Israelite law as 'rhetorical' in the narrow definition of the term, that is, as persuasive speech. According to the texts discussed in the previous chapter, law was read aloud to affect an audience orally. One may reasonably expect that texts composed for such use would display a concern for oral delivery and aural reception in their structure and contents.

The word 'rhetoric' also describes the manner in which texts govern the reading process through the manipulation of the cultural conventions and expectations that make up literary genre.[2] Under this broad definition, every text is rhetorical in nature and Pentateuchal law is no exception. Such a broad understanding of rhetoric emphasizes the

1. The definition of rhetoric in terms of 'persuasion' derives from classical theorists from Aristotle to Cicero; see the survey and analysis by K. Burke, *A Rhetoric of Motives* [Berkeley: University of California Press, 1950], pp. 49-55, 61-62.

2. D. Patrick and A. Scult's statement summarizes such a broad definition: 'In order to lead to a deeper penetration into the particularity and concreteness of the text, the "rhetoric" in rhetorical criticism must be broadened to its fullest range in the classical tradition, namely, *as the means by which a text establishes and manages its relationship to its audience in order to achieve a particular effect*' (*Rhetoric and Biblical Interpretation* [JSOTSup, 82; Sheffield: Almond Press, 1990], p. 12, Patrick and Scult's emphasis). Rhetoric becomes, in effect, a means for analyzing genre: 'From a rhetorical perspective, then, a text's genre becomes the code that must be broken in order to bring its word to life' (Patrick and Scult, *Rhetoric*, p. 15).

persuasive features of all texts, and alerts interpreters to their presence even in legal codes.

However, between the narrow and broad definitions lies a middle ground, in which 'rhetoric' describes the features of texts which, though not themselves intended for oral delivery, are composed under the influence of conventions and genres shaped by persuasive speech. In this sense, rhetoric describes the way oral practices influence conventions of written genres. My thesis turns on this intermediate meaning of rhetoric. Although the Pentateuch and its various parts (like all texts) are rhetorical in the broad sense, my contention is more specific: Israel's tradition of reading law in public (narrow sense of rhetoric) gave shape to literary conventions and genres (intermediate sense of rhetoric) which governed the combination of law and narrative in the Pentateuch.

1. *Rhetoric in Biblical Studies*

Attention to rhetoric in biblical scholarship has been shaped by the narrow and broad definitions of the term. The narrow definition has drawn attention to persuasive speech quoted or preserved in biblical texts, while the broad definition has provoked interest in the way biblical texts structure their communication with readers.

Until now, the treatment of law and the narrow sense of rhetoric (meaning persuasive speech) in the Hebrew Bible has generally concerned form- and tradition-critical analysis of legal speeches, mostly in narrative and prophecy.[3] Of the law codes, Deuteronomy has received the most attention for its overt rhetorical formulation as Moses' speech.[4] The Holiness Code of Leviticus has also drawn attention because of its oral formulas and motive clauses.[5] Classical rhetorical theory has been applied to prophetic texts and to the framework of

3. E.g. H.J. Boecker, *Redeformen des Rechtslebens im Alten Testament* (WMANT, 14; Neukirchen–Vluyn: Neukirchener Verlag, 1964).

4. Most famous is G. von Rad's theory of Deuteronomy's origin in the preaching of northern Levites (*Studies in Deuteronomy* [trans. D. Stalker; SBT, 9; London: SCM Press, 1953]). M. Weinfeld has argued that the book reflects the didactic rhetoric of the sages and their wisdom literature (*Deuteronomy and the Deuteronomic School* [Oxford: Oxford University Press, 1972], pp. 51-58, 171-78).

5. E.g. von Rad, *Studies in Deuteronomy*, pp. 25-36; H. Graf Reventlow, *Das Heiligkeitsgesetz formgeschichtlich untersucht* (WMANT, 6; Neukirchen–Vluyn: Neukirchener Verlag, 1961).

Deuteronomy, but not to the Pentateuchal law codes.[6]

One particular phase of study drew on the similarities between Hittite suzerainty treaties and the Sinai covenant to emphasize the role of covenant renewal ceremonies.[7] Instances of public readings of law were taken as allusions to such ceremonies. Recent decades have brought challenges to the historicity of the covenant renewal ceremonies and the antiquity of the idea of covenant itself.[8] This debate nevertheless shows that historical introductions to law codes and conclusions consisting of blessings and curses reflect the *rhetorical* nature of the compositions.[9] Deuteronomy makes this explicit by placing the whole complex of historical recital, exhortation, law, blessings and curses into Moses' farewell speech on the plains of Moab. But any public reading of law needs some sort of rhetorical introduction and conclusion.[10] In Israel that was likely to take the form of narrative, in fact of a particular narrative, because of the consistent association of law with the revelation at Sinai. Whatever the influence of suzerainty treaties, then, Mendenhall was right to claim that 'what we now call "history" and "law" were bound into an organic unit'.[11]

6.   Y. Gitay, *Prophecy and Persuasion: A Study of Isaiah 40–48* (Bonn: Linguistica Biblica, 1981); T.A. Lenchak, *Choose Life! A Rhetorical-Critical Investigation of Deuteronomy 28, 69-30, 20* (AnBib, 129; Rome: Biblical Institute, 1993).

7.   G.E. Mendenhall, 'Covenant Forms in Israelite Tradition', in E.F. Campbell, Jr, and D.N. Freedman (eds.), *Biblical Archeologist Review 3* (Garden City, NY: Doubleday, 1970), pp. 25-53.

8.   For a survey of research, see E.W. Nicholson, 'Covenant in a Century of Study since Wellhausen', *OTS* 24 (1986), pp. 54-69.

9.   Other rhetorical models besides suzerainty treaties have been proposed for this combination. C.M. Carmichael pointed out Deuteronomy's affinities with the Wisdom genres of 'instruction' and the farewell speech, both of which take the rhetorical form of a father addressing his children. This model has a set structure: 'reflections on the past lead to predictions and directions for the future' (*The Laws of Deuteronomy* [Ithaca, NY: Cornell University Press, 1974], p. 25).

10.   Indeed, such frameworks appear in many third and early second millennium law codes of the ancient Near East, though there is far less evidence for how they were meant to be read, or even their purposes, than is the case for Israel's law. Later Mesopotamian and Hittite codes lack introductory and concluding frameworks. See Paul, *Book of the Covenant*, pp. 10, 11 n. 5.

11.   Mendenhall, 'Covenant Forms', p. 45. His concluding phrase 'from the very beginnings of Israel itself' is more debatable because the antiquity of both narratives and laws is open to question.

Rhetorical study in the broad sense has concentrated on narrative and prophetic texts, and is for the most part indistinguishable from synchronic literary criticism.[12] Such methods have also, occasionally, been applied to the Hebrew Bible's legal texts, either as part of synchronic readings of the Pentateuch as a whole or through detailed literary study of particular collections of laws.[13] Synchronic studies argue that the laws are integrated components of the literary structure of the Pentateuch.

Form-critical studies have taken seriously the differences between the genres and rhetorical impact of law and of narrative, and as a result have treated them separately. Literary studies have taken seriously the common setting of laws and narratives in the same texts, and in the process have tended to blur the differences between them. Methods of analysis that recognize both the rhetorical distinctiveness of law and narrative and the rhetorical impact of their combination have so far been rare in biblical studies.[14]

12. J. Muilenburg advocated the application of rhetorical criticism to the historical and comparative study of the Hebrew Bible as a methodological complement to source and form studies ('Form Criticism and Beyond', *JBL* 88 [1969], pp. 1-18, repr. in P.R. House [ed.], *Beyond Form Criticism: Essays in Old Testament Literary Criticism* [Winona Lake, IN: Eisenbrauns, 1992], pp. 49-69). His successors have tended to limit the method to synchronic literary analysis (for a survey of developments, see T.B. Dozeman, 'OT Rhetorical Criticism', *ABD*, V, pp. 712-15). The present study addresses rhetoric not because of any prior methodological commitments but rather out of recognition of the intrinsically rhetorical nature of public law readings in ancient Israel.

13. In the former category are Mann, *Book of the Torah*; Sailhamer, *Pentateuch as Narrative*; T.E. Fretheim, *The Pentateuch* (Nashville: Abingdon Press, 1996), who calls attention to the Pentateuch's 'rhetorical strategies'. Also to be included here are literary arguments for the authorial unity of the Pentateuch, such as that by H.D. Bracker, *Das Gesetz Israels* (Hamburg, 1962). An example of the latter approach is found in Sprinkle, *'Book of the Covenant'*. Surveys of the uses of 'rhetorical criticism' in biblical studies are provided by M. Kessler, 'A Methodological Setting for Rhetorical Criticism', in D.J.A. Clines, D.M. Gunn and A.J. Hauser (eds.), *Art and Meaning: Rhetoric in Biblical Literature* (JSOTSup, 19; Sheffield: JSOT Press, 1982), pp. 1-19; by W. Wuellner, 'Rhetorical Criticism in Biblical Studies', published on the World Wide Web at: http://158.182.34.202/ ALLIANCE/JD/JD4/2.WUELLNERtxt; and by D.M. Howard, Jr, 'Rhetorical Criticism in Old Testament Studies', *BBR* 4 (1994), pp. 87-104, who called for more attention to the persuasive aspects of biblical rhetoric.

14. An exception is M. Fishbane's study of legal and narrative interpretation

2. *The Rhetoric of Story, List and Divine Sanction*

Classical rhetorical theory has contributed a great deal to the study of the literature of early Judaism and Christianity in the Hellenistic and Roman periods. Its application, however, to the pre-Hellenistic litera- ture of the Hebrew Bible and ancient Near East has been far more lim- ited, probably due to the lack, in Dale Patrick and Allen Scult's words, of a 'manifestly rhetorical culture from which the Hebrews could have borrowed the idea of artfully casting their religious texts as persuasive discourse'.[15]

At this point, another definition of 'rhetoric' confuses the issue, namely rhetoric as the *theory* of persuasive speech. There is no evi- dence of the existence of traditions of rhetorical theory prior to their development in Athens in the fifth and fourth centuries BCE. In the sense of rhetoric as rhetorical theory, there are no 'manifestly rhetorical cultures' in the pre-Hellenistic periods. That observation, however, says nothing about the *practice* of rhetoric, either narrowly defined as per- suasive speech or broadly defined as the literary forms of persuasion, in the cultures and texts of the ancient Near East. In fact, the extant litera- tures of pre-Hellenistic Near Eastern cultures show pervasive signs of the practice of oral and written persuasion, such as the admonitions of wise sages, the propaganda of kings, and the warnings and threats of priests and prophets. Indeed, it is difficult to imagine any human culture in which rhetoric does not play a crucial role, though the degree to

which at one point led him to comment on 'rhetorical strategy': 'For by contrast with its *traditum*, an aggadic *traditio* often proceeds with different goals of com- munication, with different methods of communication, and with different assump- tions about what is in fact communicated. Moreover, these two triadic series—of literary style, form and context, and of rhetorical goal, method, and assumption— are not static and unrelated elements of an abstract analysis. Indeed, they dynami- cally interpenetrate with every occurrence of the fundamental formal triad—a *traditum*, its aggadic *traditio*, and the real or intended situation-audience. For what is fixed and received in the *traditum*, and fluid and receptive in the situation- audience, is connected and mediated by the *traditio—which uses literary means for rhetorical effect*. Thus, in the process and event of *traditio* the literary, rhetorical and historical-situational components of aggadic exegesis come together, and the contents of the literary and rhetorical triads outlined above interfuse' (*Biblical Interpretation in Ancient Israel* [Oxford: Clarendon Press, 1985], pp. 417-18, Fishbane's emphases).

15. Patrick and Scult, *Rhetoric*, p. 30.

which it is self-consciously acknowledged may vary a great deal from one place and time to another.[16]

Rhetorical theory, then, may be applied to pre-Hellenistic literature in one way, but not in another. In so far as it speaks of general and universal characteristics of oral and literary persuasion, rhetorical theory addresses ancient Near Eastern texts as much as any others. But in so far as it speaks of the self-conscious use of theories about rhetoric, its application must be limited to the texts of cultures in which traditions of rhetorical theory are plainly present.

Does rhetorical theory provide insight into the general issue of how narrative and law interact for purposes of persuasion? As it happens, classical and modern rhetorical theory has been quite concerned with the combination and relative merits of narrative and non-narrative modes of persuasion.

Theories of List and Story

Theorists of rhetoric have argued since classical times over the use of narrative as a persuasive strategy, with story usually being subordinated to more analytical modes of argumentation. J.D. O'Banion chronicled the debate over the rhetorical use of narrative from classical to modern theory. He blamed Aristotle for the de-emphasis on narration in Western thought in general and in rhetorical theory in particular:

> Since to him the essence of an argument was 'to state a case and to prove it', Aristotle accordingly considered narratio and all 'introductory' matters to be 'superfluous' or for 'weak' audiences (*Rhetoric* 3.13-14). ...Such concerns were unfortunate tasks preliminary to proceeding with what, at least to him, really mattered—the reasons and the evidence.[17]

The importance of narrative was re-established by the Roman orators, Cicero and Quintilian, who argued that the narrative of events was essential to establishing one's case. O'Banion summarized, '[Aristotle] did not see, or explicitly state, what Cicero and Quintilian were later to argue for—the extent to which narratio, together with enthymemic proof, comprise the dialectical "soul" of a speech'.[18] O'Banion

16. For discussions of classical theory as descriptive of universal and especially biblical rhetorical phenomena, see G.A. Kennedy, *New Testament Interpretation Through Rhetorical Criticism* (Chapel Hill: University of North Carolina Press, 1984), pp. 10-12; Lenchak, *'Choose Life!'*, pp. 72-77.

17. J.D. O'Banion, *Reorienting Rhetoric: The Dialectic of List and Story* (University Park, PA: Pennsylvania State University Press, 1992), p. 52.

18. *Reorienting Rhetoric*, p. 54

supposed that narration required more discussion by the Romans because, in the increasingly literate culture, storytelling capacity could no longer be taken for granted.[19]

> The Romans…developed 'the method of *mythos*' as a counterpoint to 'the method of *logos*'. They made explicit the dialectic that was, in Greek rhetoric, used but not explicitly recognized. To be more precise, Cicero developed the method of mythos giving new significance to nar-ratio, and Quintilian recognized that the arts of mythos and logos consti-tute a dialectic.[20]

O'Banion demonstrated, however, that the influence of Aristotle per-sisted in Western culture, with the result that the narrative methods of argumentation were disassociated from the analytical methods of reason and proof, and usually isolated within the separate discipline of literary theory. (Because biblical criticism compares more closely to literary theory than to philosophical logic, the valuation of list over story which O'Banion deplored has been reversed in Pentateuchal studies: the stories have received more attention and interest than the lists. Though characteristic of much modern criticism, this tendency is naturally most obvious when literary critics discuss the Pentateuch. J.C. Powy's remark exemplifies this dismissive attitude towards lists: 'Exodus, Leviticus, Numbers, and Deuteronomy…are by far the least inspiring and the least interesting books in the whole Bible.')[21]

O'Banion championed the case for the dialectic of narrative and logic against the prevalent presuppositions of modern rhetorical theory. Drawing heavily on the works of K. Burke, he argued that logic is but one manifestation of the *list*, which 'underlies all modes of systematic expression'.[22]

> Rendered as tallies, recordings of the movements of the stars, word lists, dictionaries, or codified laws, the list is a powerful tool for arranging and disseminating isolated pieces of information. It also comes to arrange and, to a considerable degree, dictate the nature of the lives of those who are affected by lists.[23]

But the list is not self-explanatory. It requires justification and explana-

19. *Reorienting Rhetoric*, p. 59.
20. *Reorienting Rhetoric*, p. 96.
21. *Enjoyment of Literature* (New York: Simon & Schuster, 1938), p. 16.
22. *Reorienting Rhetoric*, p. xiv.
23. *Reorienting Rhetoric*, p. 12. Cf. the narrower definition of list employed by B.E. Scolnic, *Theme and Context in Biblical Lists* (Atlanta: Scholars Press, 1995).

tion from narrative. 'With the additional perspective of narration, one is able to comprehend not only any items listed but also possible reasons for and implications of a list's very existence.'[24] The list, in other words, requires the context of a story in order to be convincing. Stories also requires lists, as Patrick and Scult noted:

> It is, from this [rhetorical] perspective, impossible for a 'narrative' to 'stand alone' as it may in literature or drama. All rhetorical narratives necessarily require interpretation and are incomplete until arguments and proofs are marshalled to advise readers and audience members what it is they must do or believe as a result of the story they have heard. If there appears to be a naked narrative, we should understand that arguments, proofs, and actions are implicit, for narratives either recommend and promote or condemn and repress the action they portray.[25]

Persuasion depends on the combination of list and story.[26]

O'Banion's argument was prescriptive in nature, wishing to correct the disjunction in Western culture between oral thought, as exemplified by narrative, and literate thought, exemplified by lists.[27] From the perspective of the study of ancient literature, it seems doubtful that narratives are intrinsically any more 'oral' in origin than are lists.[28] The

24. *Reorienting Rhetoric*, p. 13. Burke distinguished 'dialectical order' which emphasizes the conflict of opinions from 'ultimate order' which creatively creates a progression of ideas (*Rhetoric of Motives*, pp. 183-97). The latter has 'the rhetorical advantage of an ultimate vocabulary as contrasted with a vocabulary left on the level of parliamentary conflict... Perhaps the "ultimate" order comes most natural to narrative forms' (p. 197).

25. Patrick and Scult, *Rhetoric*, pp. 113-14.

26. O'Banion, *Reorienting Rhetoric*, p. 19. R.M. Cover described the interdependence of list and story from the perspective of legal theory: 'No set of legal institutions or prescriptions exists apart from the narratives that locate it and give it meaning. For every constitution there is an epic, for each decalogue a scripture. Once understood in the context of the narratives that give it meaning, law becomes not merely a system of rules to be observed, but a world in which we live. In this normative world, law and narrative are inseparably related. Every prescription is insistent in its demand to be located in discourse—to be supplied with history and destiny, beginning and end, explanation and purpose. And every narrative is insistent in its demand for its prescriptive point, its moral' ('Foreword: *Nomos* and Narrative', *Harvard Law Review* 97.1 [1983], pp. 4-68 [4-5]).

27. O'Banion, *Reorienting Rhetoric*, p. xiv.

28. In making these distinctions, O'Banion depended on literacy studies by classicists and anthropologists which are increasingly being questioned within those fields. For a re-examination of the impact of literacy on ancient Greek culture

validity, however, of O'Banion's prescriptive agenda is irrelevant for understanding the rhetorical function of biblical law, and its evaluation can safely be left to others. For present purposes, certain *descriptive* aspects of O'Banion's rhetorical theory are most applicable.

O'Banion, following Cicero and Quintilian, defends the necessity of narrative in part because story is already juxtaposed with list in many speeches and texts. This juxtaposition is characteristic not only of the legal speeches with which the Romans were most concerned, but also of other kinds of persuasive texts from ancient Near Eastern and Mediterranean cultures. Thus the rhetorical theory espoused by O'Banion and his Roman predecessors describes and explains a prominent feature of ancient literary traditions. It also explains why the juxtaposition of law and narrative, list and story has been met with consternation by Western interpreters trained by Aristotelian rhetoric to separate one from the other, a tendency amply attested in modern Pentateuchal studies, among other disciplines. It is this descriptive and explanatory aspect of O'Banion's rhetorical theory which applies most readily to Pentateuchal law and narrative.

Story and List in Ancient Literature

O'Banion and other proponents of story as essential to list point out a frequent feature of ancient rhetoric and of persuasive texts: the juxtaposition of historiography or story or account of origins with lists of instructions, stipulations or laws. Story and list are combined, not just in one particular genre or one literary tradition, but in a variety of genres from many different cultures. The combination is so prevalent because it contains a basic rhetorical strategy aimed at persuasion. The theoretical insight of the Roman orators, Cicero and Quintilian, that argument requires both narrative and analytic elements, describes much older rhetorical practices.

Well-known examples of the combination are found in Hittite treaties of the late second millennium BCE. Historical prologues emphasizing the 'benevolence' of the overlord towards the vassal usually precede the lists of stipulations to which the vassal is bound.[29] The history-stipulation sequence of the treaties functions rhetorically to remind

---

that suggests very subtle interactions between culture and literacy which defy broad generalizations, see Thomas, *Literacy and Orality*.

29. On the structure of Hittite and other ancient treaties, see McCarthy, *Treaty and Covenant*.

vassals of the past situation (whether military, legal or personal) and persuade them to remain loyal to their overlord by fulfilling the treaty's stipulations. The obviously one-sided accounts of the overlord's benevolence, which frequently in suzerainty treaties means that the overlord's threat of military attack has not (yet) been put into action, underscores the rhetorical force of the documents. By citing the overlord's benevolent past actions, they implicitly promise continued favor if the vassal upholds the treaty stipulations, but punishment if not, and thereby intend to motivate the former actions and dissuade the latter.[30]

Narrative frameworks also encase early second millennium BCE law codes from Mesopotamia, such as those of Lipit Ishtar and Hammurabi, and emphasize the king's accomplishments, justice, and religiously sanctioned authority.[31] Though one might expect their rhetorical force to be directed at the enforcement of the laws, their effect actually seems aimed in a quite different direction, as S.M. Paul noted: 'The prologue

30. 'The history, then, is no objective recounting of what has happened. It has strong paranetic interests. It exhorts rather than merely informs...this hortatory tendency extends into the expression of the terms' (McCarthy, *Treaty and Covenant*, p. 53).

31. See Roth, *Law Collections*; *ANET*, pp. 159-80. S.M. Paul described the development of this literary form: 'The prologue and epilogue represent the literary framework which encases the body of the legislation. This tripartite division is a traditional one, first occurring in the reforms of Urukagina and Gudea, and found later in legal collections, treaties, and even in late historical prisms' (*Book of the Covenant*, p. 10). V.A. Hurowitz has challenged this tripartite analysis of Hammurabi's Code, arguing instead for a command–fulfillment pattern that combines the laws with other elements to describe the king's fulfillment of a divine commission. Hurowitz nevertheless noted that 'The bilateral structure of Codex Hammurabi places the "Piety Register", which describes the king's religious achievements, as a counterbalance to the laws which illustrate Hammurabi's secular accomplishments. This structure along with the series of titles just mentioned show that in portraying the king for gods and posterity, divine service and social service were considered on an equal par' (*Inu Anum Sirum: Literary Structure in the Non-Juridical Sections of Codex Hammurabi* [Occasional Publications of the Samuel Noah Kramer Fund, 15; Philadelphia, 1994], p. 61; cf. 52-60). The combination of historiographic narrative with law for the purpose of characterizing the king appears also in medieval English legal manuscripts (M.P. Richards, 'The Manuscript Contexts of the Old English Laws: Tradition and Innovation', in P.E. Szarmach [ed.], *Studies in Earlier Old English Prose* [Albany, NY: SUNY Press, 1986], pp. 171-92 [173, 187]). This medieval practice, of course, may well have been influenced by the example of narratively inset biblical law.

and epilogue of [the laws of Hammurabi] may be understood as one grand auto-panegyric to bring the attention of that deity to bear upon the deeds and accomplishments of the king.'[32] He concluded that such religious self-characterization was the primary purpose of the law codes themselves.

In a wide variety of ancient cultures, commemorative inscriptions often use the rhetoric of story and list to persuade readers not to destroy the king's accomplishments, including the inscription itself. Thus the king of Akkad, Naram-Sin (twenty-third century BCE), celebrated his victories with a third-person battle narrative followed by a first-person command not to deface the stela.[33] A millennium later, Kurigalzu of Babylon claimed credit for building temples and guaranteeing their cult, then listed the lands and supplies for the Ishtar temple, followed by an account of granting the lands to that temple.[34] A monument, a royal letter and the 'Marduk Prophecy', all apparently from the reign of Nebuchadnezzar I of Babylon (1124–1103 BCE), follow narratives of war or travels with grants of land (the monument), commands to restore a temple (the letter) or lists of supplies for sacrifices (the 'Marduk Prophecy').[35]

Similar literary patterns appear in some Egyptian, Phoenician and Greek commemorative inscriptions. As in the cuneiform texts, these texts claim authority over the reader's performance of the mandated duties. An inscription of Seti I (c. 1300 BCE, Egyptian Nineteenth Dynasty) at Wadi Mia commemorates the digging of a well for gold-miners, offers a prayer of dedication, then records Seti's decree of a perpetual endowment for goldwashers to bring gold to his temple at Abydos.[36] The Naucratis Stela of Nectanebo I (378–360 BCE, Thirtieth Dynasty) consists of praise of the king, including narration of the goddess's support, and a list of his godly attributes, followed by an account and quotation of the royal decree granting a tithe of the Naucratis port

32. *Book of the Covenant*, p. 23; see also p. 26.

33. B.R. Foster, *Before the Muses: An Anthology of Akkadian Literature* (2 vols.; Bethesda, MD: CDL, 1993), I, pp. 52-53.

34. Foster, *Before the Muses*, I, pp. 278-79.

35. Foster, *Before the Muses*, I, pp. 297-98, 302, 304-306.

36. M. Lichtheim, *Ancient Egyptian Literature* (3 vols.; Berkeley: University of California Press, 1973, 1976, 1980), II, pp. 53-56, who noted that Seti's son, Ramses, in fact completed the temple and the endowment and commemorated that fact with an inscription at Abydos (p. 52).

taxes to the temple.[37] The Famine Stela of Sehel Island (Ptolomaic era, though attributed to Djoser of the Third Dynasty) tells the story of a famine alleviated by the god Khnum and then records the donation in perpetuity of land, personnel and supplies to the temple of Khnum on Elephantine Island.[38]

The Karatepe inscription of Azitawadda of the Phoenician city of Adana (early first millennium BCE) rehearses at length the king's accomplishments which include defense of the borders, suppression of outlaws, the building of 'this' city and the establishment in it of a Baal cult, and then describes a brief cult calendar: 'A sacrific(ial order) was established for all the molten images: for the yearly sacrifice an ox, at the [time of pl]owing a sheep, and at the time of harvesting a sheep.'[39] Azitawadda thus describes himself as the founder of city and cult, and obliges the town's citizens to support the cult which is described by the list of regular sacrifices.[40]

Another example, a fifth or fourth century BCE Greek dedicatory inscription found in Sardis in Asia Minor, demonstrates the influence of cultic instructions grounded in the story of a cult's establishment. The text records the erection of a statue of Zeus by Droaphernes, Persian hyparch in Lydia, and his command prohibiting this temple's priests from participating in the 'mysteries' of other local deities. The inscription's purpose, however, was not to commemorate the cult's founding but rather, as the final statement makes clear, to record the stipulation's fulfillment by one Dorates.[41] Though this text only alludes to the story of the cult's establishment rather than narrating it, it shows the persuasive effects on Dorates of an antecedent rhetoric of list and story.

Epic poems may also make use of the rhetoric of story and list for persuasion. The last one-and-a-half tablets (out of a total of seven) of

37. Lichtheim, *Ancient Egyptian Literature*, III, pp. 86-89.

38. Lichtheim, *Ancient Egyptian Literature*, III, pp. 94-100.

39. *ANET*, pp. 653-54.

40. The curses which conclude the inscription do not mention failure to maintain the sacrificial order, concentrating instead on future mutilation of Azitawadda's commemorative gate (*ANET*, p. 654, which therefore classifies this as a building inscription). Thus his rhetoric does not aim narrowly at the cult calendar, but more generally at the preservation of all of his accomplishments in the city, both architectural and cultic.

41. P. Frei, 'Zentralgewalt und Lokalautonomie im Achämenidenreich', in *Reichsidee und Reichsorganisation im Perserreich* (OBO, 55; Freiburg: Universitätsverlag, 2nd edn, 1996), pp. 8-131 (24-25, 90-96; Greek text on p. 24 n. 47).

Enuma Elish, the Babylonian creation epic, are devoted to the recitation and explanation of the 50 names of the god Marduk, a list derived from older traditions.[42] The epic *Anzu* ends similarly with a much shorter list of the names of Ninurta.[43] Both texts advance propagandistic purposes in the guise of celebrating the Babylonian and Assyrian national gods respectively and, in their focus on the necessity of absolute power, may aim to encourage obedience to the monarch.[44]

My point is not to argue for a necessary connection between story and list in these or any other ancient genres. Treaties may lack historical prologues,[45] many Akkadian law codes do not use narrative frames,[46] building inscriptions usually lack any stipulations or instructions,[47] inscriptions of cultic instructions may merely allude to the conditions of their establishment,[48] and epics are more likely to end with hymns than lists.[49] Rather, the above examples illustrate the persuasive force of story and list when used in combination and therefore point to the rhetorical purpose behind that combination when it does occur.

This emphasis on rhetorical strategy distinguishes my thesis from

42. Foster, *Before the Muses*, I, pp. 389-401; on the traditional nature of the 50 names, see p. 24.

43. Foster, *Before the Muses*, I, pp. 462, 483-84.

44. Foster, *Before the Muses*, I, p. 351.

45. McCarthy summarized his comparative survey of treaties: 'Thus the historical section is almost confined to the Hittite treaties, while a great emphasis on curses and the use of substitution rites characterize the treaties from Assyria and Syria' (*Treaty and Covenant*, p. 141).

46. This pattern does not appear in Middle Assyrian, Hittite or Neo-Babylonian legal collections (Paul, *Book of the Covenant*, p. 11 n. 5), and the Laws of Eshnunna, nearly contemporary with Hammurabi's, begin with only a date formula (Roth, *Law Collections*, pp. 57-59).

47. E.g. the inscriptions of Kilamuwa, Zakir and Yehawmilk (*ANET*, pp. 653-56), to mention only a few.

48. E.g. the Greek portion of the Letoon inscription of 358 or 337 BCE and the Punic tariffs found at Marseilles and Carthage begin by simply listing those who decided on the cult and/or its rules. For the former, see H. Metzger, 'L'inscription grecque', in H. Metzger (ed.), *Fouilles de Xanthos. VI. La stèle trilingue du Létôon* (Paris: Librairie C. Klincksieck, 1979), pp. 29-48 [32-33]; cf. A. Dupont-Sommer, 'L'inscription araméenne', in Metzger (ed.), *Fouilles de Xanthos*, pp. 136-37, and Frei, 'Zentralgewalt', pp. 12-13 and n. 13; for the latter, *ANET*, pp. 656-57.

49. J.W. Watts, *Psalm and Story: Inset Hymns in Hebrew Narrative* (JSOTSup, 139; Sheffield: JSOT Press, 1992), pp. 208-209, 212, 214.

attempts to establish the genre of the Pentateuch or its component parts on the basis of similar literary patterns in other ancient Near Eastern texts (such as Hittite treaties).[50] The combination of story and list appears too widely and too unpredictably to be regarded as a distinguishing feature of a particular genre (though in Israel's culture it did become a typical feature of Torah). It should rather be regarded as a strategy of persuasion employed by many cultures in a variety of literary genres for the purpose of convincing readers and hearers of the document's, and its author's, authority. The combination of story and list can serve as evidence neither of literary dependence nor of a document's date of composition. Instead, it indicates the rhetorical setting of the literature and the persuasive goals motivating its composition.

Persuasion depends, according to O'Banion and his Roman predecessors, on the correlation of the desired result with the narrative of its origins, of the proof with the statement of the case, of the list with the story. The story alone may inspire, but to no explicit end. The list alone specifies the desired actions or beliefs, but may not inspire them. It is the combination of both together which maximizes the persuasive effect of a speech or text. The texts reviewed above suggest that this practical insight shaped the composition of at least some persuasive rhetoric long before the classical theorists analyzed its nature.

The Rhetoric of Divine Sanction
In many of the above examples of persuasive texts, there is another common element besides list and story: divine enforcement is invoked through blessings and curses. Ancient texts frequently invoke the power of religion to strengthen their persuasive appeal, a rhetorical device of which the classical theorists disapproved.

Treaties typically conclude by both invoking deities as witnesses and by pronouncing blessings on those who keep the treaty's stipulations, and curses on those who do not. The blessings and curses are relatively brief in the Hittite documents, but the curses become longer and more elaborate in the Assyrian treaties of the eighth to seventh centuries

---

50. As propounded most famously by G.E. Mendenhall and elaborated by many others. See Mendenhall, 'Covenant Forms'; M.G. Kline, *Treaty of the Great King: The Covenant Structure of Deuteronomy* (Grand Rapids: Eerdmans, 1963); McCarthy, *Treaty and Covenant*; Weinfeld, *Deuteronomy and the Deuteronomic School*. For a critical survey of the issue, see Nicholson, 'Covenant'.

BCE.[51] Hammurabi's laws conclude with a long string of blessings and curses.[52] Greek laws, inscribed in the vicinity of temples to emphasize the deity's authorization of the law, threaten divine enforcement with curses.[53]

Ancient commemorative inscriptions regularly curse those who might in the future disturb the architectural or inscriptional achievements of their writer. Naram-Sin curses anyone who defaces his stela, and Kurigalzu curses those who alter his grants of land and offerings.[54] Seti I blesses future rulers and officials who honor his decree, and curses those who do not, while the second to the last sentence of the Famine Stela contains a single curse on 'him who spits (on the tablet) deceitfully'.[55] Azitawadda concludes the Karatepe inscription with a typical juxtaposition of promise and threat depending on future treatment of his stela.[56] The trilingual Letoon inscription, which records the establishment in Asia Minor under Persian authority of a temple cult and its laws in the fourth century BCE, concludes with 8 lines of curses (out of a total of 27 lines in the Aramaic portion of the inscription).[57] Greek foundation ceremonies and their written memorials usually incorporated blessings and curses as a structural element.[58]

Even epics occasionally conclude with blessings on those who revere their contents or physical form, and curses on those who do not. *Enuma Elish* ends by promising prosperity and safety on those who study the

---

51. McCarthy, *Treaty and Covenant*, p. 121; Weinfeld, *Deuteronomy and the Deuteronomic School*, pp. 116-46.

52. Roth, *Law Collections*, pp. 135-40; *ANET*, pp. 178-80.

53. New legislation was particularly likely to invoke religious threats, according to Thomas: 'The monumental stone inscription was perhaps at first an attempt to give new political and procedural laws the weight and status—and, most important, divine protection—that was already accorded the unwritten laws' (*Literacy and Orality*, p. 72; see also pp. 145-46).

54. Foster, *Before the Muses*, I, pp. 53, 279. For a summary of typical formal elements in Akkadian inscriptions, see A.K. Grayson, 'Histories and Historians of the Ancient Near East: Assyria and Babylonia', *Or* 49 (1980), pp. 140-94 [151-54].

55. Lichtheim, *Ancient Egyptian Literature*, II, pp. 55-56; III, p. 100.

56. *ANET*, p. 654; cf. the concluding blessings and curses of other inscriptions on pp. 653-56.

57. Dupont-Sommer, 'L'inscription araméenne', pp. 136-37; Frei, 'Zentralgewalt', pp. 12-13 and n. 13.

58. Summarized by M. Weinfeld, *Deuteronomy 1–11* (AB, 5; New York: Doubleday, 1991), pp. 10-12.

50 names and revere Marduk.[59] The *Erra Epic* by Kabti-ilani-Marduk (eighth century BCE?) concludes with Erra's blessings on those 'who honor this poem', and one line of curse on 'the one who neglects it'.[60] Sanctions to defend a piece of literature appear occasionally in apocalyptic works of the Hellenistic era as well (see *1 En.* 104.10-13; Rev. 22.18-19). The Letter of Aristeas (310–311) depicts a ceremony invoking sanctions against those who might meddle with the Septuagint Greek translation of the Hebrew Bible.[61]

In the dialectic of story and list, blessings and curses may look like another form of list. Their rhetorical force, however, differs considerably from that produced by lists of laws, stipulations or instructions. The latter address beliefs and behavior, whereas appeals to divine authorizations and threats aim at motivation. The Hittite terminology for a treaty, 'binding and oath', shows that this distinction was recognized in antiquity.[62]

The persuasive intent behind such texts is undisguised in the blessings and curses. J. de Romilly surveyed classical theorists' misgivings about the rhetorical use of 'sacred magic'.[63] Her analysis paralleled in many respects O'Banion's description of their subordination of narrative to logic. From Isocrates and Aristotle in the fourth century on, theorists emphasized rationality as the key to saving rhetoric from

---

59. Foster, *Before the Muses*, I, p. 400.

60. Foster, *Before the Muses*, II, p. 804.

61. Aristeas 310-311; see *OTP*, II, p. 33.

62. 'This designation refers to the two most important constituent elements of the agreements: the stipulations ("binding"), and the curses and blessings ("oath") by which the contracting parties invoked the gods as witnesses and guarantors of these provisions' (G. Beckman, *Hittite Diplomatic Texts* [ed. H.A. Hoffner, Jr; WAW, 7; Atlanta: Scholars Press, 1996], p. 2).

63. J. de Romilly, *Magic and Rhetoric in Ancient Greece* (Cambridge, MA: Harvard University Press, 1975). She used the phrase 'sacred magic' to describe rites such as incantations, curses, etc. in cultures like pre-classical Greece which do not discriminate clearly between religion and magic (pp. 4-6). Curses, of course, form a widely attested inscriptional genre on their own, ranging from magical attacks on national enemies to personal vendettas (for Egyptian examples, see *ANET*, pp. 326-29; for Greco-Roman examples, see J.G. Gager [ed.], *Curse Tablets and Binding Spells from the Ancient World* [New York: Oxford University Press, 1992]; for Phoenician, Aramaic and Hebrew examples, see T.G. Crawford, *Blessing and Curse in Syro-Palestinian Inscriptions of the Iron Age* [New York: Peter Lang, 1992]).

being only a technique for manipulating emotions.[64] They felt that sacred magic, like narrative, threatens to overwhelm an audience's capacity to reason by arousing irrational and supernatural concerns.[65] The rhetorical power of sacred magic is thus evident in the writings of classical theorists, not from their use of it, but from the their antipathy towards it.[66]

So a full description of the rhetorical force of most of the above texts should emphasize three interdependent elements: story, list and divine sanction.

Conclusion

Classical rhetorical theory is valuable to the study of biblical and other ancient Near Eastern documents because it preserves an ancient perspective on the forms and uses of persuasion. The classical theorists presuppose various rhetorical practices and though they may evaluate many of them negatively, such as story and sacred magic, in doing so they preserve evidence for their existence and nature. The influence of the theorists' arguments on subsequent Western thought has blinded many moderns to how consequential these issues were in the ancient world, and have made pre-classical rhetorical forms appear inexplicable. From the ancient theorists' perspective, however, such forms were all too explicable—as attempts to pander to emotions and delude hearers and readers, thus endangering the body politic.

64. De Romilly, *Magic and Rhetoric*, pp. 70-75.

65. For Plato, sophistic rhetoric generated illusions just like magic, and his hatred of the former expressed itself in the terminology of the latter (e.g. *Euthydem.* 288b). This accusation of magical practices was a serious charge in fourth-century Greece, when activities associated with witchcraft, incantations and 'immoral cults' were prosecuted (de Romilly, *Magic and Rhetoric*, p. 27). Plato's views on the negative effects of magical curses appear in the *Rep.* 2.364b-c, and the *Laws* 11.933a (Gager, *Curse Tablets*, pp. 249-50).

66. The modern rhetorical critic, K. Burke, provided an analysis of magic as rhetoric (*Rhetoric of Motives*, pp. 40-43): 'Originally, the magical use of symbolism to affect natural processes by rituals and incantations was a mistaken transference of a proper linguistic function to an area for which it was not fit. The realistic use of addressed language to *induce action in people* became the magical use of addressed language to *induce motion in things*' (p. 42, Burke's emphases) and concluded 'now that we have confronted the term "magic" with the term "rhetoric," we'd say that one comes closer to the true state of affairs if one treats the socializing aspects of magic as a "primitive rhetoric" than if one sees modern rhetoric simply as a "survival of primitive magic"' (p. 43).

Their prescriptive agenda therefore preserves descriptive evidence of forms of ancient rhetoric that often combined narratives and divine sanctions with various kinds of lists. Sufficient examples of these combinations appear in ancient Near Eastern literature to demonstrate that such rhetorical forms were not unique to Hellenistic civilization but were known throughout the Mediterranean and Near Eastern world.

3. *Pentateuchal Rhetoric*

The Pentateuch presents laws in three separate collections. This triple depiction of law is evident in a literary survey and has been re-emphasized by historical research into the differences and relations between them. The story of covenant-making at Mt Sinai (Exod. 19–24) contains the Ten Commandments (Exod. 20.2-17) and a collection of laws usually termed the Book of the Covenant (Exod. 20.22–23.33).[67] Then follows, in the distinctive style of the priestly writer (P), three large sets of lists interwoven with narratives: instructions for constructing the Tabernacle (Exod. 25–31), cultic instructions and communal laws (Leviticus), and census and genealogical lists with instructions on organizing the Israelite camp and miscellaneous religious rules (Num. 1–9). The rest of the book of Numbers mixes legal rulings into its narratives at various points. The book of Deuteronomy then provides the third major legal collection (Deut. 12–26) as part of Moses' farewell speech to the Israelites before his death. Each of these presentations exhibits the characteristic features of ancient persuasive rhetoric surveyed above, namely the juxtaposition of story, list and divine sanction.

Sinai Covenant
Exodus 19–24 contains two collections of law. After arriving at Sinai, the people of Israel agree to a covenant with YHWH (Exod. 19). Then God gives the Ten Commandments (Exod. 20.1-17), and the frightened people ask Moses to mediate (vv. 18-21). Moses returns to the mountain to receive more extensive legal instructions, starting with ritual rules (20.22-26), then civil and criminal laws (21.1–23.19), and concluding with promises of divine support for Israel's invasion of Canaan (23.20-33). Moses ratifies the covenant, in the process of which he

---

67. The name derives from Exod. 24.7.

reports to the people the laws, then writes them down and reads aloud this 'book of the covenant' (24.1-11; see Chapter 1 above).

The rhetoric of persuasion structures Exodus's presentation of the Sinai covenant. Narrative introductions and conclusions emphasize speeches specifying YHWH's past benevolence towards Israel (19.4-6) and the people's repeated agreement to the covenant's obligations (19.8; 24.7), while a narrative interlude points out that Moses' role as mediator and hence his authority as law-giver comes at the people's request (20.18-20). These stories serve to (1) establish YHWH's legitimacy on the basis of past and present events, (2) ground Israel's legal obligations on communal self-committal, and (3) explain and authorize Moses' role as mediator on the basis of the people's request. Story thus legitimates the origins and the application to Israel of the lists of laws.[68]

68. Strong challenges to the presence of historical overviews in the Sinai pericope have been mounted by D.J. McCarthy and L. Perlitt, who argued that Exod. 19 emphasizes YHWH's present theophany, rather than God's past actions. McCarthy noted that the present form of Exod. 19–24 contains 'element[s] corresponding to prologue, stipulations, and blessing...but only remotely' (*Treaty and Covenant*, p. 245), and they are missing in earlier forms of the text entirely (p. 247; cf. Perlitt, *Bundestheologie im Alten Testament* [WMANT, 36; Neukirchen–Vluyn: Neukirchener Verlag, 1969], pp. 95, 164, 179).

Both McCarthy and Perlitt focused their attention on the origins of the treaty/covenant forms, and therefore paid little (McCarthy) or no (Perlitt) attention to the text as it stands. This produced some exaggerations, such as McCarthy's conclusion that 'the relation created by the appearance of the LORD (theophany) through the awe it inspires is what is important in J and E and the final text. The mere amount of space expended on its description is enough to establish this, and this is not the world of the treaties with their basis in forensic persuasion and oath' (*Treaty and Covenant*, p. 276). This comment overlooked the rather larger amount of space devoted to law in Exod. 19–24, which casts a heavy forensic tone on the whole. Perlitt argued that in P, the covenant represented not obligation, but pure promise (*Bundestheologie*, pp. 232-33), a conclusion which ignored the present text's combination of priestly and deuteronomistic understandings of covenant.

Methodological differences produce the contrast between my rhetorical analysis Exod. 19–24 and the compositional studies of McCarthy and Perlitt. First, the rhetorical strategy of story, list and sanction, as well as the covenant idea with which it often appears, may well be a late overlay to Exod. 19–24, absent from earlier versions of the Sinai story. My claim that the strategy structures the entire Pentateuch (below) supports its association with later layers of the Pentateuch's redaction. But this should not blind interpreters to its role in the present text. Second, the presence of the rhetorical strategy in a broad range of ancient Near Eastern and Mediterranean texts should act as a warning against comparing biblical

The laws specify the nature of Israel's obligations. The structures of both the Decalogue and the Book of the Covenant suggest that the thrust of these obligations is dual: religion and ethics. The Decalogue begins with religious requirements (Exod. 20.3-11), then turns to ethical obligations (vv. 12-17). Prohibitions of images and rules for altars similarly begin the Book of the Covenant (20.23-26), but ritual calendars also conclude its stipulations (23.10-17, with three ritual laws appended in vv. 18-19). In between come casuistic laws governing civil and criminal behavior, with only an occasional ritual stipulation mixed in (22.19, 27-30 [Eng. 22.20, 28-31]). The lists thus specify the implications of the story: the people of Israel have obligated themselves to an exclusive relationship with YHWH and to ethical dealings with each other and with strangers.

The concluding divine sanctions motivate the people's compliance with the covenant stipulations. Exod. 23.20-33 makes obedience to the messenger of YHWH a condition of Israel's success in conquering and settling the land of Canaan. Occasional threats (vv. 21, 33) do not disrupt the overall theme of promise in this exhortation. The fact that the object of obedience is YHWH's messenger, rather than the law as in Leviticus and Deuteronomy (see below), has occasioned theories of diachronic development in this text.[69] As the text stands, however, these promises contingent on obedience to YHWH refer to the previous and subsequent stories of deliverance, summed up in the figure of YHWH's messenger (cf. Exod. 14.19), and thus ground the promise of future success in the experience of past deliverance. Since the stories of past deliverance are used to legitimate the law (19.4-6), the effect is the

---

examples with too narrow a range of genres (such as Hittite treaties). The ancient parallels, like the biblical texts, show great varieties of formulation and genre. The rhetorical strategy was capable of many mutations which should not obscure the rhetorical impact of combining story, list and sanctions together.

69. G. Beer, *Exodus* (HAT, 3; Tübingen: J.C.B. Mohr [Paul Siebeck], 1939), p. 121; Noth, *Exodus*, p. 192; B.S. Childs, *The Book of Exodus: A Critical, Theological Commentary* (OTL; Philadelphia: Westminster Press, 1974), p. 486. McCarthy and Perlitt challenged the comparison of Exod. 23.20-33 with covenant sanctions, regarding them rather as part of the supplementary Book of the Covenant (McCarthy, *Treaty and Covenant*, p. 245; Perlitt, *Bundestheologie*, p. 165). The ancient parallels show, however, that the sanctions may play the same rhetorical role in law codes and various inscriptional genres as in treaties. The lack of an exact match to the treaties does not deprive Exod. 23.20-33 of its rhetorical force as sanctions.

same as if the promise was conditioned directly on obedience to the law: obedience to YHWH's messenger and obedience to YHWH's law (related through the mediator, Moses) are implicitly equated.[70] When read together, the divine sanctions join the stories and lists of laws in a rhetoric of persuasion to motivate assent and compliance.

Exodus 19–24 thus falls generally into the pattern observed in some other ancient texts of persuasion: stories introduce lists that conclude with divine sanctions. The major difference is that in Exodus, stories surround the lists and sanctions rather than just introducing them. Third-person narration encompasses the other genres which are cast as direct speech. This difference shows once again that the combination of story, list and divine sanction is not characteristic of any one genre or literary convention, but is rather a rhetorical strategy adapted to various ancient genres and literatures. Here, Israel's writers adapted this typical strategy to the conventions of Hebrew literature, which uses direct speech to incorporate inset genres within a narrative frame.[71] The rhetorical force of the combination of story with list and divine sanctions does not depend on any set structure or pattern of combination, but rather on the intrinsically persuasive power of these juxtaposed elements.

Levitical Law

The rhetorical context of the priestly legislation is more difficult to describe because the unit's literary boundaries are less obvious. Its usual delineation as Exodus 25 to Numbers 9 makes sense on grounds of style and content, but ignores the fact that this material shares the same temporal and physical setting as the preceding chapters. The priestly legislation continues the description of the Sinai event which begins in Exodus 19–24.[72] P's Sinai material in its present form seems

70. An old interpretive tradition has equated the מלאך 'messenger', not with an angel as usually translated, but with Moses. Childs summarized the arguments of Maimonides to this effect (*Guide for the Perplexed* 2.34; Childs, *Exodus*, p. 487). Most recent commentators, however, find the parallel usage of the phrase for a supernatural messenger in Exod. 32.34 and 33.2 too strong a precedent to deny that meaning in Exod. 23.

71. For the application of this convention to genres of inset poetry, see Watts, '"This Song"', pp. 345-58; *idem*, *Psalm and Story*.

72. As a result, the literary structure of these books lends itself to a variety of analyses. Cf., e.g., the description, which takes seriously the divisions between books, of Exod. 25–31 as the cultic laws matching the civil legislation in Exod. 21–

to have been shaped with the content of the entire Pentateuch in mind, so its rhetorical force depends more heavily on the wider context than is the case with either the earlier Exodus legislation or with Deuteronomy. Nevertheless, the following observations concentrate on the P material, leaving P's rhetorical role in the larger composition for the discussion of the whole Pentateuch's rhetoric below.

The dominant organizing principle in the priestly legislation is list, not story. Three kinds of lists follow each other in succession: instructions for building the Tabernacle (Exod. 25–31), continued and partially repeated by the listlike narrative of the fulfillment of these instructions (chs. 35–40); laws and regulations, which themselves divide into three literary blocks consisting of sacrificial regulations (Lev. 1–7), purity rules (Lev. 11–16), and laws of the holy community (Lev. 17–27); and census lists and rules for religious personnel (Num. 1–9). Two narrative complexes find places between sets of lists: the story of the golden calf and its consequences (Exod. 32–34, which itself incorporates another list, the 'ritual decalogue' of 34.10-26) appears between the building instructions and the account of their fulfillment (itself mostly narrative repetition of the earlier list of instructions), and the story of the inauguration of cultic worship in the Tabernacle (Lev. 8–10) sits between the sacrificial rules and the purity regulations. The third legal list in Leviticus, usually called the Holiness Code, concludes with divine sanctions in the traditional form of blessings promised to those who obey the laws and threats against those who do not (Lev. 26; ch. 27 seems to be an appendix of miscellaneous regulations).

The lists describe the ideal cult and ideal community; that is, they describe Israel as it should be. The whole complex of lists bifurcates into those pertaining to the cult, whose physical description (Exod. 25–31; 35–40) precedes the rules for its operation (Lev. 1–7), and those pertaining to the whole community, whose rules for operation (Lev. 11–27) precede its physical description (Num. 1–7).[73] The lists' rhetorical force derives from a constant focus on the ideal, that is, from the persuasive power of a vision of cult and people structured for communion with God. Among the lists, the laws of Leviticus distinguish

23 (so Mann, *Book of the Torah*, pp. 102-103) with the analysis, based on the stylistic distinctives of the priestly source, of Exod. 25–31 as the physical description of the cult matched, in Lev. 1–7, by the rules for its operation (so Blum, *Studien*, pp. 300-301).

73. Blum, *Studien*, p. 302.

themselves by their normative force: whereas the Tabernacle instructions and the census lists describe past achievements only, the laws and
ritual instructions bind readers to the task of maintaining the ritual cult
and community which were first created at Sinai. The laws thus hold
out to readers the hope of achieving the ideal in their own day. According to the lists of Leviticus, a well-ordered Temple service and holy
community remain the necessary and sufficient conditions for God's
presence in the midst of Israel.

Amid the lists' dominant rhetoric of ideals, interposed narratives
warn of dangers that threaten the divine–human communion. The story
of the golden calf (Exod. 32–34), placed between the Tabernacle's
building instructions and the account of their fulfillment, narrates the
subversion of Israel's cult into idolatry even before its institutions have
been constructed. The incident threatens the existence of the people as a
whole (Exod. 32.9-14) and the less dire outcome nevertheless emphasizes the close connection between ritual observances and Israel's
endurance as a people (e.g. in the 'ritual decalogue', 34.10-26). The
story of the cult's inauguration (Lev. 8–10), placed between sacrificial
regulations and the community's rules of purity, narrates the fulfillment
of the priestly ideal in the Tabernacle worship. The achievement is
authenticated by divine fire on the altar (9.24), and then is immediately
threatened by priestly malpractice and YHWH's fiery retribution (10.1-
3). Thus both sets of narratives emphasize that observant maintenance
of the cult preserves the people's standing before God, and thereby also
the community's social and political viability. Threats to this divine–
human communion, however, appear immediately and persistently, and
resistance requires the vigilance of priests and people alike (Exod.
34.11-16; Lev. 10.8-11).[74]

Divine sanctions play a major structural role at the end of Leviticus,
repeating the idealistic promise of the lists but emphasizing even more
the dangers highlighted by the narratives. Leviticus 26 specifies the
blessings resulting from observance of the commandments (vv. 3-13),
summing them up in the promise of God's dwelling with Israel (vv. 11-
12). But the curses resulting from disobedience receive more space and

74. J. Blenkinsopp noted that both Exod. 32–34 and Lev. 8–10 'follow the by
now well established pattern of a new beginning followed by a deviation' (*The
Pentateuch: An Introduction to the First Five Books of the Bible* [ABRL; New
York: Doubleday, 1992], p. 219).

chronicle the various disasters that can afflict individuals and nations, up to and including exile (vv. 14-39). Unlike the story of the golden calf, however, Leviticus 26 explicitly excludes the ultimate threat of nullifying Israel's covenant relationship with YHWH: repentance will always be met by God's mercy, even in exile (vv. 40-45). The blessings and curses that conclude Leviticus thus encapsulate the rhetoric of ideals and threats emphasized by the preceding lists and stories respectively, but end by synthesizing this dialectic into a vision of YHWH's eternal faithfulness to the covenant. As a result, the idealism of the priestly legislation becomes more than a statement of obligations enforced by threats; it unveils a vision of hope grounded in YHWH's covenant commitment to Israel.

The material from Exodus 25 through Numbers 9 thus uses the rhetoric of story and list to develop a dialectical tension between the idealistic vision of a divine–human communion and realistic warnings of its dissolution due to popular disobedience and official malpractice. The persuasive intent behind this pattern aims to inspire compliance with the legislative program by describing ideal communion with God and to discourage noncompliance by detailing past and future threats. The divine sanctions of Leviticus 26 combine both elements of the dialectic and transcends them with a wider promise of God's covenant faithfulness. The priestly writers and editors thus used the rhetoric of list, story and divine sanction to persuade their readers and hearers of both the serious consequences of human actions and the constancy of divine mercy.

Deuteronomy
The book of Deuteronomy presents the most obvious biblical example of the rhetorical use of story, list and divine sanction. Cast for the most part as a speech by Moses to the Israelites prior to his death, Deuteronomy is not only explicitly rhetorical (in the narrow definition of the term), it alone of the Pentateuchal books combines story, list and divine sanction in a single voice. Whereas previous texts reserved most narration and some non-legal lists (e.g. census information) for the anonymous third-person narrator while placing all laws and divine sanctions in direct speech, Moses' voice commands all the major genres of Deuteronomy. The interplay of the various rhetorical elements is therefore most apparent in this book, as is its evident structural similarity to

other ancient Near Eastern texts that employ the rhetoric of list, story and divine sanction.[75]

Moses' speech begins by recalling the events experienced by Israel in the wilderness and the exodus, interspersing exhortations to faithfulness to the law, which is summarized in various formulations including the Decalogue (Deut. 5.6-21), and foresees a future ceremony of blessings and curses (11.26-32). Laws and regulations follow (chs. 12–26), with religious regulations (chs. 12–16, 26) bracketing a core dominated by civil and criminal laws (chs. 17–25). Then curses on those who break the laws and blessings on those keeping them (chs. 27–28) anticipate again a future ceremony of covenant renewal when Israel has entered the land (27.2-12). The speech concludes finally in exhortations to faithfulness (chs. 29–30).

The rhetoric of persuasion is obvious throughout Deuteronomy. The mix of narrative and exhortation that begins and ends Moses' speech constantly grounds the people's present and future obedience in Israel's past experience, which illustrates not only YHWH's acts of mercy but also God's punishing judgments. The recital of past events thus anticipates the list of possible blessings and curses, so that the latter become a description of the entire speech: 'I set before you today a blessing and a curse' (11.26; cf. 30.15, 19). As in the past, so in the future, Israel holds the key to its own fortunes in its observance of the law.[76]

The lists of laws specify the obedient life in terms not only of ritual observances and of civil laws, but also in the regulation of institutions such as monarchy, temple and prophecy (12.1–13.5; 17.14-20; 18.15-22). Such rules seem less interested in the legal form of the institutions themselves than in their ability to model the obedience to the commandments mandated of all the people.[77] So the king's role is defined largely in terms of studying the law, and prophets are evaluated on their support for the law. Thus the laws themselves aim to persuade readers

---

75. E.g. McCarthy argued that Deuteronomy, but not the Sinai traditions of Exodus, exhibits the influence of the treaty genre (*Treaty and Covenant*, pp. 157-205, 243-76, 292).

76. For analyses of the introductory frame of Deuteronomy, see the commentaries and additionally A. Menes, *Die vorexilischen Gesetze Israels im Zusammenhang seiner kulturgeschichtlichen Entwicklung* (Giessen: Alfred Töpelmann, 1928), pp. 126-41, and Mann, *Book of the Torah*, pp. 147-52.

77. Note the utopian sense conveyed by Deut. 15.4: 'There shall be no poor among you' (Blenkinsopp, *Pentateuch*, p. 213).

and hearers to follow the whole law in general, as well as to teach specific provisions.

The blessings and curses conclude the speech by drawing the consequences of obedience and disobedience starkly, but the speech goes even further by institutionalizing their recital in a future ceremony at Shechem. Deuteronomy obliges Israel not only to legal obedience but also to repetition of the book's own rhetoric of persuasion through re-enactment, both by individuals (6.20-25; 17.18-20) and by the nation as a whole (11.29; 27.12; cf. 31.10-13). The choice between blessing and curse extends through time to the readers and hearers, whom Deuteronomy obliges to observe the covenant and to transmit the stories, laws and sanctions to present and future generations.

The rhetoric of Deuteronomy employs the elements of story, list and divine sanction more obviously than any other part of the Pentateuch, but it also integrates their effects more thoroughly.[78] Past and future mirror each other in the stories and blessings/curses, emphasizing the stark consequences confronting the people in every time and place. The laws specify the nature of obedience and disobedience, but also are concerned with how obedience must be modeled by religious and government leaders alike. The result of this unitary rhetoric is a document that drives home to readers and hearers the validity and urgency of the deuteronomic program.

The Pentateuch
The blocks of literary material discussed above are large and complex, and the rhetoric of story, list and divine sanction cannot do justice to all of their contents. All the more complicated is the larger body of literature in which they are placed. The Pentateuch's intricate structure, varieties of genres, and range of themes force any attempt at synthetic description to a high level of abstraction. Nevertheless, the overall shape of the Pentateuch betrays the now-familiar rhetoric of stories (Genesis through Exod. 19), lists (Exod. 20 through Numbers) and divine sanctions (Deuteronomy).

The employment of this rhetorical strategy appears most clearly at

---

78. As Mann concluded: 'The reciprocity of law and story is now transparent: obedience to law is rooted in the recital of and identification with a story, an identification that is vacuous without obedience to the law' (*Book of the Torah*, p. 151).

the end of the Pentateuch, in Deuteronomy. Despite its various materials, that book describes itself in the stark language of blessing and curse (Deut. 11.26; 30.19) and depicts its contents as Moses' hortatory recapitulation of earlier laws and experiences. Its emphasis in narration, sanctions, and even in some of the legal lists, falls on obedience to the law as a whole more than on the particulars of the legislation. Deuteronomy thus lends itself to the persuasive role of emphasizing the ultimate consequences of urgent choices, in other words, to the rhetoric of divine sanctions, of blessings and curses.

The shift from a preponderance of narrative to a preponderance of list in the middle of Exodus has long been noted by biblical interpreters.[79] Exodus, Leviticus and Numbers not only contain many lists; they also exemplify the rhetoric of list by specifying the nature of the ideal. Here universal principles are manifested by particular actions, and by requiring the latter, the lists point the people of Israel towards the former.[80] The rhetoric of list usually finds its justification in story, and the central books of the Pentateuch are no exception. Besides allusions to preceding narratives in scattered motive clauses (see Chapter 3 below), the lists interact with stories on a more fundamental level. For example, the construction of the Tabernacle, related in lists of instructions and listlike narratives of their fulfillment (Exod. 25–31; 35–40), depicts a re-creation of the world whose degradation the stories of Genesis have chronicled. The account concludes in Exodus 39–40 with language evocative of the first creation story in Genesis 1.[81] Specific stipulations, for example, regarding the Sabbath, the blood prohibition and Passover, echo themes already emphasized in narratives. The blessings promised to the obedient (especially Lev. 26.9-13) evoke earlier divine promises in the narratives (e.g. Exod. 6; Gen. 9; 17) that are now attainable to those who observe the law.[82] The lists of laws thus provide

79. Blenkinsopp estimated that, whereas lists (primarily genealogies) compose only 14% of Genesis, in the whole Pentateuch lists of various sorts occupy one-third more space than do stories (*Pentateuch*, p. 34).

80. For discussion of how the most specific rules may point to universal principles, see J. Milgrom, 'The Biblical Diet Laws as an Ethical System', *Int* 17 (1963), pp. 288-301.

81. J. Blenkinsopp, 'The Structure of P', *CBQ* 38 (1976), pp. 275-92 (280-83); *idem*, *Pentateuch*, p. 218; Blum, *Studien*, pp. 306-11; M.S. Smith, 'The Literary Arrangement of the Priestly Redaction of Exodus: A Preliminary Investigation', *CBQ* 58 (1996), pp. 25-50 (34-35 and the literature cited in n. 40).

82. Blum, *Studien*, pp. 325-29.

the solutions to problems and issues detailed by the narratives, which in turn demonstrate the necessity of the law.

Pentateuchal stories, especially those of Genesis, may seem to have the least connection to the rhetoric of story, list and divine sanction. Their structure and scope invites independent treatment from interpreters, and this they have usually received. The above observations, however, point to themes in the narratives that find their resolution only in the lists that follow: themes such as the degradation of creation, the nature of the divine–human relationship, and the identity of Israel as YHWH's people. Connections between stories and lists appear most noticeably in the material usually credited to P. Discussion of the levitical legislation above noted the unusual dialectic of list and story in Exodus 25 through Numbers 9. Within the larger context of the Pentateuch, however, this material takes its place as list in a more typical pattern of story, followed by list, concluding with divine sanctions. The close relationship between P's narratives and lists suggests that the priestly writers and editors worked with the larger context in mind and intentionally structured the whole to highlight levitical legislation as the central list in the Pentateuch's rhetoric.[83]

The resulting Pentateuch is a complex document, far removed in size and scope from the texts published through public law readings in Judah's late monarchic period. Yet its form shows that the rhetoric of story, list and divine sanction still shapes its priestly redaction, though now it is probably no longer the primary rhetoric of oral readings but rather the intermediate rhetoric of a literary genre shaped by oral conventions.[84] The goal, however, remains the same: to persuade hearers and readers to observe the law by describing its extraordinary origins in

83. This shaping of the whole Pentateuch was recognized by B.S. Childs: 'In a real sense, Genesis serves as a prologue and Deuteronomy as an epilogue to the canonical corpus, but the heart of Torah lies in its three central books' (*Biblical Theology of the Old and New Testaments* [Minneapolis: Fortress Press, 1992], p. 680). R.P. Knierim was more specific: 'The Sinai pericope aims at the book of Leviticus. This book is the center of the Pentateuch' (*The Task of Old Testament Theology: Method and Cases* [Grand Rapids: Eerdmans, 1995], p. 367). Blenkinsopp argued for the same conclusion on the basis of the fivefold division of the Pentateuch (*Pentateuch*, p. 47).

84. On the literary effect of the Pentateuch's adaptation and expansion of the ancient genres of treaty, law and grant, see J. Nohrnberg, *Like Unto Moses: The Constituting of an Interruption* (Bloomington: Indiana University Press, 1995), pp. 69-95.

a story stretching back to creation, by specifying the ideal divine–human relationship that it makes possible, and by promising great blessings and threatening worse curses contingent on the audience's response. The rhetoric of story, list and divine sanction unifies the Pentateuch for the overriding purpose of persuasion.

Conclusion

Greco-Roman theorists of rhetoric pointed out the persuasive force of story, list and divine sanction in combination and considered it dangerous. That practical insight, if not that evaluation, was shared by writers throughout the ancient world who on that basis structured inscriptions of various types to maximize their rhetorical power. In ancient Israel, where law was published through public readings of entire documents, the need to maximize the texts' persuasive force led writers to employ the same rhetorical strategy.[85] Thus law finds itself in the company of story and divine sanctions in almost all of Israel's extant legal traditions until the late first millennium BCE. As these traditions were combined into ever-larger blocks of material, the setting in public readings of whole documents may have become increasingly anachronistic. The resulting complex, the Pentateuch, is truly *sui generis*, without parallel in size, scale and contents in Israel's or any other culture's earlier or contemporary literature. Yet the rhetoric of story, list and divine sanction still shapes its maze of genres and traditions. The pre-eminent place and influence of the Pentateuch in all subsequent forms of Judaism shows the enduring power of that rhetorical strategy.

85. Patrick and Scult generalized the observation about the persuasive intent of law to the Bible in general: 'The words of the Bible were meant to persuade its audience to right action, or what the Biblical authors considered to be right action, and so it is the success of the text as persuasive discourse which is most likely to account for the power of these words to endure through time… The Bible assumes the narrative shape that it does, not because it is most beautiful or most truthful, but rather because this is the form that is most persuasive' (*Rhetoric*, p. 104; cf. Fretheim, *Pentateuch*, p. 40).

Chapter 3

INSTRUCTION

The rhetoric of persuasion not only shapes the large-scale structures of the Pentateuch, it also influences the wording of sentences within the legal collections. Persuasion cannot depend only on the hearers' or readers' ability to comprehend the shape of the whole.[1] The words must regularly remind the audience of the laws' importance and of reasons for observing them. They must take memorable forms and they must hold the audience's attention. Thus one would expect that the standards of legal writing and codification with which we are familiar in the modern world would not apply to legal collections governed by such a different rhetorical and literary setting. The tradition of reading law publicly would result in an emphasis on effective expression and mnemonics, in addition to rhetorical structure, in the composition of biblical law.[2]

The texts that describe public law readings emphasize instruction as much as persuasion. Nevertheless, interpreters have attempted to distinguish didactic from persuasive rhetoric in order to discover the nature of the groups that authored the legal collections. For example, G. von Rad argued that the hortatory addresses in Deuteronomy and the

1.   The distinction between hearers and readers, which has been so fruitful for studies of orality and literacy, is blurred by the practice of reading aloud for aural reception. Since Israel's legal texts and law-reading tradition do not differentiate between readers and hearers, I do not distinguish them either, regarding both as part of the text's 'audience'.

2.   Roman theorists classified rhetoric in four parts, three of which were structure and organization (*collocutio*), word choice and arrangement (*elocutio*), and mnemonics (*memoria*). In relation to Pentateuchal law, Chapter 2 above dealt with the first of these, while this chapter addresses the other two. The discussion here, however, is not directed or limited by the categorical divisions of classical rhetoric. For discussion of the classical divisions, see Kessler, 'Methodological Setting', p. 2.

Holiness Code (Lev. 17–27) revealed the material's origins in the preaching of the Levites.[3] M. Weinfeld and others have contended that the legal rhetoric is more didactic than sermonic and thus has more in common with wisdom than with priestly traditions.[4] The tradition of public law readings, however, suggests that ancient Israelite law emphasized persuasion *and* instruction. Both knowledge of the law and motivation to do the law are required to attain the goal of an obedient people of YHWH. The discovery that the Pentateuch uses a rhetorical strategy that combines and transcends particular genres (see Chapter 2) also supports the notion that the writers did not limit themselves to the linguistic forms of only one literary tradition.[5] Whatever the traditional origins of the language might have been, the extant collections of ancient Israel's laws aim both to instruct and to persuade, and use a variety of means to do both.

Several stylistic traits of biblical law seem intended to further its aural reception. Previous studies in Pentateuchal law have devoted considerable attention to two such devices: hortatory addresses and motive clauses. Other prominent features of the legal collections, such as repetition and variation, also make rhetorical sense as didactic devices.

1. *Address*

The most obvious hortatory feature of biblical law is its frequent 'apodictic' formulation as direct second-person address: 'you shall/you shall not'. Formulations of law addressed directly to 'you' dominate not only the various decalogues (Exod. 20.3-17/Deut. 5.7-21; Exod. 34.11-26) but also distinct sections of the major legal and instructional collections. In the Book of the Covenant, apodictic laws (Exod. 20.23-26; 22.21–23.19, usually second-person singular, but occasionally plural—

3. Von Rad, *Studies in Deuteronomy*, pp. 25-36, 60-69.
4. Weinfeld, *Deuteronomy and the Deuteronomic School*, pp. 51-58, 158-71, 177-78, 244-319; Carmichael, *Laws of Deuteronomy*, p. 25.
5. As H. Gese pointed out with particular reference to P: 'In Israel…wisdom thought and Torah traditions were merged to form theology' ('The Law', in *idem, Essays on Biblical Theology* [trans. K. Crim; Minneapolis: Augsburg, 1981], pp. 60-92 [76]). One of Weinfeld's arguments for Deuteronomy's origins in wisdom circles derived from the book's wide variety of component genres, which must have been authored by 'persons who had at their command a vast reservoir of literary material…' (*Deuteronomy and the Deuteronomic School*, pp. 177-78).

20.23; 22.20-21, 30 [Eng. 22.21-22, 31]) surround a central core of third-person casuistic ('if...then...') legislation.[6] The instructions for building the Tabernacle (Exod. 25–31) are addressed to Moses in the second-person singular, but conclude with the second-person plural Sabbath command addressed to the people (31.12-17). The sacrificial regulations of Leviticus 1–7 generally take the form of third-person casuistic law, but the rules for the grain offering take a second-person casuistic form that alternates between singular and plural (Lev. 2.4-16) and dietary prohibitions on fat and blood appear in second-person plural apodictic form near the end of the collection (7.22-27). Second-person plural address shapes the dietary rules (ch. 11) but the following purity regulations (chs. 12–15) take third-person casuistic form. In the Holiness Code, sections dominated by laws in the second-person (Lev. 18–19; 23–24) and third-person (chs. 17; 20.1-16; 27) are interspersed with sections that mix third-person casuistic formulations with second-person apodictic commands (20.17–22.33; 25). Alternation in address and legal form continues between blocks of instructions in Numbers. Deuteronomy, however, maintains a second-person form of address throughout that is consistent with its setting as a speech, but it varies between singular and plural and between apodictic and casuistic formulas.[7]

The rhetorical force of second-person legal address was recognized by A. Alt, who located the original setting of apodictic language in cultic liturgies rather than the legal settings suggested by casuistic laws.[8] Alt considered the apodictic form unique to Israel because Mesopotamian law collections contain only casuistic formulations, but subsequent studies have pointed out the presence of apodictic statements in ancient Near Eastern liturgical and wisdom texts.[9] Alt's

6. Even this is interrupted four times by second-person address: Exod. 21.2, 14, 24; 22.17. See W. Morrow, 'A Generic Discrepancy in the Covenant Code', in Levinson (ed.), *Theory and Method*, pp. 136-51.

7. For discussion of the variation from singular to plural in Deuteronomy, the Book of the Covenant, and ancient Near Eastern treaties, see Weinfeld, *Deuteronomy 1–11*, pp. 15-16.

8. 'The apodeictic law provides the central text for a sacral action involving the whole nation, and those who proclaim it are the mouthpiece of Yahweh, the levitical priests...' (Alt, 'Origins', p. 125).

9. Mendenhall cited apodictic parallels in Hittite treaties as further evidence that the treaty form shaped Israelite law ('Ancient Oriental and Biblical Law', in E.F. Campbell, Jr, and O.N. Freedman [eds.], *Biblical Archaeologist Review 3*

classification of all Israelite law into two categories has also been challenged as too simplistic.[10]

The form-critical debate over the legitimacy of Alt's reconstruction
does not detract from the rhetorical observation that underlies it.
Second-person address gives commandments a sense of immediacy and
urgency lacking in the hypothetical formulation of (usually) third-
person casuistic laws. The 'you' addressed by Yahweh and Moses is
typified by but not limited to the Israelites in the wilderness. Hearers
and readers are likely to feel directly addressed and therefore obliged to
respond.[11] Second-person address thus highlights the rhetorical function
of law, a function closely related in form and aim to passages of
proverbial wisdom.[12] Both law and wisdom seek to persuade hearers/
readers of the urgency of practising their teachings. Both, in other
words, aim to instruct their audience in a way of life.

Some law collections, like wisdom, reinforce their second-person
address with exhortations to listen and obey. The *Shema* ('Hear,
Israel...' Deut. 6.4) is only the most famous of many imperatives of
attention that punctuate Deuteronomy: 'hear, listen' (Deut. 5.1; 6.3-4;
9.1); 'keep, observe, take heed' (Deut. 4.1, 9, 15; 27.1; also Exod.
34.11-12); 'remember' (Deut. 8.2; 9.7).[13] The Holiness Code couches
its exhortations in the indicative: 'you shall keep my commandments
(and do them)' (Lev. 18.5; 19.37; 20.22; 22.31; 25.18).

These exhortations make explicit the didactic purpose behind the

[Garden City, NY: Doubleday, 1970, pp. 1-24 [4]). But the treaty parallels tend to
be isolated statements or else repetitive sequences dealing with a single subject
matter, not a wide-ranging list of moral imperatives as in the decalogue (McCarthy,
Treaty and Covenant, pp. 60-62, 250-52). Better parallels can be found in ancient
Near Eastern cultic liturgies and wisdom collections (McCarthy, *Treaty and Covenant*, p. 250 n. 12; see E.S. Gerstenberger, *Wesen und Herkunft des Apodiktischen
Rechts* [WMANT, 20; Neukirchen–Vluyn: Neukirchener Verlag, 1965]).

10. For brief surveys of the form-critical debate over Alt's theory, see Childs,
Exodus, pp. 389-91; D. Patrick, *Old Testament Law* (Atlanta: John Knox Press,
1985), pp. 21-24; and R. Sonsino, 'Law: Forms of Biblical Law', *ABD* 4, pp. 252-
54.

11. For further discussion of how law 'specifies' a reader, see Chapter 4 below.

12. Cf. Prov 3.3-12, 25-31; 4.13-15, 21-27; 22.22–23.25, etc., but note that the
prohibitions of the sages use the milder negative particle אַל expressing dissuasion
rather than the stronger negative particle לֹא which is characteristic of the laws.

13. Cf. Prov. 3.1; 4.1, 10, 20; 5.1, 7; 7.1-3, 24; 23.19, 22. For a survey of
rhetorical phrasing in Deuteronomy, see Weinfeld, *Deuteronomy and the Deuteronomistic School*, pp. 171-78.

law. The text aims to instruct its readers, and through second-person address and exhortations calls upon them to pay careful attention to its contents. The Israelite tradition of reading law publicly provides a plausible explanation for the rhetorical phrasing of so much biblical law.

2. *Motivation*

Another stylistic feature of Pentateuchal law that has frequently been cited as unique or at least distinctive is its use of motive clauses. B. Gemser defined these as 'grammatically subordinate sentences in which the motivation for the commandment is given'.[14] The contents of the clauses vary from practical explanations (Deut. 20.19) through ethical (Deut. 24.6) and religious reasons (Lev. 17.4) to historical motivations (Exod. 23.14).[15] Motive clauses appear in all the Pentateuchal legal collections, but are not distributed evenly: R. Sonsino estimated that the percentage of motivated regulations ranges from 13–20 per cent (in the cultic decalogue of Exod. 34.10-26, the book of the Covenant, and the priestly legislation) up to 45–51 per cent (in the Decalogue, Deuteronomy and the Holiness Code).[16] He noted that political and moral laws are more likely to be motivated than cultic and civil laws.[17]

Mesopotamian law collections employ motive clauses much less frequently than does biblical law. When they do appear, they tend to be repetitive and focus on the justice of the king.[18] Biblical law's emphasis on motivation has been explained by several interpreters on the basis of its public and didactic character. Gemser called attention to the rhetorical setting of Israelite law in public recitations,[19] and S.M. Paul observed that 'These explanatory, ethical, religious, and historical comments appeal to the conscience of the people and pedagogically aid and motivate them to observe the law.'[20] Their didactic character

14. B. Gemser, 'The Importance of the Motive Clause in Old Testament Law', in G.W. Anderson *et al.* (eds.), *Congress Volume: Copenhagen* (VTSup, 1; Leiden: E.J. Brill, 1953), pp. 50-66 (50).

15. Gemser, 'Motive Clause', pp. 55-56.

16. R. Sonsino, *Motive Clauses in Hebrew Law: Biblical Forms and Near Eastern Parallels* (SBLDS, 45; Chico, CA: Scholar's Press, 1980), p. 221.

17. Sonsino, *Motive Clauses*, pp. 222-23.

18. Sonsino, *Motive Clauses*, p. 225.

19. Gemser, 'Motive Clause', p. 62.

20. Paul, *Book of the Covenant*, p. 39.

becomes even clearer when compared to wisdom literature, which contains numerous parallels to the legal motive clauses.[21] The laws aim to instruct as well as to command, and by providing rationales for some of the regulations, the motive clauses enhance the persuasiveness of the law as a whole.

The comparisons with wisdom literature, however, should not obscure the communal nature of Israel's Torah: whereas Wisdom's stereotypical setting is private instruction within the family, reading law is usually depicted as a public activity addressing the whole people.[22] The laws frequently appeal to collective motivations, such as Israel's history with God, as well as the more universalistic concerns of wisdom. The legal motive clauses reflect individual, communal and universalistic concerns, demonstrating once again the variety of traditions which the Pentateuch combines to present law as persuasively as possible.

Motive clauses create links between the lists of laws and the stories of the Pentateuch.[23] Such links are obvious in historical motivations

21. Gemser ('Motive Clause', pp. 64-66), Carmichael (*Laws of Deuteronomy*, pp. 37-40) and Sonsino called attention to the close correspondence between biblical law and wisdom literature in this regard, the latter arguing that 'In the Bible, among all the literary genres outside of law, wisdom instructions have the highest concentration of number and kind of motive clauses. These motive clauses are in many respects very similar to those found in laws. This similarity, along with the recognized influence of wisdom upon law, suggests that the motive clauses in wisdom instructions constituted the basic models for the formulation of the legal motive clauses. A teaching function (as in the case of wisdom instruction) rather than an alleged cultic preaching seems to be reflected best in the use of the legal motive clauses' (*Motive Clauses*, p. 225). An overemphasis in past scholarship on covenant and history has been corrected by the increased attention being given to wisdom influences in biblical law. See J.D. Levenson, 'The Theologies of Commandment in Biblical Israel', *HTR* 73 (1980), pp. 17-33.

22. Gemser, however, pointed out that proverbs play a decisive role in public and especially legal proceedings in many African traditional societies, and speculated that this was also the case in ancient Israel ('Motive Clause', pp. 65-66). In that case, the stereotypically 'private' settings of wisdom may be literary constructs rather than reflections of Israelite life.

23. S. Amsler summarized these links as follows ('Les documents de la loi et la formation du Pentateuque', in A. de Pury [ed.], *Le Pentateuque en question* [Geneva: Labor et Fides, 1989], pp. 235-57 [242-43]): Deuteronomic law makes reference to the exodus (Deut. 15.15; 24.18), the wilderness wandering (23.5-6 [Eng. 23.4-5]; 25.17-19), and the settlement (19.14). So does the Holiness Code,

that explicitly cite incidents from Israel's experiences in Egypt and the wilderness (e.g. Lev. 19.34; Deut. 5.15). However, cosmological and cultic motivations also allude to the larger narrative context, such as the Sabbath command's grounding in the creation story (cf. Exod. 20.11 with Gen. 2.2-3) and the blood prohibition's repetition in both narrative and law (cf. Lev. 17.10-16 with Gen. 9.4-6). Motive clauses thus contribute to the Pentateuch's rhetoric of persuasion not only by explaining the laws, but also by tying story and list more closely together. They reinforce on a small scale the effect of the larger rhetorical structure that presents the *torah* of God in both narrative and law.

Some repetitive motive clauses provide thematic unity to lists of extremely diverse material. The phrase 'for it is an abomination to YHWH' and its variants punctuate the laws of Deuteronomy (12.31; 17.1; 18.12; 20.18; 22.5; 23.19 [Eng. 23.18]; 24.4; 25.16) and even extend into the introductory oration (7.25) and the concluding curses (27.15). 'Abomination' clauses also show up in the Holiness Code (Lev. 18.22; 20.13), but another refrain appears much more often: 'I am YHWH'. This phrase, usually without a conjunction, appears around 45 times in Leviticus 17–27, with the result that it seems to motivate the entire collection.[24] Gemser suggested that 'this refrain can…be understood as a kind of antiphon to the recital of the laws by the priests at the assembly'.[25] Both motive phrases recall the attention of hearers and readers to the religious foundation of the various stipulations and the thematic unity of the lists, stories and divine sanctions.

Thus motive clauses, like hortatory addresses, have called interpreters' attention to how the individual laws and the legal collections of the Pentateuch have been shaped by rhetorical concerns. The motivations attached to laws point out the didactic intent in their formulation, wishing to instruct hearers/readers not only in specific regulations but also in the law's foundations in Israel's communal experiences and religious ideas.

---

though more briefly (Lev. 19.34, 36; 20.24; 22.23; 23.43; 25.38, 42, 55). The Covenant Code has only three such references (Exod. 22.20 [Eng. 22.21]; 23.9, 15), but these may be Deuteronomistic glosses. Only the P legislation (aside from the Holiness Code) lacks any narrative references (but note the exceptions in Gen. 17 and Exod. 12), though its position within the Sinai pericope nevertheless supplies them.

24. Gemser, 'Motive Clause', pp. 51, 55, 63.

25. Gemser, 'Motive Clause', p. 63.

3. *Repetition*

Less attention has been paid to the role of repetition in biblical law than to the roles of hortatory addresses and motive clauses. Repetition plays a decisive role in many forms of narrative literature, including the stories of the Hebrew Bible.[26] But its presence is even more pronounced in Pentateuchal law, with distinct codes overlapping in their subject matter and re-presenting laws that are elsewhere found in narratives. The resulting repetitions over the span of all five books include, for example: the twelvefold repetition of the Sabbath command,[27] seven regulations regarding murder and its punishment,[28] and, most famously, two renditions of the whole Decalogue.[29] For the most part, different versions of commandments do not make explicit mention of each other. But there are exceptions and one whole code, Deuteronomy's, depicts itself as a re-presentation of laws already recorded in Exodus, Leviticus and Numbers.

Critical interpretation has usually viewed repetition in law as well as

26. Studies of repetition in biblical narrative include: W. Baumgartner, 'Ein Kapital vom hebräischen Erzählungsstil', in H. Schmidt (ed.), *EΥΧΑΡΙΣΤΗΡΙΟΝ: Studien zur Religion und Literatur des Alten und Neuen Testaments* (Göttingen: Vandenhoeck & Ruprecht, 1923), pp. 145-57 (150-55); M. Sternberg, *The Poetics of Biblical Narrative: Ideological Literature and the Drama of Reading* (Bloomington: Indiana University Press, 1985), pp. 365-440; R. Alter, *The Art of Biblical Narrative* (New York: Basic Books, 1981), pp. 88-113; G.W. Savran, *Telling and Retelling: Quotation in Biblical Narrative* (Bloomington: Indiana University Press, 1988), pp. 1-12 and *passim*.

27. Exod. 16.22-30; 20.8-11; 23.12; 31.12-17; 34.21; 35.2-3; Lev. 19.3b; 19.30a; 23.3; 25.2-7; 26.2; Deut. 5.12-15. In addition, there are three references to aspects of Sabbath observances: the creation of the Sabbath (Gen. 2.1-4), punishment for Sabbath breaking (Num. 15.32-36), and the Sabbath sacrifices (Num. 28.9-10).

28. Gen. 9.5-6; Exod. 20.13; 21.12, 14, 21; Lev. 24.17, 21; Num. 35.16-21, 30-34; Deut. 5.17; 19.11-13. Note the greater concern with retribution for murder than for Sabbath breaking: whereas only one Sabbath text mentions punishment (Num. 15.32-36), all the murder texts address the subject except for the command contained in the two versions of the Decalogue (Exod. 20.13; Deut. 5.17).

29. Or perhaps three, if the 'ritual decalogue' of Exod. 34.11-26 is intended (v. 28) as an alternative version of the Decalogue in Exod. 20.2-17 and Deut. 5.6-21. But their contents differ so much that it is difficult to consider this an example of repetition.

narrative as a product of multiple sources being combined together, in other words, of the diachronic development of the text. Therefore each code and decalogue was assigned to a different source.[30] Some repeated commandments, such as the twelvefold Sabbath commandment, appear so often and have such strong thematic consistency that distribution of each instance to a different source became implausible, and so the repetition was credited instead to the writers' desire for emphasis.[31]

Recent redactional theories of the Pentateuch's composition, which generally posit two reworkings of the material by Deuteronomistic and then by Priestly editors, confront multiple repetitions within a single redactional layer. Such theories have therefore highlighted repetition as a literary strategy employed consciously by the Pentateuch's editors.[32] W. Johnstone, for example, understood the doublet of Exod. 23.12-19 and 34.17-26 (usually divided between J and E) as an intentional repetition by Deuteronomistic editors:

> Ex 34,17-26 picks up the beginning of the Decalogue and the end of the Book of the Covenant to mark by a kind of merismus (in this case, totality indicated by extremes) the entire contents of Decalogue and Book of the Covenant on the conjoined basis of which the covenant was made (Ex 20,1-23,19).[33]

Other interpreters have increasingly recognized repetition as a literary device in Pentateuchal law similar in its effect on readers to repetition in narrative or wisdom texts. Thus B.M. Levinson listed repetition

---

30. Noth, for example, described the various blocks of legal material in the Pentateuch and observed: 'All these were once independent units, subsisting in their own right, each having its own purpose and sphere of validity, and having been transmitted individually for its own sake in the first place' ('The Laws in the Pentateuch', in *idem, The Laws in the Pentateuch and Other Studies* [trans. D.R. Ap-Thomas; Philadelphia: Fortress Press, 1967 (1940)], p. 7).

31. Thus Kent commented regarding Exod. 34.10-26: 'This primitive decalogue is repeated in the same or expanded form elsewhere in other groups of laws. That most of the regulations are reproduced four or five times in successive codes, indicates how great was the authority and importance attributed to them by late lawgivers' (*Israel's Laws*, p. 16).

32. So Blum, *Studien*, pp. 197-200; T.B. Dozeman, *God on the Mountain: A Study of Redaction, Theology and Canon in Exodus 19–24* (SBLMS, 37; Atlanta: Scholars Press, 1989), pp. 145-76.

33. 'Reactivating the Chronicles Analogy in Pentateuchal Studies with Special Reference to the Sinai Pericope in Exodus', *ZAW* 99 (1987), pp. 16-37 (28).

among law's 'literary' characteristics,[34] Carmichael compared Deuteronomy's 'repetitive use of previously given material' with the style of
proverbial wisdom,[35] and T.B. Dozeman combined redaction criticism
of the Sinai texts with literary theories of repetition.[36]

Because of Israel's tradition of public law readings, literary analyses
of repetition should be supplemented by investigations of the rhetorical
and didactic function of laws and narratives. A full description of repetition in biblical law requires the employment of both synchronic and
diachronic methods of interpretation. Regardless of its origins, repetition must be acceptable to the text's first audience or else it would not
be preserved. The function of repetition thus requires literary description, but this does not preclude finding the origins of repetition in the
historical development of the text. My rhetorical analysis intends,
therefore, not to replace historical investigation of the origins of Israel's
legal literature, but rather to account for the success of its Pentateuchal
form.[37]

Repetition is a prominent feature of public speech, used to emphasize
important points and make the contents memorable. Its importance for
rhetoric and instruction has been widely emphasized, from, for example,
Quintilian's comment: 'Our aim must be not to put him in a position to
understand our argument, but to force him to understand it. Conse-
quently we shall frequently repeat anything which we think the judge
has failed to take in as he should',[38] to the Marine Corp's dictum 'Tell
them what you're going to tell them, then tell them, then tell them what
you just told them.' During a public reading of law, repetition would
provide thematic unity, emphasis and mnemonic effect.

34. 'The Right Chorale: From the Poetics to the Hermeneutics of the Hebrew
Bible', in J.P. Rosenblatt and J.C. Sitterson, Jr (eds.), *'Not in Heaven': Coherence
and Complexity in Biblical Narrative* (Bloomington: Indiana University Press,
1991), pp. 129-53 (148).
35. *Laws of Deuteronomy*, p. 255
36. *God on the Mountain*, pp. 145-76.
37. So Crüsemann: 'The reconstruction of prehistory cannot replace an understanding of what happened. Thus far, the questions of "how," "why" and "by what
means" different law books were combined into the one Torah, one Pentateuch, the
one canon have only been addressed with inadequate tools' (*The Torah: Theology
and Social History of Old Testament Law* [trans. W. Mahnke; Edinburgh: T. & T.
Clark; Minneapolis: Fortress Press, 1996], p. 8).
38. *Inst. Orat.* 8.2.22-24

The repetition of individual commandments obviously enhances their mnemonic force, but it also serves to emphasize certain themes.[39] For example, the widespread injunctions to honor and obey parents and to respect the rights of resident aliens color the tone of the legal collections as a whole with the themes of orderly family relationships and just dealings with foreigners.[40] Similarly, the frequent prohibitions on the use of images and on various kinds of magic firmly establish a theme of strict conformity in religious practice.[41] In Leviticus 17 and 20, the same punishments ('cut off', 'put to death') are attached to many different laws; the regular repetition of these sentences unifies diverse material by emphasizing identical consequences. Repetition thus serves to unify at the thematic level particular legal collections and Pentateuchal law as a whole. It establishes emphases which by their frequent reappearance come to represent the whole. Repetition makes law memorable and persuasive.

The relationship between the larger legal collections is partly characterized by repetition as well. At this level, the juxtaposition of different collections whose contents overlap serves to identify them with each other. Thus P's legislation in Leviticus appears from its narrative setting at the mountain to be another version of the Covenant Code, as does in a different way Deuteronomy, which casts itself as a reminder of previous events and covenants. This depiction of Pentateuchal law in the form of a threefold (at least) repetition creates the impression of a unified Mosaic law and obscures the contradictions contained within it (see below). The rhetorical force of this large-scale repetitive structure thus motivates allegiance and obedience to the law while hiding but not harmonizing the different traditions that it contains.

The repetitive cast of Deuteronomic law has attracted a great deal of attention because of its overt claim to recapitulate the Sinai laws. Blum argued that Deuteronomy equates itself with the Covenant Code of

---

39. As has frequently been recognized. See Kent's comment quoted in n. 31 above.

40. Regarding duties to parents, see Exod. 20.12; 21.15, 17; Lev. 19.3a; 20.9; Deut. 5.16; 21.18-21; 27.16. Regarding relations with aliens, see Exod. 22.21 (Eng. [English verse numbers] 22.20); 23.9; Lev. 19.33-34; 24.22; Num. 9.14; 15.14-16, 29-30; 35.15; Deut. 1.16; 24.14, 17-18; 27.19.

41. For prohibitions on images, see Exod. 20.4-6, 23; 34.17; Lev. 19.4; 26.1; Deut. 4.15-28; 5.8-10; 7.5; 12.1-4; 16.21-22; 27.15. On magical practices, Exod. 22.17 (Eng. 22.18); Lev. 19.26b, 31; 20.6, 27; Deut. 18.9-14.

Exodus 21–23, giving the Pentateuch a mirror structure in which the proportions of narrative to inset law in Genesis to Numbers (without P) are inverted in Deuteronomy's law collection within its paranetic framework.[42] Carmichael suggested that Deuteronomy imitates the Covenant Code's structure.[43] Childs depicted Deuteronomy 'as an authoritative commentary on how future generations are to approach the Law and how it functions as a guide for its interpretation'.[44]

Note, however, the relative rarity in Deuteronomy of statements such as 6.1: 'Now this is the commandment, the statutes and the ordinances that YHWH your God commanded (me) to teach you...' The book more often emphasizes the present moment of law-giving ('Keep all these commands that I command you today', 11.8; cf. 11.26; 12.28; 13.19 [Eng. 13.18]; etc.) and 28.69 (Eng. 29.1) casts the laws of Moab as additional to, rather than a repetition of, the laws of Sinai. Deuteronomy's use of law resembles its use of quoted direct speech, which has attracted literary-critical analysis. G. Savran discovered that direct quotations serve different purposes in Deuteronomy's narratives than they do in other books from Genesis to Kings:

> It would appear that the idea of verifiability in Deuteronomy is different from that of other books, in which quotation and original statement are compared for accuracy. In this sense Deuteronomy is essentially self-referential, and the authenticity of its quotations depends not upon comparison with prior speech but upon the authoritative voice who quotes them, that is, Moses.[45]

Similarly, despite their many parallels in other parts of the Pentateuch, Deuteronomy's laws present themselves as a self-contained, free-standing collection. The book in its historical rehearsals explicitly acknowledges earlier instances of law-giving, just as its quotations refer to earlier speeches. Nevertheless, the laws like the quotations address the current audience and base their appeal on the authority of their speaker, Moses.

Thus the Pentateuch's use of large-scale repetition cannot be analyzed

---

42. *Studien*, pp. 197-201. He added that by emphasizing repetition of law, Deuteronomy opened the door for further multiplication of such 'Mosaic' codes, of which the later insertion of priestly laws took advantage.

43. *Laws of Deuteronomy*, p. 255.

44. *Old Testament Theology in a Canonical Context* (Philadelphia: Fortress Press, 1985), p. 56.

45. *Telling and Retelling*, p. 116.

simply on the basis of content and structure, but also depends on the characterization of the speakers of law. I will therefore return to the subject of repetition when discussing the voicing of Pentateuchal law in Chapter 4.

4. *Variation*

Repetitions of law in the Pentateuch frequently involve variation as well, ranging from differences in wording and alternative motive clauses to contradictory instructions and differences in punishments mandated for the same offense. For example, the Sabbath commandment is motivated by references to creation in Exod. 20.11, by the practical necessity of rest in 23.12, as a sign of the covenant in 31.13-17, by reference to YHWH's identity in Lev. 19.3; 19.30 and 26.2, and by reference to the exodus in Deut. 5.15. In Exod. 21.37–22.3 (Eng. 22.1-34), reparations for theft range from 200 per cent to 500 per cent, depending on circumstances, whereas in Lev. 6.5 they are set at 120 per cent. Again, Exod. 20.24 envisions multiple altars for the worship of Yahweh, Deut. 12.13-15 endorses sacrifice on only one altar but allows profane slaughter elsewhere, while Lev. 17 restricts all sacrifice and slaughter to the Tabernacle altar alone. And, of course, there are the numerous differences in detail that point to conflict over the roles of priests and Levites.[46]

Variation amid repetition is also a prominent feature of Hebrew narrative style. Quotations and allusions rarely reappear exactly the same way, but are regularly shortened and paraphrased. According to Savran, the significance of this cannot automatically be deduced from the nature of the change but depends entirely on the context.[47] The law codes also show an appreciation for variety: even in detailed renditions of cultic law (e.g. Lev. 1–3), exact repetition of entire rituals is rare. Slight variations in wording or content relieve the tedium of duplication and reveal a flair for rhetorical style.[48] Variety preserves interest and

46. For a longer list of contradictions, see Blum, (*Studien*, pp. 333-34), who noted that the vast majority concern cultic and priestly issues. Crüsemann suggested that massive juxtapositions of conflicting themes and details seem to have been a 'compositional principle of the Pentateuch' (*The Torah*, p. 329).

47. *Telling and Retelling*, pp. 29-36.

48. D. Damrosch suggested that the threefold structure in Lev. 1–3 'gives these chapters a certain lyrical aspect' ('Leviticus', in R. Alter and F. Kermode [eds.],

attention in publicly read law, as it does in narrative. Israel's tradition of public reading can be expected to have encouraged variety for rhetorical effect even, perhaps especially, in the midst of didactic repetition.[49]

The more severe contradictions require further explanation, however. For the most part, these occur between the major law collections, that is, the Book of the Covenant, the Priestly legislation, the Holiness Code and Deuteronomy.[50] But conflicts of tone, and occasionally of content, also occur within collections.[51] Such differences provide the evidence for various theories of the collections' historical development and their temporal relationship to each other. Developmental hypotheses, however, leave half the question unanswered: though they account for the origins of the contradictions, they do not explain why such differences were acceptable to the earliest hearers and readers of the Pentateuch. The latter problem requires that attention be paid to the literary and rhetorical conventions shaping contradictions in the law collections.

First Explanation: Fixed Written Law

A common explanation for ancient Israel's tolerance of legal contradictions argues that social conventions forbade the emendation of *written* laws. Whereas oral law developed and changed according to circumstances, the reduction of law to writing fixed its form so that changes could only be made through supplementation, not emendation. As a result, the legal collections expanded with additional cases and

The Literary Guide to the Bible [Cambridge, MA: Harvard University Press, 1987], pp. 66-77 [67]). S.E. McEvenue noted that 'variety within system' is the essence of P's narrative style (*The Narrative Style of the Priestly Writer* [AnBib, 50; Rome: Biblical Institute Press, 1971], p. 50), and this observation applies to priestly legislation as well.

49. Lenchak noted the interplay of repetition, variation and direct address as evidence for the aural nature of Deuteronomy (*'Choose Life!'*, p. 18).

50. Or one can find five different codes by dividing Leviticus between the sacrificial laws (chs. 1–7), the purity laws (11–15) and the Holiness Code (17–26), as S. Amsler did ('Les documents', p. 239).

51. P.D. Hanson pointed out the tension in the Book of the Covenant between casuistic laws designed to protect property owners and apodictic decrees concerned with the poor and disadvantaged ('The Theological Significance of Contradiction within the Book of the Covenant', in G.W. Coats and B.O. Long [eds.], *Canon and Authority: Essays in Old Testament Religion and Theology* [Philadelphia: Fortress Press, 1977], pp. 110-31).

harmonizations.[52] A variant form of this theory credits the refusal to modify written law to a particular period of Israel's history. F. Crüsemann traced the convention of unalterable written law to the supposedly Persian custom, mentioned in Est. 8.8, of irrevocable royal edicts that can only be counterbalanced by contrary edicts. He suggested that Jewish editors of the Persian period applied the same principle to divine law, with the result that variant and contradictory laws were preserved together.[53] From a rhetorical perspective, this theory can be rephrased to suggest that Persian-period readers and hearers would not accept the alteration of written law. The rhetorical situation therefore reinforced a literary convention with social pressures to produce an acceptable document—pressures familiar to all writers who wish to have their work published and read.[54] Yet the notion that written law is immutable does not explain why so many variant traditions were included in the first place. The mere fact of a law collection being written as divine speech was surely not enough to grant it irrefutable authority. Prophets challenged the validity of some written laws that claimed divine authority (Jer. 8.8, which explicitly refers to writing; Ezek. 20.25-26). Crüsemann himself noted the exclusion from Pentateuchal law of aristocratic interests and the views of eschatological prophets,[55] which makes it very unlikely that the Pentateuch includes *all* written laws extant in Judah in the postexilic period. Other factors besides law's textualization must also have encouraged the audience to tolerate contradictions.

Second Explanation: Plot Development
A second explanation for contradictions between the legal collections points to the narrative framework of Pentateuchal law. The narrative setting suggests that repetition of law may affect its meaning, just as repetition within narrative provides thematic unity to disparate events.[56]

52. 'The redactional preservation of discrepant yet equally authoritative texts leads to editorial attempts at their harmonization, which in turn introduces additional inconsistencies that further break down the text's (literal) authority' (Levinson, 'Right Chorale', p. 147).

53. Crüsemann, 'Der Pentateuch als Tora', pp. 260-61; *The Torah*, pp. 349-51.

54. For a discussion of the particular pressures that produced the compromise text of the Pentateuch in the Persian period, see Chapter 5 below.

55. *The Torah*, pp. 340-43.

56. Savran summarized the role of repetition in narrative: 'Recurrent themes and motifs are the stuff that binds together the longer work, be it Genesis or Joyce's

The Pentateuch marks the boundaries between collections of law not only by differences in theme and style, but also by narrative indicators such as physical setting (Mt Sinai, the Tabernacle, Moab) and speaker (Yahweh, Moses). A reading of the whole Pentateuch in sequence presents these contexts along with the laws. As with quotations in narratives, then, the interpretation of variation within law may depend on the narrative context.

By its position and subject matter, the story of the Golden Calf incident (Exod. 32–34) seems particularly likely to influence the meaning of the various collections of Sinai laws. Placed between the instructions for building the Tabernacle (Exod. 25–31) and the narrative of their fulfillment (chs. 35–40), the story also divides the laws of the Book of the Covenant (chs. 20–23) from the priestly legislation in Leviticus. This story of a broken covenant and divine retribution threatens the complete annihilation of the Israelites, a result avoided only because Moses appeals to YHWH's promise to the ancestors (32.7-14). The incident concludes with the delivery to Moses of the 'cultic decalogue' (34.10-28) which differs significantly from the decalogue previously given in ch. 20. J.H. Sailhamer argued that

> When viewed within the context of the differences between the laws of the Covenant Code and those of the Code of the Priests... the arrangement of this material appears to reflect a definite strategy ...Israel's initial relationship with God at Sinai, characterized by the patriarchal simplicity of the Covenant Code, is now represented by the complex and restrictive laws of the Code of the Priests.[57]

He suggested that the idolatrous sins of the priest, Aaron, and the people with the Golden Calf required the development of more detailed cultic rules for priests (Lev. 1–16) and people (Lev. 17–27) alike.

Examination of the Golden Calf story and the priestly legislation, however, does not bear out Sailhamer's conclusions. The story highlights the faithful action of the Levites as well as the sins of the Aaronide priesthood, yet the legislation of Leviticus reinforces the

---

Ulysses, and that allows the reader to reflect upon the sameness of human experience in the face of constantly changing circumstances' (*Telling and Retelling*, p. 5). But repetition of an incident or a law, precisely because it is repeated, also adds to and alters what is repeated (Sternberg, *Poetics*, p. 390). Dozeman therefore concluded, 'At best we can only discuss near-repetition in literature' (*God on the Mountain*, p. 148).

57. Sailhamer, *Pentateuch as Narrative*, p. 48.

Aaronides' authority over the cult and over the Levites.[58] Furthermore, the sacrificial and purity regulations of Leviticus 1–7 and 11–15 are directed to the people as a whole (though some parts show signs of having originated as priestly instructions).

Any interpretation of Exodus 34 as containing a 'new' covenant which governs what follows fails for a similar reason: the close parallels between the instructions of chs. 25–31 and their execution in chs. 35–40 emphasize continuity, not change in Israel's relationship with God.[59] The subsequent law collections do not develop the expectations raised by the Golden Calf story. Thus the relationships between legal collections do not seem to be governed primarily by narrative considerations.[60] As Alt pointed out, the narrative setting seems decisive for the interpretation of law only when the laws are relatively isolated from each other.[61] The relationships between the larger legal collections, however, break the conventions of narrative plot development.

58. Lev. 8.1-36; 10.8-11; 16.1-34; cf. Exod. 38.21 for Aaronide authority over Levites (Blum, *Studien*, p. 334).

59. This criticism applies to the structural analysis of Exod. 19–40 into two covenants (the first in chs. 19–31, the second in chs. 32–40), advanced by J. Fokkelman ('Exodus', in Alter and Kermode [eds.], *Literary Guide*, pp. 56-65 [58]) and M.S. Smith ('Literary Arrangement ', pp. 38, 46-49).

60. Sailhamer subordinated the laws to narrative constraints, that is, he reduced list to story. This interpretive tendency has dominated modern Pentateuchal criticism, though it has taken various forms: e.g. the subordination of law as secondary accretions to a prior narrative, or as stipulations of the narratively described covenant. This emphasis on story over list gains strength from Christian tendencies, first, to focus on biblical stories as theologically primary and, second, to minimize the relevance of Pentateuchal law. The criticism by J.D. Levenson is apropos: 'We see here a hallmark of biblical theology in our century, the subordination of norm to narrative, of *ethos* to *mythos*, or, if you will, of law to gospel' ('Theologies of Commandment', p. 19). Patrick suggested instead that the rhetoric of Exodus 'super-imposes' one story of covenant-making on the other, which is why interpretive traditions have rarely regarded the Decalogue as superseded by Exod. 34: 'The narrative cannot be and has not been read sequentially in the case of the decalogue' (*The Rhetoric of Revelation* [OBT; Minneapolis: Fortress Press, forthcoming]).

61. Alt, 'Origins', pp. 81-82. He suggested that Deuteronomy is the principle exception to this rule because of its narrative depiction as Moses' farewell speech. The case of Zelophehad's daughters and their inheritance rights (Num. 27.1-11; 36.1-12) is an example of an isolated ruling developed in close dependence on narrative.

Third Explanation: Re-emphasis

The placement of Exodus 32–34 between the Tabernacle instructions and their fulfillment emphasizes that the priests' and people's apostasy did not derail the divine plan.[62] These chapters therefore do not point to plot developments between law collections, but rather the role of repetition and its accompanying variations in *re-emphasizing* the law. Such re-emphasis is obvious in the listlike narrative of the Tabernacle's construction and dedication (Exod. 35–40), though the details and arrangement vary from the previous instructions (Exod. 25–31).[63] But re-emphasis, that is, repetition in altered form, also describes the relationship between the laws of Leviticus and the Book of the Covenant, and between Deuteronomy and the entire complex of Sinai legislation. The Holiness Code and Deuteronomic laws reproduce the overall form of the Book of the Covenant: each begins with cultic, especially altar, laws (Exod. 20.22-26; Lev. 17; Deut. 12); each ends with calendrical regulations (Exod. 23.10-19; Lev. 25; Deut. 26).[64] Their narrative settings, however, distinguish them from the revelation on Mt Sinai: Moses receives the regulations of Leviticus in the Tabernacle (Lev. 1.1), and in Deuteronomy he reminds Israel on the plains of Moab of previously heard laws. Thus repetition in new circumstances does not supply a narrative rationale for variation in plot development, but rather in the situation of the speaker and the audience. This rationale obviously governs Deuteronomy. Its application to Leviticus is obscured by the ambiguity of the setting that leaves open the possibility that the priestly legislation is another account of the original revelation on Mount Sinai.[65]

The near-verbatim repetition of the Decalogue in Exodus 20 and Deuteronomy 5 contrasts dramatically with the considerable differences

62. As Mann noted: 'This is the final movement of the divine presence, culminating in the enthronement of Israel's exalted king, but now that enthronement takes place "in the midst of" a "stiff-necked" people stained by "iniquity" and "sin" (34.9)' (*Book of the Torah*, p. 111).

63. For discussion of the differences, see Childs, *Exodus*, pp. 529-30, 633-34.

64. Note that the annual ritual calendar appears earlier in Lev. 23 and Deut. 16. The return to calendrical issues at the end of these collections suggest deliberate shaping to emphasize a form reminiscent of the Book of the Covenant despite the varying contents.

65. Leviticus is inconsistent in locating the place of revelation: 7.37-38; 25.1; 26.46 and 27.34 place it on Mt Sinai, thus equating the priestly legislation even more closely with Exod. 20–23.

between the Book of the Covenant, the Priestly and the Deuteronomic legislations. The Ten Commandments are reproduced carefully, with only minor divergences of wording and a different motive clause on the Sabbath commandment, well within the standards of direct quoted speech in the Hebrew Bible.[66] By its position at the head of the collections, the Decalogue is clearly privileged in both Exodus and Deuteronomy, and the latter emphasizes YHWH's *unmediated* delivery of the Ten Commandments to the people at Sinai.[67] On the other hand, the laws from the mountain (Exodus), the Tabernacle (Leviticus and Numbers) and the plains of Moab (Deuteronomy) are mediated to the people through Moses and therefore are in a certain sense secondary. Mediation through Moses apparently allowed for much greater variation in content, as comparison of the unmediated Decalogue of Exodus 20 and Deuteronomy 5 with the mediated 'ritual decalogue' of Exodus 34 shows.

The effect of Moses' mediation, however, is tempered for readers of the Pentateuch by the fact that, unlike the people in the narrative, they read the law collections of Exodus and Leviticus as YHWH's direct speech. Only Deuteronomy uses Moses' voice to mediate the law it contains. Whereas Moses mediates all the law except the Decalogue to the Israelites in the wilderness, he mediates only Deuteronomic law to readers. This textual mediation through Moses' voice isolates

---

66. Savran, *Telling and Retelling*, pp. 35-36.

67. Deut. 4.12-13, 33, 36, and especially 5.4: 'Face to face YHWH spoke with you', but note that the following verse immediately emphasizes Moses' role as mediator. Such discomfort with the notion of unmediated revelation may account for the odd introduction to the Decalogue in Exod. 19.25–20.1: ויאמר אלהם וידבר אלהים את כל־הדברים האלה לאמר '[Moses] said to them and God spoke all these words saying'. The phrase וידבר...לאמר is P's standard introduction to legislation marking it as direct discourse (see S.A. Meier, *Speaking of Speaking: Marking Direct Discourse in the Hebrew Bible* [VTSup, 46; Leiden: E.J. Brill, 1992], pp. 153-56). But 19.25 also provides a marker of Moses' direct discourse, but without a following speech, unless one takes the decalogue and its direct discourse marker as part of Moses' mediation of the law (so Sailhamer, *Pentateuch as Narrative*, p. 55 n. 89). Such a construction is unparalleled in biblical Hebrew, and may be a redactional attempt to mark the Decalogue as mediated law. Or it may be a product of the editorial insertion of the Decalogue into an older text during which the contents of Moses' speech were displaced, as the source critics have usually maintained— e.g. M. Noth: 'Verse 25 is a fragment' (*Exodus*, p. 160). The translations usually render the Decalogue as YHWH's direct speech, not Moses' quotation of it.

Deuteronomy as the sole example of law re-emphasized in a new situation, while it unifies the law collections of Exodus and Leviticus as
YHWH's revelation at Sinai. Thus once again, full evaluation of repetition and variation in the laws depends on analysis of the characters who
voice Pentateuchal law (Chapter 4 below).

Fourth Explanation: Mixed Audiences
Re-emphasis through variation, like narrative development and venera-
tion of written law, only partly explains the contradictions in Pentateuchal law. While each of these explanations seems to fit certain texts
and features of the Pentateuch, the complexity of the whole defies cate-
gorization under any of these headings. In addition to such author- and
text-centered explanations, Israel's tradition of public law readings
should draw attention to the audience's influence on the shaping of a
speech.[68] Rhetorical theory highlights the intended audience as the key
to understanding a speech or text.[69] A mixed audience of people with
diverse and perhaps opposed interests may account for the nature and
extent of contradictions within a speech addressed to them all.[70]

68. Thus Mullen, who also emphasized that the texts were intended to be read
publicly, explained variation as due to 'the plurality of groups that might have constituted the intended audience for the materials' (*Ethnic Myths*, p. 315).

69. 'All rhetorical forms, monologic in their compositional structure, are
oriented toward the listener and his answer. This orientation toward the listener is
usually considered the basic constitutive feature of rhetorical discourse' (M.M.
Bakhtin, *The Dialogic Imagination* [ed. M. Holquist; Austin: University of Texas
Press, 1981], p. 280).

70. Bakhtin's description of multiple and contradictory voices ('polyphony') in
modern novels has stimulated attempts to apply his theories to tensions and contradictions in the Pentateuch. Bakhtin, however, distinguished the rhetorical genre's
use of 'authoritative discourse' from the novel's avoidance or parody of it, and
rhetoric's formal use of multiple voices for purposes of persuasion from the novel's
emphasis on 'the mutual nonunderstanding represented by people *who speak in
different languages*'. 'For this reason it is proper to speak of a distinctive *rhetorical*
double-voicedness, or, put another way, to speak of the double-voiced rhetorical
transmission of another's word (although it may involve some artistic aspects), in
contrast to the double-voiced *representation* of another's word in the novel with its
orientation toward the *image of a language*' (*Dialogic Imagination*, pp. 356, 354;
also 284, 342-44 [Bakhtin's emphases]). My rhetorical analysis therefore points
to a unified persuasive intention behind the multiple voices of the Pentateuch, in

The problems posed by mixed or multiple audiences have received little attention from theorists of rhetoric and communication.[71] Nevertheless, the few discussions of the issue are suggestive for understanding the rhetorical role of contradictions in the Pentateuch. Politicians regularly address multiple, and frequently opposed, audiences. Court decisions usually address individuals or social groups in conflict with each other. Analyses of these modern texts point out that, among other strategies employed to deal with multiple audiences, the separate treatment of the concerns of each audience can be effective in gaining their acceptance even when other parts of the speech may offend them.[72] Separation of the different audiences' concerns may be buttressed by integrating some of them into a common goal or vision.[73] Thus a text

contrast to some literary analyses which, in novelistic fashion, have emphasized irreconcilable tendencies in its discourse (e.g. R. Polzin, *Moses and the Deuteronomist: A Literary Study of the Deuteronomic History* [New York: Seabury, 1980], pp. 38-39; D.T. Olson, *Deuteronomy and the Death of Moses: A Theological Reading* [OBT; Minneapolis: Fortress Press, 1994], pp. 178-82; Stahl, *Law and Liminality*, pp. 21-24, who noted Bakhtin's objections and commented, 'where the Bible is concerned, one must first refute Bakhtin in order to apply him' [p. 24 n. 25]). Attempts to use Bakhtin's theory of polyphony while ignoring his analysis of genre undermine one of the major goals of his work, namely his explanation for the *distinctive* nature of the modern novel.

71. 'Aristotle does not discuss varieties of audience with the systematic thoroughness which he brings to the classification of opinion in general. And both Aristotle and Cicero consider audiences purely as something *given*' (Burke, *Rhetoric of Motives*, p. 64, Burke's emphasis).

72. W.L. Benoit and J.M. D'Agostine pointed out that offensive rhetoric may even help win over those offended by distracting them from their other, more substantive, disagreements with the speaker or writer. On Chief Justice Marshall's written decision in *Marbury v. Madison*, they concluded: 'Thus, Marshall neither limited himself to arguments, evidence, and positions acceptable to his audience, nor kept his incompatible statements vague and inoffensive. In fact, it is arguable that his offensive attacks on Jefferson were instrumental in achieving his long-term goal of establishing the power of judicial review. However, his strategies seem calculated to appeal to each audience (e.g., it was important to the Anti-Federalists to deny Marbury's commission; it was important to the Federalists, who had little power, to save face by attacking the Anti-Federalists). Thus, it appears that rhetors facing multiple audiences may also use the strategy of separation' ('"The Case of the Midnight Judges" and Multiple Audience Discourse: Chief Justice Marshall and *Marbury V. Madison*', *Southern Communication Journal* 59 [1994], pp. 89-96 [95]).

73. C.R. Smith commented on a speech by Richard Nixon: 'Where there was

may juxtapose conflicting points of view because they are representative of the views of its audience, and appeal to all sides by projecting a
vision inclusive of major points of view.[74] Needless to say, such a
speech or text leaves many points unreconciled. Its aim, however,
depends on contradiction. The speech can succeed only by convincing
the opposed groups in the audience that their views are represented in
the speaker's or writer's program, that is, only in so far as it contradicts
itself.[75] Thus self-contradiction becomes a rhetorical device for promot-
ing support of a speaker's or writer's aims.[76]

   Much evidence suggests that Pentateuchal law addresses mixed and
conflicting points of view within its intended audiences. Source-critical
theories of composition may account for contradictions on the basis of
divergent authorship, but they do not explain why these contradictions
were preserved. The Pentateuch's juxtaposition of contradictory points
of view indicates that they represented influential constituencies among
the first hearers and readers of the legal collections. The existence of
such groups may have contributed to contradictions within some legal
collections, such as the divergent emphases on personal liberation and

division in either audience, Nixon did not exacerbate it; he was either vague or he
skirted the crucial point. Where there was consensus, where a plurality could be
formed, he was specific' ('Richard Nixon's 1968 Acceptance Speech as a Model of
Dual Audience Adaptation', *Today's Speech* 19 [1971], pp. 15-22 [20]).

   74. Juxtaposition of contradictory appeals is apparently more effective at gain-
ing audience support than vague statements that offend no one, as comparison of
analyses of two keynote speeches shows (W.N. Thompson, 'Barbara Jordan's
Keynote Address: The Juxtaposition of Contradictory Values', *Southern Speech
Communication Journal* 44 [1979], pp. 223-32; C.R. Smith, 'The Republican
Keynote Address of 1968: Adaptive Rhetoric for the Multiple Audience', *Western
Speech* 39 [1975], pp. 32-39).

   75. Burke emphasized identification as the key to persuasion and noted that
'Persuasion by flattery is but a special case of persuasion in general. But flattery
can safely serve as our paradigm if we systematically widen its meaning, to see
behind it the conditions of identification or consubstantiality in general. And you
give the "signs" of such consubstantiality by deference to an audience's
"opinions"' (*Rhetoric of Motives*, p. 55). If an audience contains groups subscrib-
ing to contradictory opinions, deference to those opinions necessarily leads to self-
contradiction, but also makes the speaker persuasive.

   76. I state the case more bluntly than do any of the studies listed above, but the
charge of self-contradiction is so common in modern political discourse that this
conclusion seems self-evident.

preservation of property in the Book of the Covenant.[77] Certainly the large-scale amplifications of law in Leviticus and in Deuteronomy represent the divergent ideological interests of deuteronomists and a 'priestly' group. The preservation of their legal collections side by side in the Pentateuch indicates that these two groups did not follow each other historically but that both remained influential in Israel at the time of the Pentateuch's completion.[78]

Thus the mixed nature of the audience addressed by Pentateuchal law encouraged a rhetorical strategy that juxtaposed divergent points of view and contradictory legislation within a vision of the unitary law of Sinai. The political and literary success of this strategy is apparent from the acceptance of the Pentateuch as the foundational law of Second Temple and later Judaism, and from the acceptance of Moses as the only mediator of divine law. It is also clear that such juxtaposed contradictions require further explication, so the work of interpretation and harmonization grows naturally from the form of Pentateuchal law itself. Thus the rabbinic tradition of the equal antiquity of oral and written law makes sense as an observation on the demands created by the shape of the written law.[79] Attention to the intended audience therefore indicates that the editors of the Pentateuch achieved their rhetorical goal of presenting a unifying vision of Israel's law not just in spite of but largely *because* the law contradicts itself.[80]

77. Described by Hanson, 'Theological Significance of Contradiction', pp. 110-31.

78. Friedman suggested that the writing of law was a competitive venture: 'The priestly houses of Judah were each engaged in the composition of Torah literature and…the writings of each received a less-than-cordial welcome from the other' (*Exile*, p. 75; similarly Amsler, 'Les documents', p. 239, also 255). Crüsemann argued that the shared views outweighed the differences, making a 'coalition' between the groups possible (*The Torah*, p. 361). Stahl concluded, 'It is as if biblical law encapsulated the dissonance of the competing voices of the culture that enunciated it' (*Law and Liminality*, p. 17). For discussion of the historical circumstances surrounding the Pentateuch's redaction and promulgation, see Chapter 5 below.

79. See Fishbane, *Biblical Interpretation*, pp. 231-32, 264-65, and esp. 276-77; Crüsemann, *The Torah*, pp. 342, 363-64; and also the comments of Levinson, quoted in n. 52 above.

80. Bakhtin described this common situation: 'Very often, especially in the rhetorical forms, this orientation toward the listener and the related internal dialogism of the word may simply overshadow the object: the strong point of any concrete listener becomes a self-sufficient focus of attention, and one that interferes

   This rhetorical analysis of contradiction points once again to the persuasive intent behind the shaping of Pentateuchal law. The need for
instruction in law encourages repetition and variation, hortatory
addresses and motive clauses, in order to hold the attention of hearers
and readers and make the laws memorable, but the goal of persuasion
remains paramount. The contradictions within the law impede its
didactic aims, but remain in place because they help persuade all the
parties in Israel to accept this law as the foundation of their religious
life. In the Pentateuch, the idea of Mosaic law has become even more
important than its contents; so long as the idea is accepted, the contradictions in detail can be reconciled later.

5. *Narration*

The above discussion has shown that narrative devices such as repetition and variation shape non-narrative material in the Pentateuch, but it
has also emphasized that story does not completely determine the
arrangements of and relationships between legal collections. To
describe fully the relationship between list and story in Pentateuchal
law, the degree of law's influence on narrative conventions must also
be evaluated. That influence would appear to be considerable, if the
designation *Torah* 'law, instruction' for the whole Pentateuch is taken
seriously.[81] The results of this evaluation will once again point to the
didactic and persuasive goals behind Pentateuchal law.

Boundaries
Unlike stories, with their emphasis on beginnings and endings, lists
tend to be unconcerned with boundaries and to invite supplementation:
laws generate more laws which are added to their predecessors. These
qualities have infected Pentateuchal narrative as well. The stories, no
matter how distinct and self-contained they may be, always seem to
require predecessors and successors that stretch forward and backward

---

with the word's creative work on its referent' (*Dialogic Imagination*, p. 282). On
'intentional discontinuities' in the redaction of the Pentateuch, see the comments of
Blum, *Studien*, p. 382.

   81. Interpreters have increasingly emphasized the combination of law with narrative as determinative for understanding the Pentateuch. See Blum, *Studien*, pp.
207, 288; Amsler, 'Les documents', p. 241.

in narrative time almost without end. As a result, Pentateuchal narrative, like law, has difficulty finding beginnings and endings. Ultimately it settles on the beginning of everything as the default start of its story. Its ending eludes such easy definition, however. Moses' death brings the Pentateuch to a close, but without settling a host of outstanding issues, including the major Pentateuchal themes of the promise of the land and Israel's fidelity to the covenant. Interpreters' postulate of an original 'Hexateuch' (Genesis through Joshua) reflects unease with the Pentateuch's abrupt cessation, as does ancient Israel's addition of a four-volume continuation, the Deuteronomistic History (Joshua through Kings).[82]

The tendency to combine all of Israel's stories into one long story developed under the influence of Mosaic law, which similarly attracts all Israelite law to itself.[83] Because law lies at the center of Israel's defining story, stories must be related to law by being placed within the single, overarching narrative. This is true even (or especially) of stories that contain no reference to the law and that may even contradict its teachings (e.g. the stories of Jacob, Joseph, David, etc.). The larger narrative establishes a temporal connection between the stories and laws, and thereby offers interpreters various ways to overcome the contradictions (e.g. 'before the law', 'the law was forgotten', etc.). Israel's stories are treated like items on a list. Each takes its proper place in the list which, in this case, is organized by the time-line of history. That is not to say that, in individual books or even larger literary complexes, thematic and plot considerations do not play decisive organizational roles. My claim is simply that by collecting most of Israel's stories into a single huge narrative sequence, redactors were following a convention of lists—the amassing together of material—that is exemplified by the non-narrative texts at the center of that story, the Mosaic laws.[84]

Non-Sequential Narrative
Even narrative's time-line is affected by the atemporal lists in its midst. For example, the introduction to the Sinai legislation suffers

82. On the Hexateuch as a redactional attempt to provide more closure, see Blum, *Studien*, p. 365.
83. Amsler, 'Les documents', pp. 256-57.
84. '[The Sinai story] establishes a critical juncture between covenant and *narrative*... Covenanting is an action that has determined the form that the past has taken as a story' (Nohrnberg, *Like Unto Moses*, pp. 69-70).

chronological confusion for the sake of topical arrangement. The story of Jethro (Exod. 18) presupposes a physical setting (at the mountain) and religious practices (altars and sacrifices) to which the Israelites are introduced only later in the narrative sequences: they reach the mountain in 19.2 and first receive cultic instructions in ch. 20.[85] This story, however, summarizes the exodus events and introduces the theme of Moses' mediation of divine law, thus tying together the two halves of Exodus. As T.L. Thompson observed, 'In its present place, ...it offers a narrative context as well as a reason for the giving of the law by Yahweh on the mountain.'[86] The Jethro story, then, seems to have been placed here because of its topical relationship to the laws that follow rather than taking its temporal place in the narrative.

Leviticus 16 contains another, more ambiguous, example of temporal displacement for the sake of topical arrangement. The chapter contains YHWH's instructions mediated through Moses to Aaron for the sacrifices of the Day of Atonement. It begins by dating the instructions to a time immediately following the events narrated in Leviticus 10, and it concludes with the narrator's comment that the instructions were fulfilled.[87] If this means, as seems most likely, that the Israelites observed the Day of Atonement at Sinai, it creates a conflict between the stipulation that it be observed annually on the tenth day of the seventh month (16.29-30) and the chronological notices that do not place the Tabernacle at the mountain on that day.[88] The arrangement, however,

85. These problems have been discussed by interpreters since the Middle Ages. For a review of research, see Childs, *Exodus*, pp. 321-26.

86. *The Origin Tradition of Ancient Israel. I. The Literary Formation of Genesis and Exodus 1–23* (JSOTSup, 55; Sheffield: JSOT Press, 1987), p. 183. He argued that, in its context, 'The function of the Jethro story is to inform the audience that the law of Israel, the Torah, is superior to laws which have been made up by men, even by such a one as Moses...Moses' proper role is that of mediator. Before the people, he is to be not a judge but a teacher of the Torah, teaching them the statutes and the decisions which are of God' (T.L. Thompson, *Origin Tradition*).

87. The phrase, ויעש כאשר צוה יהוה את־משה 'he did what YHWH commanded Moses' (16.34), does not name its subject. The most natural antecedent is Aaron (so J. Milgrom, *Leviticus 1–16* [AB, 3; New York: Doubleday, 1991], p. 1059; J.H. Hartley, *Leviticus* [WBC, 4; Dallas: Word Books, 1992], p. 224).

88. The Tabernacle is completed on the first day of the first month (Exod. 40.2, 17) and the people leave the mountain on the twentieth of the second month of the same year (Num. 10.11).

follows topical logic: the day's ceremonies presuppose both the sacrificial instructions of Leviticus 1–7 and the purity regulations of chs. 11–15, and they form a climactic conclusion to the entire complex of cultic law. So the logic of list overrides the chronology of story.

Floating Narratives in Law

Other stories become so defined by their legal contexts that they lack all temporal connections with the overarching narrative. These stories tend to be 'case studies' that develop legal rulings on the basis of particular incidents. The case of the half-Egyptian blasphemer (Lev. 24.10-14) becomes an occasion to emphasize the universal application of not just the laws on blasphemy, but the criminal statutes as well (vv. 15-22). The petition of the daughters of Zelophehad (Num. 27.1-11) and the counter-petition of the elders of Manasseh (36.1-12) generate rulings permitting, but also limiting, women's inheritance rights.

The surrounding lists partly determine the positions of these stories. The census lists note Zelophehad's lack of male heirs (Num. 26.33), so the narrative follows to settle the problem of inheritance. The designation of Manasseh's tribal territories (32.39-42) raises the elders' concerns for the continuing integrity of the tribal lands, which must again be resolved with the story of their petition (ch. 36). The reasons for placing the blasphemy case in Leviticus 24 are less apparent, but probably derive from a wish to restate in summary fashion at this point in the Holiness Code the universality of the most basic religious and criminal laws.[89] All three stories further the didactic concerns and issues of the lists, rather than the plots and themes of the larger narrative.

Conclusion

The rhetorical aims of instruction and persuasion shape various details of the Pentateuch's laws and narratives. The laws address and exhort

---

89. The structure of the main body of Holiness legislation falls into three parts (Lev. 18–20; 21–22; 23–25), of which the first and third consist of two chapters of thematically unified legislation (chs. 18 and 20 on sexual relationships, chs. 23 and 25 on the religious calendar) surrounding chapters of more diverse legislation (chs. 19 and 24). The story therefore may have been placed in ch. 24 because the resulting ruling supplies the broad summary needed for the structure of the lists. C.R. Smith suggested that the story plays a role in structuring Leviticus through alternating lists of laws with stories in Lev. 8–10; 16 and 24 ('The Literary Structure of Leviticus', *JSOT* 70 [1996], pp. 17-32).

the audience/readers directly and offer various kinds of reasons for obeying their provisions. The repetition of laws makes them memorable and emphasizes crucial aspects of Israel's religious and civil life, while variation maintains readers' interest. Variety to the point of contradiction serves to hold together opposed ideological camps and persuade the people that this is YHWH's law for Israel, not simply the program of a single faction.

Both list and story use repetition to achieve their purposes. Variation may appear to be a device more natural to story, and its prevalence in Pentateuchal law indicates the degree to which narrative concerns have shaped the legal collections. The conventions of list, however, also influence biblical stories, as shown by the temporal discontinuities around the laws and by the use of some stories for purely legal purposes. The influence of list on narrative is most apparent in Israel's tendency to amass most of its stories into a single time-line stretching from creation to the exile, with the law at its center.

The rhetoric of list and story explains this influence by arguing that biblical law and narrative are two parts of a persuasive strategy that depends on both to make its case. Their mutual aim, persuasion, naturally causes them to influence each other's literary conventions. Neither, however, dominates the other. In other words, Pentateuchal law cannot be analyzed successfully as simply narrative, nor can biblical stories be reduced entirely to legal case studies. The strategy of persuasion requires that both, together with divine sanctions, function on their own terms to state the conditions of Israel's existence as a people (stories), the possibility of an ideal divine/human community (laws), and the consequences of the people's actions (sanctions). Together, these distinct literary complexes create the rhetorical force of Torah, the original expression of a religion of Scripture.

Chapter 4

COMMANDMENT

The force of law depends on the authority of its promulgator. When law takes the form of a commandment, the transaction between speaker and audience becomes most explicit. The power to command depends on the identities of both speaker and hearer, and the nature of their relationship. Thus the characterization of the law-giver plays a vital role in persuading hearers and readers to accept law and in motivating them to obey it. It is equally crucial, however, that the law specify its intended audience. Hearers and readers must identify themselves as being addressed by the commandments. Patrick pointed out that 'a commandment...effects something between the speaker and audience...[It] creates the reality it describes'.[1] The Pentateuch therefore characterizes law-speakers and specifies the law's audience as part of its rhetoric of persuasion.[2]

Characterization of law-speakers may have been more than a means to an end, if Israelite law preserved the overall goals of the Mesopotamian legal traditions with which it was familiar.[3] S.M. Paul and others have noted that the purpose of some of the Mesopotamian codes seems to be to characterize the king's divine election, accomplishments and establishment of justice.[4] The possibility exists, therefore, that

1. D. Patrick, 'Is the Truth of the First Commandment Known by Reason?' *CBQ* 56 (1994), pp. 423-41 (426-27).

2. As Jackson put it: 'We have some access to the pragmatics as well as the semantics of biblical law... Biblical law probably provides us with a richer range of acts of enunciation of norms than the legal literature of any other people of antiquity' ('Ceremonial and Judicial', p. 120).

3. For comparisons of Israelite and Mesopotamian law, see the essays and literature cited in Levinson (ed.), *Theory and Method*.

4. 'The prologue and epilogue of [the Code of Hammurabi] may be understood as one grand auto-panegyric to bring the attention of that deity to bear upon the deeds and accomplishments of the king' (*Book of the Covenant*, p. 23); Paul

Pentateuchal law not only characterizes its speakers in order to validate law, but also that it promulgates law in order to characterize its speakers.

Comparison with Mesopotamian codes points, however, to a distinguishing feature of biblical law: the Pentateuch presents two speakers of law, one divine (YHWH) and the other human (Moses), and depicts all law as direct speech quoted by a third-person narrator. Whereas the Code of Hammurabi unites law and narration in the first-person voice of the king, the major blocks of the Pentateuch's discourse are divided among three voices. On the surface, it would seem that voicing has little effect, for only YHWH and Moses give the law (the narrator never does), and Moses acts as God's messenger. So YHWH is really the only source of law.[5] But characterization derives not only from explicit descriptions but also implicitly from the character's speech, as Savran noted:

> Characterization is accomplished not by simple description but by drawing analogies between the repeated words and behaviors of various figures in the text and by judging the constancy of identity in the replication of thoughts and actions in speech, and the reverse.[6]

Thus questions about the law's consistency become questions regarding the character of both the divine law-giver and the messenger, and the nature of their law. Does, then, the varied and occasionally contradictory nature of Pentateuchal law undermine Moses' stature as God's messenger? Or does divine authority override such considerations, validating Mosaic law regardless of any incoherence?

concludes that this is the primary purpose of the Old Babylonian law codes (p. 26). J.J. Finckelstein pioneered this interpretation of Mesopotamian law in 'Ammisa-duqa's Edict and the Babylonian "Law Codes"', *JCS* 15 (1961), pp. 91-104.

5. 'God…is not merely the guarantor of the covenant, as the deities are in the epilogues to the Mesopotamian legal collections and treaties; he is the author of the covenant who directly addresses his people' noted Paul (*Book of the Covenant*, p. 37), adding that 'Only in biblical legal corpora are there to be found prescriptions by the deity addressed in the first person' (p. 37 n. 2). Crüsemann noted the uniqueness of divine voicing of law in comparison not only with Mesopotamian but also with Greek and Roman law (*The Torah*, pp. 14-15). B.M. Levinson explored the hermeneutical implications of this innovation in 'The Human Voice in Divine Revelation: the Problem of Authority in Biblical Law', in M.A. Williams, C. Cox, and M.S. Jaffee (eds.), *Innovations in Religious Traditions* (RelSoc, 31; Berlin: Mouton de Gruyter, 1992), pp. 35-71.

6. *Telling and Retelling*, p. 5.

Previous chapters have already highlighted many aspects of characterization in Pentateuchal law. The stories that introduce lists of Mesopotamian and Israelite laws characterize the identity and authority of law-speakers through their past accomplishments, and the sanctions that conclude them characterize the speaker's willingness to enforce their provisions. Direct second-person address within the codes reminds hearers and readers of their relationship to the speaker, while motive clauses link laws to the stories that precede them and the sanctions that follow. Repetition highlights the issues of most importance to the law-speakers, but contradiction raises questions about the speakers' reliability.

What remains to be discussed is the overall effect that the disparate voicing of law has on the characterization of its speakers and, through them, on the nature of the Pentateuch itself. We must therefore explore the triangular relationship between narrator, law-speakers and their audiences within and beyond the story.

1. *YHWH as Law-Giver*

YHWH is a major character in the narratives of the Pentateuch. God's character is developed in stories of divine creation and destruction, promise and fulfillment, battle and redemption. These accounts rarely describe God directly, providing at most short epithets to characterize the major actor. Instead, as M. Sternberg observed, 'the complex of features making up God's portrait emerges only by degrees and only through the action itself, starting with the creation of light by terse fiat'.[7] The lack of introductions forces readers to infer YHWH's character from the stories, though Patrick noted that God's unannounced entry presumes prior acquaintance. By simply narrating the speech and actions of 'God', Genesis implies a reader who already knows this character. The process of characterization thus becomes a matter of elaborating and correcting the reader's impressions of a 'God already known'.[8]

---

7. *Poetics*, p. 322.

8. 'Yahweh is always already known in the tradition. There is no real beginning to the knowledge of the biblical God. There is no moment when he enters human consciousness for the first time' (D. Patrick, *The Rendering of God in the Old Testament* [OBT; Philadelphia: Fortress Press, 1981], p. 32).

The stories of YHWH's deeds form a biography that shapes God's characterization. YHWH is 'the God of Abraham, Isaac and Jacob' and the one 'who brought you out of Egypt'. The name YHWH gets attached to the biography by continuous usage and by explicit identification in Exod. 3.13-16 and 6.2-8.[9] In this way, the Pentateuch's stories build a coherent picture of the character of YHWH.

The laws explicitly evoke YHWH's biography in historical motive clauses (see Chapter 3 above) and ground their prescriptions by invoking the divine name. The laws of Exodus, Leviticus and Numbers supplement such direct characterization by the impressions provided by YHWH's speech. Speeches always indirectly characterize their speaker by providing readers the basis for inferring the kind of person who talks this way.[10] So the law codes voiced directly by God provide a powerful impression of the divine character.[11]

Literary analyses of the Pentateuch have tended to downplay the significance of direct quoted speech for divine characterization, subordinating it to narrative. D.J.A. Clines, for example, suggested that, because the narrator transmits direct quoted speech, 'the words in the mouth of God have no privileged status compared with words spoken directly by the narrator in describing God's motives and actions'.[12]

9.   On the use of name and biography in the characterization of God, see Patrick, *Rendering of God*, pp. 31-37.

10.   On implicit characterization by quoted direct speech in other parts of the Hebrew Bible, see Savran, *Telling and Retelling*, pp. 79-94; Watts, *Psalm and Story*; M. Cheney, *Dust, Wind and Agony: Character, Speech and Genre in Job* (ConBOT, 36; Lund: Almqvist & Wiksell, 1994); and E. ben Zvi, 'Twelve Prophetic Books or "The Twelve": Preliminary Considerations', in P.R. House and J.W. Watts (eds.), *Essays on Isaiah and the Twelve in Honor of John D.W. Watts* (JSOTSup, 235; Sheffield: Sheffield Academic Press, 1996), pp. 125-56 (152-54).

11.   'Even the legislator appears in the text. He does not claim to be anonymous, impersonal or above the law. He chooses entirely different forms of legitimation from modern law' (Jackson, *Ceremonial and Judicial*, p. 120).

12.   'God in the Pentateuch: Reading Against the Grain', in *Interested Parties: The Ideology of Writers and Readers of the Hebrew Bible* (JSOTSup, 205; Sheffield: Sheffield Academic Press, 1995), pp. 187-211 (187). Similarly Savran: 'Narration through quotation by a character in the story is not meant to compete with the impersonal narrator, for the reader must be aware that a character acts and speaks only at the behest of the narrator' (*Telling and Retelling*, p. 13; cf. Sternberg, *Poetics*, p. 476). L. Eslinger admitted that YHWH's evaluation may conflict with that implied by the narrator, but still insisted that the narrator's evaluation remains decisive, despite a history of interpretation to the contrary, which he

Such reasoning rules out in advance the possibility of tensions between a narrator's description and a character's self-presentation.[13] It also produces literary 'biographies' of God that pay little attention to God's own words.[14] In contrast, classical theorists of rhetoric recognized self-characterization, the speaker's *ethos*, as crucial to persuasion. Aristotle argued that 'Persuasion is achieved by the speaker's personal character when the speech is so spoken as to make us think him credible... This kind of persuasion, like the others, should be achieved by what the speaker says, not by what people think of his character before he begins to speak.'[15] When characters' speeches dominate a text, as God's words do in Exodus 20 to Leviticus, and as Moses' do in Deuteronomy, they may overwhelm the narration's characterizations of the speakers with their own.

Commandment and Character
In Hebrew stories, YHWH's speeches characteristically emphasize transactions with the addressee(s). Patrick observed that 'God normally divulges his name, promises, commands, expresses his state of mind,

summarized ('Freedom or Knowledge? Perspective and Purpose in the Exodus Narrative [Exodus 1–15],' *JSOT* 52 [1991], pp. 43-60; repr. in J.W. Rogerson [ed.], *The Pentateuch: A Sheffield Reader* [Sheffield: Sheffield Academic Press, 1996], pp. 186-202).

13. Polzin provided a more nuanced evaluation of a narrator's reliability in the face of a dominant speaking character, in this case, Moses (*Moses*, pp. 25-29). He too eventually ceded dominance to the narrator (p. 72). Olson disagreed, arguing that it is YHWH who emerges dominant at the end of Deuteronomy (*Deuteronomy*, p. 181).

14. Thus J. Miles defends his scant attention to the books of Leviticus (5 pages), Numbers (7 pages) and Deuteronomy (11 pages) on the grounds that, in comparison with Genesis and Exodus, 'God changes less in the biblical books that immediately follow, and the literary biographer has less need to talk about them' (*God: A Biography* [New York: Knopf, 1995], p. 127). Here the isolation of *change* as the crucial issue in characterization inevitably subordinates all other genres to narrative. Closer attention to self-characterization through instruction provokes the more balanced evaluation of T.W. Mann: 'When we consider the complementary functions of instruction (*torah*) and narration we shall find that the book [of Leviticus] represents an indispensable development in the characterization of Yahweh and Israel' (*Book of the Torah*, p. 113).

15. *Rhet.* 1.2.1356a. For an application to Deuteronomy, see Lenchak, '*Choose Life!*', p. 58 and *passim*.

and/or pronounces judgment when he speaks.'[16] God 'exerts his influence', as Sternberg put it, 'less through words than deeds or through words as substitutes for or preliminaries to deeds: performatives, forecasts, commands, admonitions'.[17] Laws framed as commandments thus exemplify a divine characteristic already established in the preceding stories, but bring it to even greater prominence. YHWH is the one who gives the law and commands Israel to obey it.

A commandment is a performative utterance that does not describe reality, but rather creates it.[18] The command invokes the speaker's authority and establishes an obligation on the addressee(s). Therefore commandments presume and reinforce the speaker's authority and characterize the speaker as someone who orders these kinds of activities.

The authority to command may stem from several sources. The Pentateuch does not emphasize inherent divine right, based in the act of creation, as much as one might expect.[19] Occasionally, God's creative acts are cited to motivate imitation (Exod. 20.11) and the law's wisdom is extolled (Deut. 4.4-8). Such references are remarkably rare around Pentateuchal law when compared with prophetic and psalmic texts that describe law and covenant in terms of cosmology and wisdom (e.g. Pss. 19; 119.1-16, 89-105; Jer. 33.19-21, 25-26; Sir. 24.23).[20]

For the most part, the Pentateuch's laws derive their authority

---

16. D. Patrick, 'The Rhetoric of Revelation', *HBT* 16 (1994), pp. 20-40 (24), adding 'These utterances cannot be reduced to declaratory statements about God and creatures without doing violence to their rhetoric... Rather they create a social reality between God and the humans he addresses whose truth can only be known in response.' See also *idem, Rendering of God*, pp. 90-100.

17. Sternberg, *Poetics*, p. 157.

18. Performative statements were described in the speech-act theory of J.L. Austin (*How to Do Things with Words* [William James Lectures, 1955; Cambridge, MA: Harvard University Press, 2nd edn, 1975]), which has been invoked by many interpreters to describe divine commands in biblical literature. In literary theory, M.M. Bakhtin emphasized a speaker's utterance as the essential defining element in the novelistic genre, a point of view that his editor, Michael Holquist, compared to speech-act theory (*Dialogic Imagination*, p. xxi). Bakhtin argued that the 'authoritative discourse' of commandment is foreign to the dialogical nature of prose art and belongs among the rhetorical forms instead (*Dialogic Imagination*, pp. 342-44, and Holquist on pp. xxxii-xxxiii).

19. Patrick, 'Is the Truth', p. 431.

20. On these, see Levenson, 'Theologies of Commandment', pp. 25-33.

...m more immediate relationships. Autobiographical references
...ng past actions on Israel's behalf introduce the Ten Com-
...nts ('I am YHWH your God, who brought you out of the land
...out of the slave house,' Exod. 20.2) and the Sinai legislation
...You have seen what I did to the Egyptians, how I carried
...wings and brought you to myself,' Exod. 19.4; 'You
...seen that I spoke with you from heaven', 20.22). A
...reater actions in the future introduces the 'Cultic
...do wonders that have never been done in all the
...ations', Exod. 34.10). Such references evoke the
...biography and promises contained in the preced-
...ound YHWH's authority to command in Israel's
...God. Because YHWH has done and will do these
...l owes YHWH obedience.[21]

...source of God's authority to command law lies in
...lationship with Israel, that is, the covenant. This
...plicitly described as including Israel's obedience to
...19.5), and the people's acceptance of the covenant
...at point (v. 8). God's authority therefore derives in part

...proclamation of Yhwh's saving deeds, the exodus above all, is not
...produce a philosophical generalization, but an existential claim. Yhwh
...onstrated his power and good will, and Israel owes him its praise and
s... (Patrick, 'Is the Truth', p. 433). A rabbinic midrash makes this same
o... ation on the persuasive influence of biography on the acceptance of law in
the ...rm of a parable:

> A king who entered a province said to the people: May I be your king?
> But the people said to him: Have you done anything good for us that you
> should rule over us? What did he do for them? He built the city wall for
> them, he brought in the water supply for them, and he fought their
> battles. Then when he said to them: May I be your king? They said to
> him: Yes, yes. Likewise, God. He brought the Israelites out of Egypt,
> divided the sea for them, sent down the manna for them, brought up the
> well for them, brought the quails for them. He fought for them the battle
> with Amalek. Then He said to them: May I be your king? And they said
> to Him: Yes, yes.

(Translation in J.Z. Lauterbach [ed.], *Mekilta de-Rabbi Ishmael* [Philadelphia: Jewish Publication Society, 1933], II, pp. 229-30, as modified by J.D. Levenson, *The Death and Resurrection of the Beloved Son: The Transformation of Child Sacrifice in Judaism and Christianity* [New Haven: Yale University Press, 1993], pp. 168-69, 245).

from a prior agreement establishing YHWH's role as law-giver.[22] The rhetoric of covenantal authority has 'the power to persuade subsequent generations to accept responsibility for incurring the obligation; the narrative engages the audience in a performative act'.[23] The deity engages in rituals of covenant-making that are shaped by rhetorical conventions and social norms, as the much-studied parallels between the laws and treaties of the ancient Near East and Bible show.

This conclusion contradicts that of Sternberg who, in commenting on speech-act theory, argued that 'the biblical convention of divine performative works against convention, deriving its affective force from the infringement or the transcendence of all the norms that would govern a human equivalent'.[24] Whether or not this observation is true of some Hebrew narratives, it does not describe the heavy use of traditional contents and forms in biblical law and the stories that describe covenant making. From its use of Mesopotamian legal traditions through its modification of international treaty forms to its overarching application of the conventional persuasive strategy of story, list and sanctions, the Pentateuch depicts YHWH as using and being bound by human social and rhetorical norms.[25] The narratives thus depict YHWH's authority to command as partly due to Israel's delegation to YHWH of a socially established role, that of law-giver. They characterize YHWH as the kind of God who accepts and abides by such conventions.

Despite these biographical and social claims of authority, it remains possible for those addressed by commands to reject them. Authority is not real unless it is acknowledged. Though the people immediately acquiesce to the divine commandments (Exod. 20.19; 24.3, 7), the warnings that punctuate the law collections anticipate less positive responses, and the narratives bear them out. So the characterization of YHWH as authoritative law-giver must be completed by the characteri-

22. Patrick noted that the Hebrew Bible derives much of its legal authority from 'actual or putative performative transactions', i.e., covenant making in Exod. 19–20, 24, 34, and Josh. 24 ('Is the Truth', p. 431).

23. Patrick, 'Is the Truth', p. 432.

24. *Poetics*, p. 108. Similarly, D.J.A. Clines: 'The God of the Pentateuch is a complex and mysterious character, passionate and dynamic but by no means conformable to human notions of right behavior' ('God in the Pentateuch', p. 211).

25. So Miles: 'The giving of laws has an effect on the lawgiver as well as on the law receiver…[God] will move out of the realm of the purely arbitrary and into the realm of the bounded and lawful' (*God*, p. 121).

zation of Israel and the readers as obliged to obey God's laws (see below).

Contents and Character

Commandments characterize not only the authority of their speaker, but also illustrate by their contents other aspects of character. Patrick pointed out that the First Commandment (Exod. 20.3; Deut 5.7) heightens YHWH's position to a unique level, something not presupposed by prior covenantal commitments.[26] Other laws may less directly address YHWH's role in the community, but all serve to establish through direct discourse the issues of concern to God.

We must therefore consider the emphases established by repetition of contents not just for their mnemonic value, as in Chapter 3 above, but also as a means of characterizing the speaker of law.[27] The character of YHWH as law-giver that emerges from the laws and commandments of Exodus, Leviticus and Numbers shows similarities to the characterizations of their sponsors provided in many ancient Near Eastern law collections, treaties, and commemorative and dedicatory inscriptions. Just as the forms of Pentateuchal law and some of these texts were shaped by similar persuasive strategies (Chapter 2 above), so also their parallel contents depict similar characterizations of their speakers.

Prologues to Mesopotamian law-collections usually emphasize the king's divine election, accomplishments, and intent to establish justice. The latter depends on the king's god-given ability to perceive immutable truth and apply it fairly. The lists of laws that follow are intended therefore to demonstrate the king's claims to a just rule.[28]

The case (or casuistic) laws of the Pentateuch show a similar interest for fairness and equity, and thereby characterize their promulgator as just. The repetition of particular issues elevates them to paradigmatic illustrations of YHWH's concerns. For example, laws protecting the welfare of resident aliens (Exod. 22.20 [Eng. 22.21]; 23.9; Lev. 19.33-34; 24.22; Num. 9.14; 15.14-16, 29-30; 35.15) establish in the divine speeches the theme of YHWH's equal justice for all. YHWH's emphasis on the community's punishment of murderers (Exod. 20.13; 21.12, 14,

---

26. Patrick, 'Is the Truth', p. 427.
27. Mann, *Book of the Torah*, pp. 116-17.
28. Paul, *Book of the Covenant*, pp. 5-7, 17; J. Hengstl, 'Zur Frage von Rechtsvereinheitlichung im frühaltbabylonischen Mesopotamien und im griechisch-römischen Ägypten: Eine rechtsvergleichende Skizze', *RIDA* 40 (1993), pp. 27-55.

21; Lev. 24.17, 21; Num. 35.16-21, 30-34) demonstrates that God shares judicial authority with the leaders of the community. These texts, together with the rest of the Pentateuch's civil legislation, paint a portrait of YHWH that exemplifies the ancient Near Eastern ideal of the just king.

The considerable overlap in the contents and themes of biblical and Mesopotamian civil laws has prompted numerous theories of legal history and composition.[29] To these we may now add a rhetorical explanation: the parallel contents reflect the similar goals of biblical and Mesopotamian law, namely the characterization of the law-giver as just according to internationally recognized standards of law.[30] Deuteronomy 4.6-8 shows Israel's awareness of this widespread judicial ideal and its judgment that Pentateuchal law demonstrates the superiority of the divine law-giver as measured by international standards.

Many interpreters have found that superiority not in the similarities but in the differences between Pentateuchal and other ancient Near Eastern laws. M. Greenberg, for example, explained the absence in biblical law of a husband's or king's usual right to pardon an adulterous wife or a murderer as due to the law's divine authorship: 'the injured party is God, whose injury no human can pardon or mitigate'.[31] Similarly, E. Otto suggested that the divine voicing in the Book of the Covenant serves to limit human rule.[32] In these and other ways, the idea that YHWH is Israel's king and overlord impacts the details of criminal law.[33] Thus in their distinctive details, as well as their overall similari-

29. For recent overviews, see the essays edited by Levinson in *Theory and Method*.

30. R. Westbrook denied the parallel: 'by no stretch of the imagination can the chapters following the legal corpus (however widely defined) in Exodus and Deuteronomy be described as *apologia* of the lawgiver; there is therefore no evidence from their present textual context that the codes originated in a royal inscription' ('Biblical and Cuneiform Law Codes', *RB* 92 [1985], pp. 247-64 [250]). But the Pentateuch has appropriated the genres of royal inscription to portray the divine king, YHWH; thus the present context is in fact a kind of royal inscription.

31. M. Greenberg, 'Some Postulates of Biblical Criminal Law', in *idem, Studies in the Bible and Jewish Thought* (Philadelphia: Jewish Publication Society, 1995 [1960]), pp. 25-41 (29-30).

32. E. Otto, 'Gesetzesfortschreibung und Pentateuchredaktion', *ZAW* 107 (1995), pp. 373-92 (377).

33. Greenberg describes this 'double metaphor' for God: 'God is at once a

ties to ancient standards, the civil codes of the Pentateuch characterize God as king.

Pentateuchal codes include religious as well as civil laws, a mixture unparalleled in the ancient Near East.[34] Many of the religious provisions resemble those found in non-Israelite inscriptions commemorating the founding of a temple or cult. Such documents may include instructions or accounts of the (re)building of a sanctuary,[35] provision for a cult's supplies through land grants or taxes,[36] instructions for or descriptions of (especially the amounts of) sacrifices,[37] and requirements on the priesthood of exclusive service to this temple and its god.[38] The purpose of such inscriptions is to characterize the cult founder as a devout ruler who makes wise provisions guaranteeing perpetual service to the gods.

These themes dominate large portions of YHWH's speeches to Moses in the Pentateuch. Detailed instructions for constructing the Tabernacle

treaty partner and the proper King of Israel' ('Three Conceptions', p. 15). However, both are royal characterizations: kings make treaties as well as laws. It is really Israel who is cast in multiple roles, as vassals, as citizens and as priests (below and Greenberg, 'Three Conceptions', pp. 15-16) of the one king, YHWH.

34. Hurowitz noted, however, that in Hammurabi's Code the juxtaposition of a list of the king's contributions to various temples with the list of laws 'show[s] that in portraying the king for gods and posterity, divine service and social service were considered on an equal par' (*Inu Anum*, p. 61).

35. E.g. a letter of Nebuchadnezzar I to the Babylonians (Foster, *Before the Muses*, I, p. 302) and the 'Marduk Prophecy' (*Before the Muses*, I, pp. 304-306); cf. the mortuary stela of Amenhotep III (Lichtheim, *Ancient Egyptian Literature*, II, pp. 43-47).

36. E.g. Kurigalzu's land grant to the Ishtar temple (Foster, *Before the Muses*, I, pp. 278-79), Seti I's endowment of goldwashers for his Abydos temple (Lichtheim, *Ancient Egyptian Literature*, II, pp. 55-56), Nectanebo's grant of a portion of Naucratis's taxes to a temple (*Ancient Egyptian Literature*, III, pp. 86-89), the Famine Stela's record of grants of land, personnel and supplies to a temple (*Ancient Egyptian Literature*, III, pp. 94-100).

37. E.g. Kurigalzu's inscription: '3 kor of bread, 3 kor of fine wine, 2 (large measures) of date cakes, 30 quarts of imported dates, 30 quarts of fine(?) oil, 3 sheep per day did I establish as the regular offering for all time' (Foster, *Before the Muses*, I, pp. 279); similarly the 'Marduk Prophecy' (*Before the Muses*, I, p. 307) and the Karatepe inscription (*ANET*, pp. 653-54).

38. A rare feature found in a Greek inscription from Sardis prohibiting the priests of Zeus from participating in·the 'mysteries' of other local gods (Frei, 'Zentralgewalt', pp. 19-20).

sanctuary in Exodus 25–31 are matched by the narrative of their execution in Exodus 35–40. YHWH repeatedly mandates various means for
the support of the sanctuary in perpetuity, such as taxes and tithes
(Exod. 30.11-16; Lev. 27.30-33; Num. 18.25-32) and first-fruits offerings (Exod. 23.19; 34.26; Lev. 19.24; 23.10-14; Num. 15.17-21; 31.25-
29), and specifically delineates the priesthood's sources of income
(Lev. 6.16-18, 26, 29; 7.6, 8-10, 14, 31-36; 23.20; Num. 18.8-32;
31.25-29). YHWH stipulates the nature of the sacrifices (most
specifically in Lev. 1–7) and establishes the annual calendar of religious festivals and sacrifices (Exod. 23.10-19; 34.22-23; Lev. 23; 25;
Num 28–29), with special emphasis on the Sabbath (Exod. 16.22-30;
20.8-11; 23.12; 31.12-17; 34.21; 35.2-3; Lev. 19.3b; 19.30a; 23.3; 25.2-
7; 26.2). YHWH's claim on Israel's exclusive worship (Exod. 20.3;
22.19 [Eng. 22.20]; 23.13; 34.14) may depend in part on the depiction
of the entire people as a priesthood consecrated to YHWH's service
(Exod. 19.6; cf. 22.30 [Eng. 22.31]; Lev. 19.2; 20.26). It includes
repeated prohibitions on certain kinds of religious practices, such as
divination (Exod. 22.17 [Eng. 22.18]; Lev. 19.26b, 31; 20.6, 27) and
the use of images (Exod. 20.4-6, 23; 34.17; Lev. 19.4; 26.1).

Of course, these Pentateuchal laws do not praise the accomplishments of a human ruler but rather describe God's own establishment of
religious institutions and practices. This difference does not, however,
alter the resulting characterization very much. Like the royal sponsors
of dedicatory inscriptions, YHWH guarantees the sacred equilibrium
between heaven and earth by establishing the cult that mediates
between them and by mandating perpetual means for its support. The
speeches cast YHWH as the ruler who founds and sponsors the cult, and
thus as the guarantor of cosmic order through royal authority. Like the
dedicatory inscriptions, the speeches also help legitimate that authority
by showing the beneficial use to which it is put.

Law codes and dedicatory inscriptions do not exhaust the list of
ancient Near Eastern genres which share concerns with the Pentateuch's legal collections voiced by YHWH. For example, treaties
between imperial overlords and vassal rulers stipulate some similar
provisions, notably demands for exclusive loyalty and the payment of
taxes. These comparisons simply reinforce the characterization of
YHWH as protective overlord, cult founder and equitable judge, that is,
as the ideal ruler.[39] Though such depictions are typical of royal inscrip-

39. Mann, *Book of the Torah*, pp. 102-105.

tions throughout the region, only the Bible combines them together in a single text.[40]

Yet this royal portrayal never becomes explicit. Unlike the inscriptions that tend to predicate the names of their sponsors with glorious titles, the Pentateuch's laws never call YHWH a 'king'.[41] At most, adjectives describe God's attitude as judge ('I am compassionate', Exod. 22.26 [Eng. 22.27]) or as religious competitor ('I am a jealous God', Exod. 20.5; 34.14), but such emotional self-characterizations are rare. Throughout YHWH's speeches, however, the law collections of Exodus, Leviticus and Numbers implicitly depict their speaker as fulfilling the ancient ideal of a good monarch.

The Pentateuch's restraint contrasts with psalms that celebrate YHWH's rule explicitly (Pss. 43; 93; 95; 96; 97; 98; 99). In the Pentateuch, only poems declare 'YHWH rules' or 'YHWH is ruler' (Exod. 15.18), or that YHWH is 'king' (Num. 23.21 and, if YHWH is the subject, Deut. 33.5). Inset Hebrew poetry typically states themes explicitly that are implicitly developed in the surrounding prose.[42]

Yet the narrative's restraint still requires explanation. The old theory that, with these poetic exceptions, the Pentateuch knows nothing of the kingship of God must be rejected in light of its implicit yet thoroughgoing characterization of God as royal law-speaker.[43] More likely is the suggestion of S. Kreuzer that many biblical texts distinguish between God's 'lordship' over Israel and God's 'kingship' over nature and over the divine realms (i.e. other gods).[44] Pentateuchal lists and stories may

---

40. Paul, *Book of the Covenant*, p. 37.

41. Moses comes closer to an explicitly royal description in Deut. 10.17-18, but still avoids the root מלך 'king, royal rule': 'For YHWH your God is God of gods and Lord (אדני) of lords (האדנים), great, mighty and awesome, who does not show partiality and does not take a bribe, who executes justice for the orphan and the widow, and who loves strangers by giving them food and clothing.'

42. Watts, *Psalm and Story*, pp. 38, 96, 116-17, 190-91.

43. For the notion that divine kingship was a late addition to Israel's theology, see G. von Rad, 'מלך and מלכות in the OT', *TDNT*, I, pp. 565-71 (570), and the survey by Childs, *Biblical Theology*, pp. 633-34.

44. S. Kreuzer, 'Die Verbindung von Gottesherrschaft und Königtum Gottes im Alten Testament', in J.A. Emerton (ed.), *Congress Volume: Paris 1992* (VTSup, 56; Leiden: E.J. Brill, 1995), pp. 145-61. Kreuzer argued that God's rule over Israel is therefore expressed not by the title מלך 'king' but rather by אדון 'lord', though the name YHWH incorporates into itself the notion of rule to such an extent that it 'requires no further title' (p. 158).

avoid the language of divine kingship in order not to invoke the existence of other gods.[45] Yet YHWH's commandments powerfully assert
God's rule over Israel and thereby implicitly characterize their speaker
as lord and king.

Most of YHWH's explicit self-characterizations focus instead on
divinity. They take two forms. One form claims title to divinity: 'I am
YHWH your God' (28 times in Exodus–Numbers, not counting frequent third-person self-references to '[YHWH] your God'). The other
describes the divine condition with an adjective, 'I am holy' (Lev.
11.44, 45; 19.2; 20.26; 21.8). Other uses of the word 'holy' appear
throughout Leviticus, making the characterization of YHWH by this
term a major theme of the book.[46] By combining these explicit claims
to divinity with the laws' implicit royal characterization, the YHWH
speeches of Exodus–Numbers combine the two patterns into a self-
portrait of the divine ruler.

All of these connotations become associated with the divine name,
YHWH, so that it can be used alone to justify commandments ('for I am
YHWH', Lev. 18.5, etc.). At the point in the Pentateuch where this
phrase echoes through the Holiness Code, the name has become richly
evocative of the layers of characterization provided by preceding texts:
the God of the fathers and the savior of Israel from Egypt, from
YHWH's narrative biography and autobiographical references; the fair
and merciful law-giver, from YHWH's commandments; the exacting
cult-founder, from YHWH's religious laws; the protective overlord,
from the use of the formal conventions of treaties/covenants; the holy
God, from YHWH's explicit self-descriptions. Thus most of the decisive
characterizations of YHWH in the Pentateuch are provided by the laws
and instructions of Exodus, Leviticus and Numbers (and reinforced by
Moses' repetition in Deuteronomy).

Contradiction and Character

Consistency affects characterization. Though absolute consistency produces unrealistic characters, readers still weigh inconsistencies in and
between words and actions for their understanding of a character. In the
case of YHWH, issues of divine freedom and fidelity complicate that

45. For a description of how Pentateuchal narrative presupposes a monotheistic
perspective, see D. Patrick, 'The First Commandment in the Structure of the
Pentateuch', *VT* 45 (1995), pp. 107-18.

46. Mann, *Book of the Torah*, pp. 116-17.

evaluation, but do not exempt God from the conventional workings of literary characterization.[47]

YHWH's commandments and instructions sometimes contradict each other. For example, all altars should be made of earth or unhewn stones according to Exod. 20.24-25, but God orders a Tabernacle altar built of gold-embossed wood (Exod. 27.1-8). YHWH commands the sacrifice of first-born sons as well as animals in Exod. 22.28-29 (Eng. 22.29-30), though all other laws regarding the first-born emphasize redemption of humans (Exod. 13.12-13; 34.19-20; Num. 3.11-13, 44-51).[48] Victims of theft should receive more reparations according to Exod. 21.37–22.3, 6-8 (Eng. 22.1-4, 7-9) than according to Lev. 6.5. Such inconsistencies not only complicate the teaching and application of the instructions (see Chapter 3 above), they also raise questions about this self-contradictory speaker, YHWH.

The consequences of self-contradiction for the character of God in the Pentateuch are, however, far from obvious. Stories usually explain inconsistencies on the basis of plot developments, psychological descriptions or the character's motives. Biblical narratives and prophetic texts explore such themes in YHWH's character as well, describing God as feeling a humanlike 'repentance' (e.g. Gen. 6.6) and also as claiming a non-human freedom from the constraints of consistency (Hos. 11.8-10). The stories surrounding Pentateuchal laws and instructions, however, offer no narrative rationales for the contradictions in YHWH's commandments. The inconsistencies do not usually accord with plot developments (see Chapter 3 above), nor do they paint a coherent portrait of changing divine motives. Narratives do not explain inconsistencies in Pentateuchal laws.

Narrative techniques are not the only genre conventions at work in YHWH's commandments. Lists of laws and instructions operate by their own principles of genre which require no narrative rationale. Since legal and instructional genres dominate God's speeches, it is fair to ask how inconsistencies within them influence YHWH's *legal* characterization.

Legal and religious traditions must necessarily adapt to changing

47. On consistency in the Bible's characterization of God, see Patrick, *Rendering of God*, pp. 46-60, who summarized, 'A single identity emerges ... in a dialectical process that absorbs divergent, discrepant and polemical features into the portrait of the God already known' (p. 47).

48. See Levenson, *Death and Resurrection*, pp. 3-17, 43-52.

circumstances. Revisions and amendments are therefore characteristic features of civil laws and religious instructions of every period and society. The Pentateuch suggests that in ancient Israel's legal understanding, God not only established laws but also founded a tradition of legal and religious interpretation and revision.[49]

Biblical scholarship has long maintained that Pentateuchal laws were produced through ongoing traditions of legal thought.[50] Some legal texts, however, are not only products of such traditions, but explicitly show legal interpretation and development taking place within divine law. In Lev. 24.10-23, the case of a half-Israelite blasphemer prompts YHWH to enunciate a new legal principle, 'You shall have one law for the alien and for the citizen: for I am YHWH your God' (v. 22), and to apply it to a variety of offenses (vv. 16-21). Some Israelites' predicament of being disqualified from celebrating the Passover by uncleanness leads YHWH to authorize a second celebration at a later date (Num. 9.6-14, the last verse repeating the principle from Lev. 24.22). The arrest of an offender elicits YHWH's ruling on whether gathering firewood on the Sabbath is a capital crime in Num. 15.32-36. The case of Zelophehad dying without male heirs leads YHWH to expand inheritance rights in such circumstances to daughters (Num. 27.1-11).

These cases not only illustrate the development of Israelite legal traditions.[51] They also cast God as the principal instigator of change within law. In addition to giving the laws in the first place, YHWH reacts to new circumstances by enunciating underlying judicial principles, defining the scope of the law's jurisdiction, developing alternative

---

49. Nohrnberg described the operations of Exodus's laws and stories about laws in narrative terms: 'the text of the narrative becomes its own story: that is, it becomes a case of elongation (or "dilation"), abbreviation, displacement, and interruption' (*Like Unto Moses*, p. 54), but concluded by pointing out the consequences of the generic shift: 'The end result is less a law, than an *art* of law' (p. 56, Nohrnberg's emphasis). As a result, 'laws are like texts; to be kept they must needs be searched, codified, compared, redacted, reinterpreted, and emended' (p. 60; see also p. 75).

50. The nature and development of the Pentateuch's legal thinking has been summarized by, among others, Greenberg, 'Some Postulates', pp. 25-41; P.D. Millar, Jr, 'The Place of the Decalogue in the Old Testament and its Law', *Int* 43 (1989), pp. 229-42 (233-42).

51. For formal and legal comparisons between these cases, see Fishbane, *Biblical Interpretation*, pp. 98-104; Westbrook, 'Biblical and Cuneiform Law Codes', pp. 261-64; Crüsemann, *The Torah*, pp. 98-101.

means for compliance, and expanding enfranchisement. Thus God establishes not only the laws but also the process of legal development. These case laws characterize YHWH as judge, legal interpreter and legal reformer, as well as law-giver.

God is the only source of law, according to the Pentateuchal writers. This divine monopoly does not, however, extend to the other legal functions of judicial administration, interpretation and reform. A diverse group of humans takes part in these activities. Jethro, Midianite priest and Moses' father-in-law, suggests a system of judicial appeal that Moses implements without consulting YHWH (Exod. 18.13-26). No statement of YHWH ever repeats or alters this system, though a later divine command validates the idea of delegated power (Num. 11.16-17) and other divine commandments presuppose the existence of some kind of judiciary (Exod. 23.2-3, 6-8; Lev. 19.15-16). Aaron, in his function as High Priest, wins an argument with Moses over the interpretation of certain cultic regulations (Lev. 10.16-20). Human reason, not divine fiat, plays the decisive role. In Num. 36.1-12, Moses, acting in his capacity as highest court of appeal, limits the enfranchisement granted to Zelophehad's daughters by YHWH's previous case decision in Num. 27.[52] Unlike the earlier text which quotes God directly, God does not speak in Numbers 36 but Moses reports the decision 'according to the command of YHWH'.[53] Here human mediation takes the place of divine speech in the development of legal tradition.

The placement of these three episodes relative to YHWH's laws and instructions suggests an intentional commentary on divine–human interaction in legal traditions. Jethro's advice in Exodus 18 precedes the giving of divine law at Sinai (and disrupts the temporal progression of the story: see Chapter 3). Aaron's casuistry in Leviticus 10 occurs at the climactic moment of the inauguration of Tabernacle worship, in the center of the divine lists of instructions and laws that dominate Exodus 20 through Numbers (see Chapter 2). Moses' judgment in Numbers 36

---

52. Because the inheritance would now 'revert to precisely those males who would be next in line if the father had no children whatsoever...the ruling in favour of female inheritance provided by the first adjudication (Num. 27.8) is functionally subverted by the *responsum* in Num. 36.6-9—*even though* its specific provisions remain valid (27.9-10)' (Fishbane, *Biblical Interpretation*, p. 105, Fishbane's emphasis).

53. עַל פִּי יהוה: this phrase in Numbers usually describes Moses' fulfillment of a previously quoted divine order: e.g. 3.16, 39, 51; 4.37, 41, 45, 49, etc.

follows the last of YHWH's large legal speeches in the Pentateuch, and anticipates Deuteronomy's focus on Moses' mediation and reinterpretation of divine law. Thus before, after and at the center of YHWH's instructional speeches, the Pentateuch highlights human participation in the development of Israel's legal and religious traditions.

This point should not be overstated. Biblical law remains quite reticent in showing the historical development of law. B.M. Levinson has described a 'rhetoric of concealment' in inner-biblical and later legal interpretation that camouflages change by misquoting the original laws, failing to credit them to YHWH, or reinterpreting them contrary to their plain sense.[54] This concern to conceal legal history also motives the Pentateuch's placement of all law at Sinai or in the Wilderness and the canonical tradition's description of all five books as divine Torah, which of course includes the legal contributions of Jethro, Aaron and especially Moses.[55] The Pentateuch does not, however, go so far as to deny any human involvement in the origins of Israel's law. It rather describes the origins of legal and religious instructions in the *interaction* of YHWH with Israel.[56] God gives the law, but also starts the process of interpretation and development in which the human characters participate. Legal and religious traditions necessarily require interpretation and development; this too is Torah. This realization on the part of the Pentateuch's writers leads them to depict YHWH as author, revisor and interpreter of law, and to include humans in the process as well.

These stories of development in Pentateuchal law cast the problem of YHWH's inconsistencies in a new light.[57] Explicit mention of God revising and interpreting the laws invites readers to understand other changes in the same way. Where there is no explicit basis for privileging one commandment over another that contradicts it, the stories of human mediation and interpretation of laws encourage the application of theological and legal reasoning to the problem, and to reckon the results as part of the divine Torah as well. For the justice of a ruler is

54. 'Human Voice', pp. 43-61; cf. Crüsemann, *The Torah*, pp. 102-104.
55. Num. 31.13-24 contains a narrative version of this process: Eleazar (vv. 21-24) not only expands Moses' original command (vv. 19-20) but also credits it to YHWH through Moses; see Fishbane, *Biblical Interpretation*, pp. 259-60 and n. 64.
56. Fishbane, *Biblical Interpretation*, p. 436.
57. Crüsemann noted regarding the stories in Num. 15, 27 and 36, 'The basic problem of new law, of amplification and extension of the Sinai law is treated in narrative form' (*The Torah*, p. 101).

exemplified not only by lists of laws and instructions, but also by the monarch's ability to render fair judgment in extraordinary and unforeseen circumstances (cf. 1 Kgs 3.16-28). If the occasional nature of some of YHWH's rulings seems to offend theological notions of divine foreknowledge, they nevertheless emphasize the implicit self-characterization of YHWH's speeches throughout Exodus–Numbers by exemplifying the wisdom of the just ruler.

Blessing, Curse and Character

Divine sanctions both depend on prior self-characterization by YHWH for their persuasive power and develop that characterization into its most concise and forceful expressions in the Pentateuch. The Pentateuch's stories, especially the deliverance from Egypt, establish God's power to bless and to curse. YHWH's speeches of promise, instruction and law specify God's desires for Israel. The lists of blessings and curses declare God's intention to turn those wishes into reality by enforcing the covenant.

Threats and promises attached to individual laws (e.g. 'for YHWH will not acquit those who misuse his name' Exod. 20.7, or 'so that your days may be long in the land' Exod. 20.12) punctuate the lists of instructions with the theme of YHWH's enforcement. However, the lists of sanctions that conclude the legal codes (Exod. 23.20-33; Lev. 26; Deut. 27–28) provide the most extended depictions of God's willingness to bless or curse in response to Israel's behavior. The speeches characterize their speaker as wishing to reward but willing to punish in order to maintain the covenant. Again, the self-characterization of YHWH takes the guise of the just king, who must not only promulgate and interpret law, but enforce it as well.

This unification of divine power and will in terms of sanctions produces the longest explicit descriptions of God in the Pentateuch:

> For I, YHWH your God, am a jealous God, punishing children for the parent's guilt to the third and fourth generation of those hating me, but showing steadfast love to the thousandth generation of those loving me and keeping my commandments (Exod. 20.5-6).

> YHWH, YHWH, a merciful and gracious God, slow to anger and great in steadfast love and faithfulness, who keeps steadfast love to the thousandth generation, who forgives guilt and transgression and sin, but who certainly does not acquit but rather punishes children for the parent's guilt and the children's children to the third and fourth generation (Exod. 34.6-7).

The royal sound of these self-descriptions of divine benevolence and discipline is confirmed by parallels that show 'love', 'hate' and multi-generational threats and promises to be stock language in ancient Near Eastern treaties.[58] These portrayals in Exodus 20 and 34, like the sanction lists that conclude the law codes, presuppose the stipulations whose enforcement they promise.

Scholarship has tended to discuss the self-characterizations in Exod. 20.5-6 and 34.6-7 in terms of their cultic origins or narrative contexts.[59] The treaty language and the mercy/punishment theme point rather to the political and legal background of this imagery. The literary position of these self-characterizations reinforces that connection: the first is a motive clause within the Decalogue, which is itself part of the covenant stipulations that continue throughout Exodus 21–23; the second precedes a short code ('decalogue'?) of ritual rules (Exod. 34.17-26). The Second Commandment and the story of the Golden Calf also contribute to the legal emphasis: they frame the issue of religious fidelity in terms of God's roles as law-giver, judge and enforcer. Because YHWH rules in Israel, fidelity and obedience is demanded and enforced.

Thus both the vocabulary and the contexts of these most explicit self-descriptions suggest that characterization of the law-speaker is, as in many Mesopotamian codes, a primary goal of biblical law. The divine identity of this law-speaker, however, turns legal characterization into theology. YHWH's self-descriptions became a fundamental point of departure for other biblical reflections on the nature of God (e.g. Num. 14.18; Deut. 7.9-10; Joel 2.13; Jon. 4.2; Nah. 1.3; Pss. 86.15; 103.8; 145.8; Neh. 9.17).[60] Their theological influence echoes throughout

58. W.L. Moran, 'The Ancient Near Eastern Background of the Love of God in Deuteronomy', *CBQ* 25 (1963), pp. 77-87; Weinfeld, *Deuteronomy and the Deuteronomic School*, pp. 81-91; Levinson, 'Human Voice', pp. 46-47.

59. On the cultic origins of 34.6-7, see the survey by R.C. Dentan ('The Literary Affinities of Exodus XXXIV 6f', *VT* 13 [1963], pp. 34-51 [36-37]) who emphasized its wisdom sources instead; cf. Van Seters, *Life of Moses*, pp. 346-51; on its relation to the Golden Calf episode, see R.W.L. Moberly, *At the Mountain of God: Story and Theology in Exodus 32–34* (JSOTSup, 22; Sheffield: JSOT Press, 1983), pp. 128-31, and J.I. Durham, *Exodus* (WBC, 3; Waco, TX: Word Books, 1987), pp. 454-55. Discussion of 20.5-6 tends to focus on God's 'jealousy' and point out the limitation of this vocabulary to contexts of worshiping other gods: see the survey by Childs, *Exodus*, pp. 405-406.

60. J. Scharbert, 'Formgeschichte und Exegese von Ex 34, 6f und Seiner Parallelen', *Bib* 38 (1957), pp. 130-50; Dentan, 'Literary Affinities', pp. 34-51; T.B.

Israel's traditions that both explicitly hail YHWH's kingship and tout
Torah as YHWH's most characteristic expression.[61]

2. *Moses as Law-Speaker*

Moses also speaks law, most fully and explicitly in Deuteronomy. Like
the divine instructions in Exodus, Leviticus and Numbers, Moses'
speeches in Deuteronomy combine genre elements from treaties, law
codes, and commemorative inscriptions into a persuasive appeal for
obedience to God's Torah. The above discussion therefore leads us to
expect that Deuteronomy characterizes Moses as a king also.

The book certainly presents a forceful characterization. The speeches
repeatedly call attention to their speaker, from Moses' autobiographical
review of his service to God and Israel and his suffering as a result
('YHWH was angry with me because of you'),[62] through his urgent
appeals for fidelity and obedience to *his* words ('that I am commanding
you today'),[63] to his threats of legal sanctions for noncompliance ('I
call heaven and earth to witness against you today...').[64] Moses recalls
the narrative setting of the speech at the end of his own life (Num.
27.12-23; Deut. 31.14-16; 32.48-52; 34.1-12) within the speech itself
(3.27-28; 4.22), evoking sympathy to reinforce the persuasive force of
his authority.[65] Deuteronomy presents one of the most powerful self-
characterizations by any speaker in the Hebrew Bible.

Does Moses depict himself in royal terms? Royal motifs shape parts

Dozeman, 'Inner-Biblical Interpretation of Yahweh's Gracious and Compassionate
Character', *JBL* 108 (1989), pp. 207-23 (218-23).

61. So Crüsemann: 'Torah became the medium in...which the unity of God and
the variety of areas of experience and reality were brought together. For that reason
the identity of the biblical God is dependent upon the connection with his Torah'
(*The Torah*, p. 366).

62. Deut. 1.37; 3.26; 4.21; cf. 1.9; 9.9, 18, 25.

63. Deut. 4.1-2, 5, 40; 6.2, 6; 8.1, 11; 10.13; 11.8, 13, 22; 12.11, 14, 21, 28, 32;
13.19 (Eng. 13.18); 15.5, 11, 15; 17.3; 19.7, 9; 24.8, 18, 22; 27.1, 4, 10; 28.1, 13-
15; 29.13 (Eng. 29.14); 30.11; 32.1-3, 46. But the book also unmistakably equates
Moses' and YHWH's commands: 'This very day YHWH your God is commanding
you...' (26.16; also 29.11 [Eng. 29.12]) and even merges Moses and YHWH in the
ambiguous first-person references of 29.1-8 (Eng. 29.2-9).

64. 4.26; cf. 8.19-20; 11.26-28; 30.1-2, 15-16, 18-19.

65. Olson traced the theme of Moses' death throughout Deuteronomy
(*Deuteronomy*, pp. 17-22 and *passim*).

of his biography, most obviously at his birth, and evoke comparisons with heroic sagas that usually include kingship.[66] Mosaic law implicitly (and Deut. 17 explicitly) sets standards for Israel's rulers. Moses fulfills the otherwise royal roles of national leader and highest court of appeal.[67] Moses can therefore be interpreted as a type or example of Israel's ideal king.[68]

The biblical tradition, however, tends to contrast kings with Moses, as J. Rosenberg noted:

> If Moses and David are in some respects parallel figures, they are, in other respects, polar opposites: Moses was a reluctant leader, David an ambitious one; Moses was humble, David self-promoting; Moses clumsy of tongue, David a maker of songs and a genius of public relations; Moses a prophet who challenged a king, David a king who subverted the institutions of the prophets. Moses' grave-site is unknown, David's is Mt. Zion; Moses yielded to a successor from another tribe, David sired a dynasty; Moses wished for collective leadership (Num. 11.29), David centralized it; Moses administered before a traveling sanctuary, David planned a permanent one.[69]

Most notably, Israel's kings never give law.[70] The law comes from

66. H. Gressmann pioneered the comparative study of Moses in light of other ancient stories (*Mose und seine Zeit: Ein Kommentar zu den Mose Sagen* (FRLANT, 18; Göttingen: Vandenhoeck & Ruprecht, 1918). For a survey of the scholarship, see Childs, *Exodus*, pp. 8-11. The approach has more recently been revived by G.W. Coats, *Moses: Heroic Man, Man of God* (JSOTSup, 57; Sheffield: JSOT Press, 1988). Van Seters offered a nuanced evaluation of the Moses story in light of ancient royal biographies (*Life of Moses*, pp. 2-3, 11, 462-63).

67. Though in Exod. 18.15, 19 Moses justifies this role on the basis of his oracular consultation with YHWH, in Deut. 1.17 he omits any reference to divine instructions. Fishbane cited this as an example of Deuteronomy's 'many new tendencies in the increasing rationalization of the juridical process' (*Biblical Interpretation*, pp. 244-45).

68. So Coats, *Moses*, p. 198.

69. *King and Kin: Political Allegory in the Hebrew Bible* (Bloomington: Indiana University Press, 1986), pp. x-xi.

70. The biblical tradition is nevertheless aware of royal law-givers in other countries: see Est. 1.19, 8.8, and compare the matter-of-fact narrative of Solomon's temple building (1 Kgs 5–6) with the decrees of the Persian kings to rebuild the Temple and enforce the law (Ezra 6.1-12; 7.12-26), complete with divine and human sanctions (6.11-12 and 7.23). On kings and biblical law, see H.J. Boecker, *Law and the Administration of Justice in the Old Testament and the Ancient East* (trans. J. Moiser; Minneapolis: Augsburg, 1980), pp. 41-43.

YHWH through Moses, a tradition that emphasizes Moses' uniqueness precisely in comparison with Israel's kings. Stories about Moses' humility (Exod. 3.11–4.17; Num. 12.3) show his lack of royal pretensions and, together with references to his mistakes (Num. 20.12; Deut. 32.51), also contrast him with that other Pentateuchal law-giver, YHWH. Though Moses' self-characterization in Deuteronomy is neither humble nor apologetic, it stops short of royal self-aggrandizement. By invoking his impending death, the speeches set a dominant tone of final admonition and self-justification.[71] Deuteronomy's testamentary view backward and forward in time suggests comparison less with the royal inscriptional genres of laws, treaties, and so on than with the ancient genres of religious autobiography and wise instruction.[72] As a result,

71. 'The text's self-echoing style reconstitutes Moses in the very hour of his falling silent' (Nohrnberg, *Like Unto Moses*, pp. 38-39). Olson suggested that Deuteronomy's genre is best depicted as 'catechesis' in light of its presentation of law in a testamentary context (*Deuteronomy*, pp. 10-11). R.P. Knierim raised the possibility that Pentateuchal editing modified Deuteronomy's genre: he argued that P's redaction of Deut. 1.3 transformed 'the genre of the deuteronomic farewell speech to the genre of the last will and testament of a dying person' (*Task*, p. 359).

72. The distinction is not clear-cut between royal and nonroyal characterizations in these genres because of the prevailing autobiographical tone of most royal inscriptions (see S. Mowinckel, 'Die vorderasiatischen Königs- und Fürsteninschriften, eine stilistische Studie', in Schmidt (ed.), *ΕΥΧΑΡΙΣΤΗΡΙΟΝ*, pp. 278-322). Nevertheless, the testamentary autobiography that reviews a life at the point of death developed in Egyptian funerary literature as a purely private genre: 'Kings had no autobiographies. Their lives were wholly stylized, and at once more public and more remote than those of their subjects' (Lichtheim, *Ancient Egyptian Literature*, I, p. 7). Persian-period autobiographies from Egypt and Israel (in Nehemiah) retain this private character (for comparisons, see G. von Rad, 'Die Nehemia-Denkschrift', *ZAW* 76 [1964], pp. 176-87; J. Blenkinsopp, 'The Mission of Udjahorresnet and Those of Ezra and Nehemiah', *JBL* 106 [1987], pp. 409-21; and J.W. Wright, 'The Legacy of David in Chronicles: The Narrative Function of 1 Chronicles 23–27', *JBL* 110 [1991], pp. 229-42 (237-41), who drew comparisons with David's temple building in 1 Chron. 23–27, though the latter account is not autobiographical). Later Hebrew literature, however, merges autobiography into the genre of royal psalms (e.g. the Septuagint's Ps. 151, etc.; see D. Flusser, 'Psalms, Hymns, and Prayers', in M.E. Stone [ed.], *Jewish Writings of the Second Temple Period* [CRINT, 2.2; Assen: Van Gorcum; Philadelphia: Fortress Press, 1984], pp. 551-77 [561-63]). The genre of wise instruction is sometimes credited to royalty in ancient Near Eastern literature, but often not. The Hebrew Bible associates it mostly with King Solomon (Prov. 1.1; 25.1; Eccl. 1.1; cf. Prov. 24.23; 30.1; 31.1). M. Weinfeld called attention to the ancient genre of wise instruction to the king as

Deuteronomy characterizes Moses less in royal terms than as prophet and teacher/scribe. The dual voicing of Pentateuchal law by YHWH and Moses has two effects: it restricts Deuteronomy's prophetic characterization of Moses to the narrower definition of prophecy presented in the preceding books, while it uses Moses' scribal role to present a unifying rhetoric of divine law.

The Voice of a Prophet
Moses in Deuteronomy agrees with the narrative of Exodus–Numbers in claiming to possess a *delegated* authority to give the law to Israel. Like the narrator, Moses notes two sources for that delegated authority, YHWH and Israel itself. On the one hand, YHWH commissioned Moses to hear and report the law (Deut. 4.14; 5.28-31; 18.15-18; cf. Exod. 19.9); on the other hand, the people asked Moses to mediate between themselves and God (Deut. 5.23-27; cf. Exod. 20.18-20).[73] Moses therefore claims double authorization to speak for God to Israel in law-giving. Perhaps this claim also grounds his authority to speak for Israel to God in intercession. Deuteronomy 27 may illustrate the mediator's double role with co-speakers to distinguish the functions: Moses and the elders (v. 1) pronounce the performative speech for Israel in the covenant ceremony, while Moses and the Levitical priests (v. 9) speak for YHWH.[74] This double delegation of authority to Moses maximizes his rhetorical power in Deuteronomy. When both God and Israel have appointed him to speak for them, who is left to challenge his words?[75]

comparable to Deuteronomy, which expands its intended audience to the people as well (Weinfeld, *Deuteronomy 1–11*, pp. 55-57).

73. Two different traditions of the Mosaic office may be conflated in these texts, as Childs has argued (*Exodus*, pp. 353-59). In the present text, however, they serve rhetorically to reinforce the impression of Moses' authority: 'There is a development within the deuteronomistic redaction from a public revelation of the Decalogue to a private revelation of the Book of the Covenant, which Moses must now promulgate for God. The result of this development is that Moses acquires authority in the deuteronomistic redaction, which mirrors his role in Deuteronomy' (Dozeman, *God on the Mountain*, p. 54).

74. So N. Lohfink, 'Bund als Vertrag im Deuteronomium', *ZAW* 107 (1995), pp. 215-39 (225), though he noted that the contents of the speech in vv. 2-8 do not support this distinction very well (p. 225 n. 38).

75. So Savran: 'Deuteronomy is essentially self-referential, and the authenticity of its quotations depends not upon comparison with prior speech but upon the authoritative voice who quotes them, that is, Moses...Moses' narrative voice has

Mediation comprises the essence of the prophetic role for Deuteron-omy.[76] In Deut. 18.15-22, Moses presents himself as the first of a line of prophets who, by virtue of the authority delegated by the people ('you') as well as YHWH (vv. 16-17), will speak for God to Israel. Deuteronomy thus defines prophets by comparison with Moses, and so turns the statement 'Moses was a prophet' into a tautology.[77]

The larger Pentateuch, however, provides a different depiction of prophecy that situates the speeches of Moses in Deuteronomy relative to the preceding words of God. The Pentateuch does not use prophetic vocabulary and rhetorical forms very often. Except for two places in Deuteronomy (18.15, 18; 34.10), it never calls Moses a prophet. One text (Num. 12.6) contrasts God's direct revelation of law to Moses with the visionary experiences of prophets.[78] When the word 'prophet' does appear, it applies to a variety of phenomena: Abraham's intercession (Gen. 20.7), Aaron's role vis-à-vis Moses (Exod. 7.1), Miriam's sing-ing the victory song at the sea (Exod. 15.20), and the ecstatic behavior of the elders (Num. 11.25-29). Balaam, the most obviously 'prophetic' character in the Pentateuch after Moses, also receives no title but describes himself as a visionary (Num. 24.3-4, 15-16). Nor does Moses

such overwhelming authority in Deuteronomy that it is capable of authenticating all its quotations, regardless of the presence or absence of an earlier "verifying" speech' (*Telling and Retelling*, p. 116).

76. G. von Rad, *Old Testament Theology* (2 vols.; trans. D.M.G. Stalker; New York: Harper & Row, 1962), I, pp. 294-95; Perlitt, *Bundestheologie*, p. 99; Childs, *Exodus*, pp. 355, 359; R.R. Wilson, *Prophecy and Society in Ancient Israel* (Philadelphia: Fortress Press, 1980), pp. 157-66; Otto, 'Gesetzesfortschreibung', p. 381.

77. Blenkinsopp, *Pentateuch*, p. 235.

78. H-C. Schmitt argued that Num. 11–12 support a pro-prophecy redaction (and therefore not P) of the final form of the Pentateuch in the early Hellenistic period. These and associated texts show 'the legitimation of the whole prophetic redaction of the Old Testament and its expectation of the eschatological transformation of Israel' ('Die Suche nach der Identität des Jahweglaubens im nachexilischen Israel: Bemerkungen zur theologischen Intention der Endredaktion des Pentateuch', in J. Mehlhausen [ed.], *Pluralismus und Identität* [Gütersloh: Chr. Kaiser Verlag, 1995], pp. 259-78 [276]). Yet the Pentateuch's very understated depiction of prophecy, compared to its massive focus on priestly issues and to the Deuteronomistic History's equally great obsession with prophecy, suggests that any pro-prophetic redaction was too modest to alter the message of the Pentateuch as a whole.

use the messenger formulas typical of prophets when he delivers laws to Israel, either in Exodus–Numbers or in Deuteronomy.[79] Moses sounds most like other Israelite prophets when his divine message consists of warnings and threats. In the plague stories, the messenger formula regularly introduces YHWH's threats against Egypt (Exod. 7.17; 7.26 [Eng. 8.1]; etc.), which Aaron 'your prophet' (7.1) delivers and implements. And in the Song of Moses (Deut. 32.1-43), Moses deploys a full complement of prophetic vocabulary and rhetorical forms to predict Israel's faithlessness and YHWH's punishment. Like the prophetic books, the Song presents a stronger characterization of YHWH (who emerges as quoted speaker in 32.20-27, 34-35, 37-42) than of Moses.[80] Nevertheless, it does place Moses *literarily* among prophets such as Isaiah and Hosea.

In Chapter 2, I argue that the rhetorical structuring of the whole Pentateuch casts Deuteronomy as the concluding sanctions to the preceding stories (Genesis to Exod. 19) and lists (Exod. 20 to Numbers).[81] A separate voice dominates each element in this very general schema: the anonymous narrator tells the stories, YHWH gives most of the lists, and Moses pronounces the sanctions. The numerous exceptions in detail[82] should not be allowed to obscure the overall rhetorical

---

79. Thus Pentateuchal rhetoric weighs against the prophetic origins of law, contra D.N. Freedman's view that the uniqueness of the *Torah* lay in its prophetic origins ('The Formation of the Canon of the Old Testament', in E.B. Firmage, B.G. Weiss, J.W. Welch [eds.], *Religion and Law: Biblical-Judaic and Islamic Perspectives* [Winona Lake, IN: Eisenbrauns, 1990], pp. 315-31 [326-31]).

80. Watts, *Psalm and Story*, pp. 72-73.

81. I do not claim that Deuteronomy's *genre* should be defined as 'sanctions'; the book also contains large amounts of narrative and law and reproduces in its own structure the pattern of stories (chs. 1–11), lists (chs. 12–26) and sanctions (chs. 27–33), all voiced by Moses (for discussion of the genre of Deuteronomy, see the above comments on autobiography and wise instruction and n. 72). My point is rather that within the Pentateuch's reproduction of this same pattern, Deuteronomy takes the position of the sanctions, a role for which its self-description in terms of 'blessing and curse' (Deut 11.26; 30.19; thus both before and after its laws) suits it well.

82. These are most obvious in Numbers, where the narrator voices lists (the genealogies) and stories, while some laws take the form of direct quotations of Moses (e.g. Num. 30.1-15; 36.5-9) and even Eleazar (31.21-24). Yet the increasing dominance of the divine voice in the latter part of the book supports linking it with Leviticus and the latter half of Exodus.

dominance of each voice within its own sphere.[83]

This Pentateuchal distribution of voices and roles categorizes Moses' speech in Deuteronomy as prophetic threat and promise, and characterizes Moses as a more typical prophet than the book read alone suggests. The Pentateuch's rhetoric appropriates elements within Deuteronomy, such as its self-description as 'blessing and curse' (11.26; 30.19) and its poetic climax in the threats of ch. 32 followed by the blessings of 'Moses Last Words' in ch. 33, for use in a pattern that emphasizes a narrower understanding of Moses' prophetic role. Deuteronomy 32–33 reminds readers of the Pentateuch of other large poems of sanction. Jacob's Blessing (Gen. 49) brings Genesis to a climax with an oracular combination of promise and threat.[84] Balaam, the only professional visionary in the Pentateuch, delivers blessings though hired to pronounce curses (Num. 22–24).[85] These poems appear before major transitions in the Pentateuch's plot: the death of Jacob and the end of the ancestral stories in Genesis 50, the death of the Exodus generation in Numbers 25–26, the death of Moses in Deuteronomy 34.[86] Together with the stories of Moses and Aaron delivering God's threats against Egypt, these Pentateuchal parallels to Deuteronomy categorize Moses'

83. As Levinson noted: 'If the convention of anonymity characterizes the narrative texts of the Bible, as Sternberg rightly stresses, what characterizes the legal texts is the convention of voice, the divine or prophetic attribution of law. Each convention—voice and anonymity—equally constitutes a claim for textual authority, strikingly in each case by disclaiming explicit human authorship' ('Right Chorale', pp. 146-47). But the human voice of Moses emerges strongly in Deuteronomy.

84. Carmichael provided a comparison between Gen. 49 and Deuteronomy and argued that the latter is modeled on the former (*Laws of Deuteronomy*, pp. 23-25).

85. Discussion of Balaam's role has focused either on what kind of Mesopotamian diviner he is (for summaries, see M.S. Moore, *The Balaam Traditions: Their Character and Development* [Atlanta: Scholars Press, 1990], pp. 98, 104-109; J. Milgrom, *Numbers* [Philadelphia: Jewish Publication Society, 1990], pp. 471-73) or how Israel's tradents, especially E and the Deuteronomists, shaped an increasingly negative characterization of him (Wilson, *Prophecy and Society*, pp. 147-50). The poem's role in the wider context of Numbers was analyzed by Olson (*The Death of the Old and the Birth of the New: The Framework of the Book of Numbers and the Pentateuch* [BJS, 71; Chico, CA: Scholars Press, 1985], pp. 153-64).

86. I am grateful to my student, Kenneth Garmen, for elucidating the significance of this pattern.

words as prophetic sanctions.[87] As a result, the larger Pentateuchal context takes Moses the law-giver found in Deuteronomy read apart from what precedes it (and also in Exod. 24 read alone) and makes him *just* a prophet—uniquely great, the exemplar of the prophetic office to be sure, but not a rhetorical competitor with the divine law-giver of Exodus, Leviticus and Numbers.[88] Moses instead completes the Pentateuch's rhetorical strategy by prophetically announcing the consequences of obeying and disobeying God's previously stated laws.

The Pentateuch then does not present itself on the whole as 'the law of Moses', but rather as 'the law of YHWH'. God speaks the law and God alone. Moses announces its consequences, as did Israel's lesser prophets.

The Voice of a Scribe

Deuteronomy's rhetoric calls attention to the Pentateuch's other dominant characterization of Moses as teacher and scribe. The language of sanctions aims at motivation, a key concern of the wisdom literature with which Deuteronomy has much in common.[89] The book also

87. Blenkinsopp noted that Deuteronomy defines prophecy institutionally, so that 'the principle function of the prophet is now to proclaim the law and warn against the consequences of nonobservance, and the same function is amply illustrated in Dtr (e.g., 2 Kings 17.13)' (*Pentateuch*, p. 233). The Pentateuch as a whole emphasizes the second element (warnings of consequences) in its shaping of Mosaic prophecy, while subordinating the first (law-giving) to the dominant divine voice of Exodus–Numbers.

88. Note that the celebration of Moses' uniqueness that concludes the Pentateuch (Deut. 34.10-12) emphasizes his miracles. The laws are not mentioned, despite the long interpretive tradition which has assumed that Mosaic law must be the implicit subject (a tradition summarized and followed by J.H. Tigay, 'The Significance of the End of Deuteronomy', in M.V. Fox *et al.* (eds.), *Texts, Temples and Traditions: A Tribute to Menahem Haran* [Winona Lake, IN: Eisenbrauns, 1996], pp. 137-43).

89. Blenkinsopp noted that in Deuteronomy, 'Moses is presented as teacher and scribe; as such, he not only enunciates the laws but provides motivation for their observance' (*Wisdom and Law in the Old Testament: The Ordering of Life in Israel and Early Judaism* [Oxford: Oxford University Press, rev. edn, 1995], p. 118; also Carmichael, *Laws of Deuteronomy*, pp. 34-52; P.D. Miller, ' "Moses My Servant": The Deuteronomic Portrait of Moses', *Int* 41 [1987], pp. 245-55 [246-47]; repr. in D.L. Christensen [ed.], *A Song of Power and the Power of Song: Essays on the Book of Deuteronomy* [Winona Lake, IN: Eisenbrauns, 1993], pp. 301-12 [302-

emphasizes learning and interpretation (1.5; 4.1, 10; 5.1; 6.6-9, 20) as necessary to obedience. Thus Deuteronomy displays law as instruction and Moses as the paradigmatic instructor. Towards the end the emphasis shifts from speaking ('that I am commanding you today') to texts ('the words of this law that are written in this book' 28.58; 30.10; 'the curses in this book' 28.61; 29.19-20, 26 [Eng. 29.20-21, 27]). Moses appears as transcriber (31.9, 19, 22, 24; a role he also plays in Exod. 24.4; 34.27-28) and urges Israel to follow his example (Deut. 17.18; 27.3, 8).

Moses thus exemplifies the ancient scribe who records, teaches and interprets. In writing, as in speaking, he repeats what he has heard, but he also interprets and composes outright.[90] Deuteronomy 31–32 provides a concise example of this lack of distinction between the scribal roles of author and transcriber: YHWH instructs Moses to write 'this song' (31.19) which Moses voices in the first person (32.1-3) yet which quotes YHWH extensively (32.20-27, 43-35, 37-42). The same process describes Deuteronomy as a whole: Moses claims authority delegated from both YHWH and the people to proclaim laws as first-person commands, yet as YHWH's commandments (thus 'Listen to the voice of YHWH your God and do his commandments and ordinances which I am commanding you today' 27.10). Author, editor and publisher unite in Moses the scribe, yet the law-giver remains YHWH alone.[91]

303]; Olson, *Deuteronomy*, p. 11). The definitive study of wisdom influence on Deuteronomy is Weinfeld's *Deuteronomy and the Deuteronomic School*.

90. The scribe's authority depends, of course, on the claim to transmit the text faithfully and is endangered by charges of overt modification (e.g. Jer. 8.8 'the lying pen of the scribes'). Yet transmission of law always requires its interpretation and application, which is a creative process. Even in the process of simply reproducing texts, editorial creativity is by necessity involved as well (both for ancient scribes and modern text critics: see J.W. Watts, 'Text and Redaction in Jeremiah's Oracles Against the Nations', *CBQ* 54 [1992], pp. 432-47 [436-42]). P.R. Davies argued that even in the literature of the late Second Temple period, 'for a scribe to read, copy and amend was part of the same process' (*In Search of Ancient Israel* [JSOTSup, 148; Sheffield: JSOT Press, 1992], p. 148). Deuteronomy employs on a massive scale both defensive rhetoric of fidelity to the tradition and creative reinterpretations of it.

91. At one point in the Sinai story, YHWH serves as scribe (Exod. 24.12; 31.18; 32.16; Deut. 5.22; 9.10), but only Moses reads the tablets before they are destroyed (Exod. 32.15, 19; Deut. 9.17). Who inscribed the second set of tablets remains curiously ambiguous (Exod. 34.1, 4, 27-28). Nohrnberg summarized the effect of this story on the characterization of Moses: 'Moses functions as the inspired author

How does this scribal characterization of Moses affect the contradictions between Deuteronomy and preceding Pentateuchal law codes?
Moses can be quite bold in his modifications of previously given narrative, legal and theological traditions. For example, he omits to mention
his own mistakes in the wilderness, blaming the people for his death
sentence instead (cf. Moses' claims in Deut. 1.37; 3.26; 4.21-22 with
YHWH's version in 32.51). Moses modifies the laws regarding the
location of altars and the possibility of secular slaughter (Deut. 12.13-
27), and provides new legislation regarding kings (17.14-20). The most
blatant theological example is his denial of multigenerational retribution in 7.9-10, a key idea for YHWH's self-characterizations in Exod.
20.5-6 and 34.6-7.[92]

It must be noted that contradictions mar Moses' own teaching and
scribal work since conflicts appear within Deuteronomy itself. For
example, one should judge the legitimacy of prophets by their predic-
tive accuracy according to 18.21-22 (Moses quoting YHWH), but by
their doctrinal orthodoxy according to 13.1-4 [Eng. 12.32–13.3] (Moses
alone). Polzin argued that God's direct discourse in ch. 18 overrules
Moses' indirect report in ch. 13, and that the two texts represent
conflicting tendencies found throughout the book.[93] This contradiction
differs, however, from those listed above in that Moses voices both
versions, only in one case quoting YHWH directly (though the original
statement goes unrecorded in the Pentateuch) while in the other he does
not.[94]

---

of both the law and the Pentateuch, that is, he stands for the keeping of the texts of
the law and the keeping of the covenant history embodied in them. Moses is the
only one who saw what the finger of God had written on the first set of tables
before they were broken; the correspondence with the second set, which he wrote at
God's dictation, presumes his faithfulness as an intermediary and scribe' (*Like
Unto Moses*, p. 60).

92. On the latter, see above; for the process of interpretation at work in Deut.
7.9-10, see Fishbane, *Biblical Interpretation*, p. 436, and Levinson, 'Human
Voice', pp. 53-56.

93. Polzin, *Moses*, pp. 63-65.

94. Deut. 18 therefore presents no exception to Polzin's observation that Deut.
12–26, unlike its framework, tends 'to raise the authority of the Mosaic voice to a
position almost indistinguishable from that of the voice of God. Conversely, in this
address the direct voice of God is almost totally silenced' (*Moses*, p. 55). Similarly,
Fishbane, *Biblical Interpretation*, p. 436 and n. 28; Savran, *Telling and Retelling*,
p. 114.

Moses in Deuteronomy, like YHWH in Exodus–Numbers, gives voice to changing and incommensurate legal traditions.[95] Contradiction in Pentateuchal law does not pose a conflict between YHWH and Moses so much as it authorizes legal change as a natural part of Torah. The very nature of Deuteronomy, a 'second law' delivered to a new generation in Moab, highlights the role of reinterpretation and reapplication in legal and religious traditions.[96] A unique introduction to Moses' speech emphasizes this function: 'Moses clarified (באר) this law, saying' (Deut. 1.5).[97] The scribal character of Moses' voice emerges precisely in his mastery of the tradition to present it in a new form, as Fishbane argued:

> The very fact that the traditions are represented on the Plains of Moab to the post-exodus generation is emblematic of the fundamental trope of instruction basic to aggadic exegesis—that the traditions have to be retaught and revised in each generation... It is *the* Torah, which for Deut. 1.5 as for Ps. 78.5...means *the entirety of the traditions*—the historical, the hortatory, and the legal.[98]

95. Olson explained the difficulties by means of a theological rationale based in Deut. 28.69's [Eng. 29.1] distinction between a Horeb covenant and a Moab covenant. The former 'deconstructs itself through the ambiguities of its own statutes and ordinances that shipwreck in the end upon the curses of Deuteronomy 28...The Moab covenant [Deut. 29–32] does not negate but decenters the Horeb covenant with an emphasis on the judging and saving action of God in the face of the failure and limitation of human obedience. Thus, Yahweh will be the one who will create obedience through the strategies of the Moab covenant, an obedience that humans could not achieve under the Horeb covenant (compare Deut. 10.16 and 30.6). Yet the Horeb covenant remains in effect and humans continue to struggle, however imperfectly, toward faithfulness' (*Deuteronomy*, p. 176). Olson's interpretation employs narrative development (from Horeb to Moab) to explain change, a strategy critiqued in Chapter 3 above. Legal explanations for differences and change accord better with Deuteronomy's instructional genre and produce a different rhetorical result: interpretation of law makes obedience very possible indeed. Lohfink provided a reading more compatible with the book's genre by arguing that Deut. 5–28 and 29–30 represent the *same* Moab covenant depicted from the two different perspectives of the covenant document and the covenant ritual respectively (Lohfink, 'Bund als Vertrag', pp. 229-33).

96. Perlitt, *Bundestheologie*, p. 99; Blenkinsopp, *Wisdom and Law*, p. 118; Polzin, *Moses*, pp. 65-67; Olson, *Deuteronomy*, p. 12.

97. In its only other appearances in the Hebrew Bible, the verb באר describes clear writing (Deut. 27.8; Hab. 2.2) and therefore probably should convey scribal overtones here. Miller commented on the unusual term and concluded, 'Moses functions as *teacher*' ('"Moses My Servant"', p. 246).

98. Fishbane, *Biblical Interpretation*, pp. 439-40 (Fishbane's emphasis).

Ironically, awareness of change creates concern for the tradition's integrity within Deuteronomy itself, which contains the only Pentateuchal injunctions against modifications (13.1, Eng. 12.32). The tension between this prohibition and the character of the book that contains it may be intended to highlight the issue, as Polzin suggested.[99] Or, since a scribe's authority depends on claims to *accurate* transmission of the tradition, the injunction may serve to camouflage Deuteronomy's innovations with a 'rhetoric of concealment', as Levinson put it.[100] At any rate, the overall force of Deuteronomy's rhetoric aims towards identifying divine law and its interpretive tradition as one and the same thing.

Thus Deuteronomy works to merge the voices of YHWH and Moses into a unifying rhetoric of authority. Yet the larger structure of the Pentateuch distinguishes them sharply and accords them separate functions, as speaker of law and speaker of sanctions respectively. Moses' scribal role bridges this discrepancy by making him the only authorized tradent of divine law. To Moses falls the responsibility not only of announcing the consequences of law, but also of writing, interpreting and applying the law. Although the structure of the Pentateuch relegates Moses to the role of commentator on all that precedes Deuteronomy, the power of the entire religious tradition derives precisely from such commentary. Moses thus becomes a 'cipher' for the 'correlation of tradition and autonomy', as Crüsemann put it.[101]

The narrative contexts of the laws reinforce this dialectic of divine

99. 'How better to focus on the absurdity of forbidding any ongoing process of interpreting the word of God than by putting such a prohibition within a lawcode whose basic style already inextricably combines word of God with commentary and response to that word?' (Polzin, *Moses*, p. 65).

100. Levinson, 'Human Voice', p. 45.

101. *Die Tora*, p. 131 (my translation; Mahnke translated Crüsemann's term, *Chiffre* 'cipher', with 'just an image': *The Torah*, p. 107). Burke described the inevitably religious ramifications of this rhetorical phenomenon wherever it is encountered: 'When a figure becomes the personification of some impersonal motive, the result is a *depersonalization*. The person becomes the charismatic vessel of some "absolute" substance. And when thus magically endowed, the person transcends his nature as an individual, becoming instead the image of the idea he stands for. He is then the representative not of himself but of the family or class substance with which he is identified. In this respect he becomes "divine" (and his distinctive marks, such as his clothing, embody the same spirit)' (*Rhetoric of Motives*, p. 277).

law and human mediation. Though Deuteronomy inflates Moses'
stature a great deal, the context of his speech is his own impending
death, decreed as punishment for his rash action at Meribah. On the
other hand, though the regulations of Leviticus and the later chapters of
Exodus elevate the role of priests and even in a few places cast Aaron
as a mediator of divine law (Lev. 10.8; 11.1), the narratives qualify this
characterization by showing Aaron and the priesthood's role in idolatry
(Exod. 32; Lev. 10.1-3). Thus the mediators of Pentateuchal law are
always flawed. Though conflicts between them are frequently settled by
divine intervention (Num. 12.1-16; 16.1-40), differences in interpretation may also be settled by human reason and compromise, as the curt
argument at the end of Leviticus 10 shows. The narrative context, then,
uses characterization of the mediators to relativize Israel's various legal
traditions while maintaining the authority of divine commandment.

Hence the ambiguity in the title 'Torah' for the Pentateuch: it is the
'law' of YHWH and also the 'instruction' of Moses. As prophet and
scribe, Moses depends on divine and human acknowledgement for his
authority. Yet there is no access to the divine law except through him.
The three dominant voices of the Pentateuch thus become interdependent and almost interchangeable: the anonymous narrator, like Moses
the scribe, requires both divine inspiration and reader acceptance for
authorization of the story; the divine law-giver requires reader acceptance of human mediation of the commandments; the prophetic scribe
depends on authority delegated by both God and readers to interpret the
stories, the laws and the sanctions. No wonder the Pentateuch's rhetoric
led tradition to claim both divine and Mosaic authorship of the whole.

3. Command and Audience

The Pentateuch leaves the unification of speaking voices incomplete,
however, and as a result divides the audience in two. God and Moses
(or, at least, God through Moses) address the people in the wilderness
and also, through the narrator, the readers who overhear their speeches.
Their audience comprises Israel throughout time, from Sinai to the present, as Deuteronomy makes explicitly clear (especially Deut. 5.3). The
narrator, by contrast, addresses only the readers through a discourse
lying outside the story being narrated. Thus the Pentateuch's use
of a third-person omniscient and impersonal narrator resists the
unifying rhetoric of the divine and human speeches that it contains. By

providing knowledge unavailable to the Israelites in the story, the narrator alienates readers from wilderness Israel at the same time that the laws identify them as the same. The resulting tension strengthens the persuasive power of the Pentateuch's rhetoric.[102]

Narrator

There is much about the Pentateuchal narrator's discourse that reinforces, and is reinforced by, the speeches of YHWH and Moses. The very technique of omniscient narration gives the discourse a semidivine aspect. The narrator's authorial control over the discourse invites comparison with YHWH's 'authorial' control over the story world. The discourse never presumes to make this comparison explicit, and in fact God and the narrator speak in quite distinct idioms on quite different subjects: YHWH exhorts and commands, but rarely tells a story; the narrator does the reverse.[103]

   This distinction occasionally blurs when YHWH's commands wander to subjects irrelevant to the wilderness generation, but very applicable to ancient (and modern) readers (for example, the Passover instructions of Exod. 12–13).[104] Even here, however, the shift remains implicit:

102. Identification lies at the heart of persuasion, according to Burke (*Rhetoric of Motives*, pp. xiii-xiv, 20-31 and *passim*). He argued, however, that at least a degree of alienation (his terms were 'standoffishness' and 'self-interference') 'is necessary to the form, because without it the appeal could not be maintained. For if union is complete, what incentive can there be for appeal? Rhetorically, there can be courtship only insofar as there is division' (p. 271, also p. 274).

103. Sternberg has argued at length for the literary and theological implications of the biblical narrator's omniscience, concluding, for example, that 'The very choice to devise an omniscient narrator serves the purpose of staging and glorifying an omniscient God' (*Poetics*, p. 89; also p. 92, and on the differences between deity and narrator, pp. 117, 123, 155-59). Patrick and Scult distinguished between the narrator's characteristics in various Pentateuchal sources, interpreting them as theological differences (*Rhetoric*, pp. 108, 116-17). N. Wolterstorff has challenged the accuracy of describing the biblical narrator as 'omniscient', as opposed to 'inspired' (*Divine Discourse: Philosophical Reflections on the Claim that God Speaks* [Cambridge: Cambridge University Press, 1995], pp. 243-52). My description of the Pentateuchal narrator as 'omniscient' does not intend to evoke theological comparisons, but simply to point out the narrators' mastery of information not normally available. Rhetorical analysis finds more differences than similarities between the narration and quoted divine speeches in the Pentateuch.

104. The conventional distinction between the roles of law-speakers and narrators encourages one to find the narrator's voice here, as Patrick does: 'the

YHWH and Moses never directly address the readers. The narrator's reticence is also best illustrated where it breaks down. In the context of God's speech to Moses, Num. 15.22-23 speaks of both in the third person while expanding the scope of a provision from Leviticus 4, thus apparently ascribing legislation to the narrator.[105] This shift in voicing is extremely subtle, however, and easily missed by readers. By its rarity, this exception emphasizes the rule that the narrator does not speak law. Narratorial commentary appears only slightly more often: see, for example, Num. 26.9-11, 63-65.[106] The first four books of the Pentateuch maintain almost without exception the distinction between God and Moses on the one hand, and the narrator on the other. Nevertheless, the voices' different roles do not divide their message. The deity's statements and actions support the narrator's omniscience, reliability and control.

This division of labor breaks down in Deuteronomy, where Moses' speeches poach on both the divine prerogative for law-giving and the narrator's monopoly on storytelling. Here the three voices sometimes meld to the point of being indistinguishable: for example, are the antiquarian notices in Deut. 2.10-12, 20-23, in a context of Moses' quotation of YHWH's commands, voiced by YHWH, Moses or the narrator?[107] Such overlapping voices unify the text's authority: as Moses relates YHWH's words, so also the narrator conveys the words of both.[108]

---

narrator steps out of the narrative world here to address the reader. This address is performative, requiring the readers to define their identity (through ritual) in relationship to this story' ('Rhetoric of Revelation', p. 39 n. 26). However, it is not the narrator, but rather YHWH and Moses who voice these laws and 'break frame'.

105. See Fishbane, *Biblical Interpretation*, p. 194, who called this 'the human voice of the legal exegete'.

106. Mann, *Book of the Torah*, p. 141.

107. It certainly *sounds* like the narrator, which prompted the observations of Polzin (*Moses*, p. 31) and Lohfink ('Die Stimmen in Deuteronomium 2', *BZ* 37 [1993], pp. 209-35). A similar situation exists in Deut. 10.6-9 (Polzin, *Moses*, p. 34) and 29.4-5 (Eng. 29.5-6) (Lenchak, *'Choose Life!'*, p. 106).

108. Polzin argued that Deuteronomy employs this strategy in order for the narrator to gain Mosaic authority to narrate the rest of the Deuteronomistic History (Joshua through Kings) (*Moses*, pp. 27-29, 70). Fishbane noted the legal and religious result: in the narrator's voice, 'the authority for the *traditio* is indistinguishable formally from the authority of a historical *traditum*' (*Biblical Interpretation*, p. 437).

However, what unifies the speakers' authority divides the identity of the audience. The use of an omniscient narrator distinguishes the readers of the Pentateuch from the Israelites who heard Moses at Sinai and in Moab. The readers are more knowledgeable but also more dependent on the narrator for their knowledge of YHWH's and Moses' words as well as the story that contains them.

Israel in the Wilderness

The Pentateuchal story describes the law's audience quite explicitly: Israel in the wilderness (Exodus, Leviticus and Numbers) and on the plains of Moab (Deuteronomy). Though only Moses in Deuteronomy directly addresses the people as a whole, God's instructions to Moses in the preceding books address the community as their ultimate, if indirect, audience ('Speak thus to the Israelites...' Exod. 20.22; 'These are the commandments that you shall set before them...' 21.1; etc.). Occasional provisions address more limited groups, such as the priests (e.g. Lev. 6.9), but their placement within the context of the larger Sinai or Moab legislation reorients their message to all Israel as well.

Israel inherits the divine promises from their ancestors, but the laws address only wilderness Israel. Exodus through Deuteronomy refer to the ancestors only to explain God's behavior, never the people's.[109] Despite the appearance of certain 'Mosaic' laws and practices already in Genesis 12–50 (e.g. circumcision in Gen. 17.10, levirate marriage in Gen. 38.8), laws and their motive clauses in later books never refer back to them. The confession mandated in Deut. 26.5-10 formalizes the distinction between those whom the worshipers call their ancestors and those with whom they identify themselves: '*My father* was a wandering Aramean...The Egyptians oppressed *us* and afflicted *us*...'

The characterization of Israel provided by the Pentateuchal laws and sanctions reflects the wilderness generation as depicted in the stories of Exodus and Numbers (1) as God's war booty, (2) as a nation sanctified by the divine covenant, and (3) as rebels against YHWH. The exodus story depicts YHWH's defeat of Pharaoh in a battle over possession of Israel, thus creating (Exod. 6.6-7) or revealing (Deut. 7.6-8) Israel's status as the people of God. This theme introduces the Sinai episode: 'You have seen what I did to the Egyptians, and how I carried you on

---

109. E.g. Exod. 2.24; 6.8; 32.13; 33.1; Lev. 26.42; Num. 32.11; Deut. 1.8; 6.10; etc.

eagle's wings and brought you to myself. Now if you listen to my voice and keep my covenant, you will be my treasured possession of all the peoples' (Exod. 19.4-5). A rehearsal of YHWH's capture of Israel from Egypt also begins the Decalogue (Exod. 20.1; Deut. 5.6; cf. 5.15), thus establishing a direct link between the divinity's victories and Israel's obligation to obey (cf. Deut. 7.7-11).

Though the exodus has obligated Israel to YHWH, the people also obligate themselves by agreeing in advance to the covenant stipulations (Exod. 19.8; 24.3; extended to future generations in Deut. 5.3-4). In Exodus and Leviticus, obedience to the law defines Israel as God's people (Exod. 19.5; Lev. 26.12), whereas Deuteronomy makes that status the precondition and motivation for obedience (Deut. 7.1-6; 14.1-2).[110] Making or keeping the covenant therefore distinguishes Israel as YHWH's, and defines the people as 'holy' in the basic sense of 'dedicated, set apart' for God ('You shall be holy to me, for I YHWH am holy and I have separated you from other nations to be mine' Lev. 20.26). The 'kingdom of priests and holy nation' (Exod. 19.6) must be trained by the covenant's laws for divine service.[111]

As a result, Pentateuchal law defines the nation of Israel, rather than the nation defining the scope and jurisdiction of its laws. Crüsemann noted that, unlike ancient or modern notions of national law, 'in Israel the function [of law] preceded the state and thus is above the state'.[112] The Pentateuch hardly conceives of Israel as a nation in the institutional sense at all (e.g. note the unrealistic treatment of the duties of the king in Deut. 17.14-20). The law describes Israel as the people in covenant relationship with YHWH. All the other trappings of nationality, most notably possession of land, depend on fulfilling the stipulations of that relationship.

Yet many of the commandments anticipate resistance from their hearers. Patrick observed that 'the wording of the first commandment projects an audience which would resist the commandment's exclusivism. It seems to assume the existence of other gods, or at least the audience's belief in them and attraction to them.'[113] Other laws also presuppose the attractiveness of the religious or civil practices that they

110. Weinfeld, *Deuteronomy 1–11*, p. 61; Childs, *Biblical Theology*, pp. 421-23.
111. Greenberg, 'Three Conceptions', p. 16.
112. *The Torah*, p. 15.
113. Patrick, 'Is the Truth', p. 429. Similarly Stahl, *Law and Liminality*, pp. 20-21.

prohibit, as intermittent exhortations make clear: for example, 'be attentive' (Exod. 23.13), 'keep and do them with your whole mind and your whole being' (Deut. 26.16). Indeed, it is a truism of legal research that one does not outlaw behavior that does not occur. Though due allowance must be made for the preservation of antiquated legal traditions, the bulk of Pentateuchal law nevertheless paints a lively picture of practices that its audience might be reluctant to give up (e.g. 'Do not do as they do in the land of Egypt where you were living, and do not do as they do in the land of Canaan to which I am bringing you...' Lev. 18.3).

The laws thus echo the narrative's characterization of Israel in the wilderness as a rebellious people. As S. Sandmel noted, 'the children of Israel, who are protagonists, are never the heroes; the Wilderness wanderings are, on the surface, an account of the *infamous* deeds of the Hebrews.'[114] Israel's complaints and misdeeds prompt miraculous rescues in Exodus 14–17 but in Numbers, after the giving of law at Sinai, they provoke divine punishments including the death of an entire generation in the wilderness (Num. 14.32-35).[115] Thus those who first make the covenant break it and die without receiving what YHWH had promised. The next generation hears Moses' rehearsal of the stories, laws and sanctions in Deuteronomy and is confronted with the same obligations.

The Pentateuch's characterization of Israel serves to enhance and to justify its persuasive rhetoric. Israel's rescue from Egypt and acceptance of the covenant obliges the people to obey the law. Israel's rebellious record demonstrates the critical need for persuasion. By depicting such an audience, the Pentateuch defends its rhetorical strategies as necessary for the people's survival.[116] Near its end, Moses' skeptical song (Deut. 31–32) suggests that even this will not be enough.

114. 'The Enjoyment of Scripture: An Esthetic Approach', *Judaism* 22 (1973), pp. 455-67 (466).

115. Smith, 'Literary Arrangement', pp. 32-33.

116. Patrick described the same effect as a form of literary suspense: though the end of the story is already known, 'a successful narrative produces new types of suspense which cannot be resolved by knowledge of the outcome. One way the exodus narrative creates suspense is by portraying Moses and Israel as less than ideals of religious piety' and thus prompting readers to self-examination ('Rhetoric of Revelation', p. 31).

Readers as Israel

Pentateuchal law identifies its readers with Israel, particularly the Israel of the exodus story: 'You were aliens/a slave in the land of Egypt.'[117] H. Nasuti demonstrated that 'whereas biblical narrative might imply (or invite) a reader, biblical law specifies a reader'.[118] Through its exhortations to obedience, the laws specify readers who will adopt as their own Israel's covenant and identity as the people of God and express that identity through obedience.

> Part of the function of the legal material in the Bible is precisely to keep the reader from 'getting on with the story.' It forces the reader to stop and consider who he or she is and what he or she does. It specifies who such a reader must be if he or she wants to read the text correctly...[119]

Deuteronomy commands its audience to recite this identification in words that connect the rescue from Egypt with obedience to the law (6.20-25; 26.1-11). Of course, readers may choose not to obey, but in that case they also place themselves outside of the story.[120] As Mann noted, 'The reciprocity of law and story is now transparent: obedience to law is rooted in the recital of and identification with a story, an identification that is vacuous without obedience to the law.'[121]

Thus Pentateuchal laws and Deuteronomy as a whole tend to equate the audience in the story, wilderness Israel, with the audience of the story, the readers. Many interpreters have noted details and themes that compound this effect. The people hear the law outside the land, like exilic and diaspora Judeans who may have been the first readers/hearers of the Pentateuch as a whole.[122] Towards the end of Numbers, the

117. Exod. 22.20 [Eng. v. 21]; 23.9; Lev. 19.34; Deut. 5.15; 10.19; 15.15; 16.12; 24.18, 22.

118. H.P. Nasuti, 'Identity, Identification, and Imitation: The Narrative Hermeneutics of Biblical Law', *Journal of Law and Religion* 4.1 (1986), pp. 9-23 (12).

119. Nasuti, 'Identity', p. 23; cf. Patrick, 'Rhetoric of Revelation', p. 39 n. 26.

120. Patrick, 'Is the Truth', pp. 432-36.

121. Mann, *Book of the Torah*, p. 151; cf. Patrick and Scult, *Rhetoric*, p. 52; Miller, 'Place of the Decalogue', p. 232.

122. Fretheim noted that 'The implied readers of the Pentateuch bear a family resemblance to the exiles in Babylon (587–538 BCE), but it seems just as clear that these exiles do not "exhaust" the identity of the implied readers...This lack of specificity leaves more room for other readers to hear themselves addressed' (Fretheim, *Pentateuch*, p. 40; so also Polzin, *Moses*, p. 72, and many others). P.R. Davies found the connection rather with the immigrant ruling class of Persian-period Judea (*In Search*, pp. 87-93).

wilderness rebels are replaced by a new generation whose potential, like that of the readers, for obedience and blessing or for disobedience and curse remains untested.[123] The rhetoric of Deuteronomy brings together Moses' hearers and readers with its emphasis on collective responsibility and its union of present and future generations (29.14-15) into an idealized vision of Israel.[124] Readers are urged to feel as if they themselves agreed to the covenant at Mt Sinai and heard Moses' sermon on the plains of Moab.

Yet other elements in the same texts put distance between the story audience and the readers. First, as Nasuti pointed out, the model for the readers' behavior is not Israel but God.[125] 'You should be holy because I am holy' (Lev. 11.45) and similar exhortations make the imitation of God the explicit standard of behavior in clear contrast to the rebellions of wilderness Israel.

Second, the dark threats that dominate the last eight chapters of Deuteronomy hold out little hope that subsequent generations will do any better, and likely reflect experiences already in the first readers' past.[126] The book then encourages readers to make a break with their predecessors' actions and not continue the practices of the past.

Third, the narrator's mediation places readers in a relationship to the law different from that of wilderness Israel. Unlike Moses' audience at Sinai and Moab, readers experience law first as direct quotation of divine speech (Exodus through Numbers) and only later as Moses' reformulation (Deuteronomy). Though the narrator mediates divine law, the dramatic differences between the narrative and legal idioms (see above) emphasize the authenticity of the divine quotations: that is, because the reticent narrator sounds very unlike YHWH, the latter's

123. Olson noted that the new generation remains untouched by rebellion and argued that the contrast between the generations, emphasized by the census lists of each in Num. 1 and 26, establishes the large-scale structure of the book (*Death of the Old*, pp. 83-125).

124. D. Patrick, 'The Rhetoric of Collective Responsibility in Deuteronomic Law', in D.P. Wright, D.N. Freedman and A. Hurvitz (eds.), *Pomegranates and Golden Bells: Studies... in Honor of Jacob Milgrom* (Winona Lake, IN: Eisenbrauns, 1995), pp. 421-36; Lenchak, *'Choose Life!'*, pp. 85-86, 90-93, 102-103.

125. He suggested a dialectic between Egyptian slavery and the imitation of God: 'The laws work to define Israel's present identity in terms of its past status and its future goal' (Nasuti, 'Identity', p. 18).

126. Fretheim, *Pentateuch*, pp. 41-42.

words sound more authentic than Deuteronomy's merging of narrative and law in Moses' voice.[127] Thus the self-characterizations of the three principal voices in the Pentateuch, like the work's overarching rhetorical structure (Chapter 2 above), draw attention to the laws of Exodus, Leviticus and Numbers as the original divine revelation and categorize Deuteronomy as a secondary revision. Unlike wilderness Israel, readers hear both YHWH and Moses through the narrator's presentation.

Thus the Pentateuch tries to persuade readers both to identify with and to alienate themselves from aspects of wilderness Israel. The readers' past becomes the exodus story which the text urges them to claim through repetition and ritual, and to identify their origins in the stories of ancestors and more universal tales stretching back through Genesis. The readers' present then becomes governed by divine laws that specify those who obey them as Israel. The sanctions describe the readers' possible futures, culminating in Deuteronomy's rousing call to 'Choose life!' (30.19) and reject wilderness Israel's death wish (Exod. 16.3). This dialectic of identification and alienation intends to persuade readers of who they are and what they should do. The Pentateuch's rhetoric aims to convince its readers to be the true Israel.

Conclusion

The power of commandment depends on the authoritative character of the speaker and the identity of the audience. The diverse genres and contents combined in the laws and instructions of Exodus, Leviticus and Numbers share a royal provenance and characterize their speaker, YHWH, as a just king and ideal ruler. Moses' use of the same genres in Deuteronomy, however, emphasizes the mediation of legal tradition through prophet and scribe. The nuanced result presents the claims of divine law and the reality of human transmission as mutually reinforcing obligations for Israel. The laws specify their audience's identity as

127. Polzin (*Moses*) and Conrad ('Heard but not seen') have detected in this presentation of divine law a strategy for enhancing the narrator's authority not only in the Pentateuch but in the books that follow as well. Though in one sense the narrator mediates everything in these books, the disparate voicing of law and narrative in the Pentateuch points rather to narratorial reticence. Unlike Moses, the narrator does not presume to be the authoritative interpreter of divine legislation. The narrator's omniscient insight into divine and human actions and motivations does not extend to legal reasoning.

Israel, thereby identifying readers with the wilderness generations who first agreed to the covenant. But the stories of rebellion in the wilderness and the narrator's idiom distinguish the readers' situation as well. Thus the Pentateuch's persuasive rhetoric actualizes the tension between law and behavior in the readers' present and emphasizes the urgency of the readers' response.

Chapter 5

LAW

This book's discussion of the Pentateuch's rhetoric has so far focused almost entirely on the text itself and has paid little attention to the people who shaped this literature and for whom it was written. Such social and historical realities must now be addressed to complete a rhetorical analysis of the Pentateuch. Previous chapters have described the persuasive intentions that shaped the text into its present form, but such intentionality remains an abstraction until one specifies *who* was intending to persuade *whom*. Rhetoric has therefore always drawn attention to the motives and ideologies of speakers or writers and to the social situation and commitments of their audiences.[1] Not only rhetorical theory but also the legal contents of the Pentateuch point to the historical and social world outside the text, for legislation aims to have real consequences on human behavior and even idealized laws propose critical standards for legal conduct. So both legal material and rhetorical method draw our attention to the historical conditions and processes that gave rise to the Pentateuch.

Despite these considerations, historical concerns have not been integrated more tightly into the previous chapters because one must read the Pentateuch first before arriving at conclusions as to its historical development. Calls for the priority of literary analysis have recently

1.   'In its essence communication involves the use of verbal symbols for purposes of appeal. Thus, it splits formally into the three elements of speaker, speech, and spoken-to, with the speaker so shaping his speech as to "commune with" the spoken-to. This purely technical pattern is the precondition of *all* appeal' (Burke, *Rhetoric of Motives*, p. 271, also pp. 38, 274). 'Orientation toward the listener is usually considered the basic constitutive feature of rhetorical discourse… The internal politics of style (how the elements are put together) is determined by its external politics (its relationship to alien discourse)' (Bakhtin, *Dialogic Imagination*, pp. 280, 284; see also W. Wuellner, 'Rhetorical Criticism', para. 2.4[1], also 2.5, 3).

been voiced by some historically oriented Pentateuchal critics.[2] Though
the training of modern biblical scholars usually introduces them to historical theories about the text before they have read most of it,
methodologically the text must be read sympathetically (i.e. described
as it stands) before historical questions and evidence can be adduced
from it.[3] Previous chapters have therefore employed many analytical
concepts (about, e.g., characterization and narration) from literary criticism. The evidence of Israel's reading practices led, however, to a fun-
damentally rhetorical orientation that understands persuasion, rather
than literary art, to be the overriding purpose of the text's composition.
The literary theorist M.M. Bakhtin distinguished the rhetorical genres'
use of 'authoritative discourse' from the novel's avoidance or parody of
it, and rhetoric's formal use of multiple voices for purposes of persuasion from the novel's emphasis on 'the mutual nonunderstanding represented by people *who speak in different languages*'.[4] Rhetorical analysis

2.   'A better understanding of the end result of the traditio-historical process
may provide some safeguards against insufficiently substantiated assumptions
regarding earlier stages of the process and, ultimately, a new basis for the study of
the tradition history of the Pentateuch itself' (Knierim, *Task*, pp. 368-69; also
Blenkinsopp, *Pentateuch*, pp. 184, 194).

3.   F. de Saussure already reflected this methodological priority of synchronic
over diachronic interpretation when he introduced the terms into linguistic study
(see J. Barr, 'The Synchronic, the Diachronic and the Historical: A Triangular Relationship', in J.C. de Moor [ed.], *Synchronic or Diachronic? A Debate on Method in
Old Testament Exegesis* [OTS, 34; Leiden: E.J. Brill, 1995], pp. 1-14 [1]). Theoretical description of the interaction between synchronic and diachronic biblical interpretation becomes quite complicated, as shown by the discussion of Barr and
D.J.A. Clines ('Beyond Synchronic/Diachronic', in de Moor (ed.), *Synchronic or
Diachronic?*, pp. 52-71). My approach simply slows down the usually rapid alternation in interpretation between systemic synthesis (synchrony) and the analysis of
change (diachrony) to show clearly the premises and conclusions that underlie each
in turn.

4.   *Dialogic Imagination*, p. 356 (Bakhtin's emphasis). 'For this reason it is
proper to speak of a distinctive *rhetorical* double-voicedness, or, put another way,
to speak of the double-voiced rhetorical transmission of another's word (although it
may involve some artistic aspects), in contrast to the double-voiced *representation*
of another's word in the novel with its orientation toward the *image of a language*'
(*Dialogic Imagination*, p. 354; also 284, 342-44). M. Holquist, Bakhtin's editor,
noted that 'Bakhtin differs from Auerbach (with whom he shares, otherwise, many
suggestive parallels, both in his life and in his work) in that the Bible could never
represent the novel in contrast with epic, since *both*, Bible and epic, would share a
presumption of authority, a claim to absolute language, utterly foreign to the

therefore emphasizes the unified persuasive intent behind the multiple voices of the Pentateuch, in contrast to some literary analyses that, in novelistic fashion, have emphasized irreconcilable tendencies in its discourse.[5] Bakhtin also argued that historical description must accompany literary analysis:

> Discourse lives, as it were, beyond itself, in a living impulse toward the object; if we detach ourselves completely from this impulse all we have left is the naked corpse of the word, from which we can learn nothing at all about the social situation or the fate of the given word in life.[6]

Intentionality provides the rhetorical connection between literary description and historical analysis. By matching the intentions found in texts with the socio-historical situations that generated the texts, a full description of the rhetorical transaction between writers and intended readers becomes theoretically possible.[7] In practice, gaps in our historical knowledge may place limits on this enterprise, but these must be delineated through the process of historical description, to which I now turn.

novel's joyous awareness of the inadequacies of its own language' (*Dialogic Imagination*, pp. xxxii-xxxiii).

5.   E.g. Polzin, *Moses*, pp. 38-39; Olson, *Deuteronomy*, pp. 178-82; Stahl, *Law and Liminality*, pp. 21-24, who noted Bakhtin's objections and commented, 'where the Bible is concerned, one must first refute Bakhtin in order to apply him' (p. 24 n. 25). Such attempts to use Bakhtin's theory of polyphony while ignoring his analysis of genre undermine one of the major goals of his work, namely his explanation for the *distinctive* nature of the modern novel.

6.   *Dialogic Imagination*, p. 292.

7.   Rhetoric's focus on the persuasive force of texts necessarily invokes the intentions that shaped the texts: 'Through the shape into which speakers cast their message they tell the audience how they mean it to be engaged and therefore to be understood. Of course, the auditors are free to interpret the language of the discourse in any way they wish, but the speaker or author attempts to constrain that freedom and direct interpretation by giving the audience cues and indicators as to how he or she means the discourse to function for them... Thus in order for the critic to comprehend the nature of a text's authority fully in this case, he or she needs to find those conventions of engagement through which the text might have originally exercised its authority over an audience. From a rhetorical perspective, then, a text's genre becomes the code that must be broken in order to bring its word to life' (Patrick and Scult, *Rhetoric*, p. 15; also Bakhtin, *Dialogic Imagination*, p. 289; cf. S.E. Fish, *Doing What Comes Naturally: Change, Rhetoric, and the Practice of Theory in Literary and Legal Studies* [Durham, NC: Duke University Press, 1989], pp. 99-100, 116-17).

The goal here is not a full discussion of the history of and in the Pentateuch, but rather simply to note the historical implications of the preceding rhetorical analysis. This chapter discusses four aspects of the history of the Pentateuch in turn: first, the social situation that shaped and that is addressed by the Pentateuch in its present macro-structure; second, the shape of earlier literary forms still discernible in the text; third, the nature of the Pentateuch's literary form; fourth, the religious effects on its early readers of the Pentateuch's promulgation as *The Torah.*

1. *Law and Religion*

Religion's use of rhetoric is more obvious than rhetoric's role in law, especially in the codification of laws. Yet modern rhetorical theorists have noted not only the rhetorical agendas of law codes, but also the common persuasive emphasis in religious and legal rhetoric on the recognition and acceptance of hierarchy.[8] In secular law the state occupies the top of the hierarchy, in religion God does, and in religious law the claims of state and divinity become identified or contrasted, or both. Rhetorical analysis of ancient religious laws has therefore emphasized their intent to build allegiance to the community. For example, C. Newsom compared the rhetoric of the prayers in the *Hodayot* and the regulations of the *Serek Ha-Yahad*, both from Qumran:

> The resources of the legal language itself, the limits it sets to what can be said, and the selection of examples all work together to create a text that persuades its reader to a belief in the authority, legitimacy, and effectiveness of the community. ...Although we are not accustomed to thinking of such legal language as rhetorical, it is every bit as much a rhetorical act as the highly charged words of the Hodayot.[9]

8.   Burke, *Rhetoric of Motives*, pp. 187-89; 275-76; *idem*, *The Rhetoric of Religion: Studies in Logology* (Berkeley: University of California Press, 1961), pp. 40-42, 178-97; cf. Wuellner, 'Rhetorical Criticism', para. 3.

9.   'Kenneth Burke Meets the Teacher of Righteousness: Rhetorical Strategies in the Hodayot and the Serek Ha-Yahad', in H.W. Attridge, J.J. Collins and T.H. Tobin, SJ (eds.), *Of Scribes and Scrolls: Studies on the Hebrew Bible, Intertestamental Judaism, and Christian Origins presented to John Strugnell on the Occasion of his Sixtieth Birthday* (College Theology Resources in Religion, 5; Lanham, MD: University Press of America, 1990), pp. 121-31 (128). On rabbinic law, see J.N. Lightstone, *The Rhetoric of the Babylonian Talmud: Its Social Meaning and Context* (Waterloo, ON: Wilfrid Laurier University Press, 1994).

For the Pentateuch then, rhetorical criticism raises questions about the political structure and tensions within the community that it was intended to address.

The Social Function of Ancient Law
Description of the Pentateuch's original function is hampered by the ambiguous social function of ancient Near Eastern laws in general. Apparently law codes did not govern actual legal procedures as they do in modern legal systems. For example, despite the widespread and long-standing publication of the Code of Hammurabi in ancient Mesopotamia, the many Akkadian texts describing legal proceedings do not refer to it or any other code of law.[10] Nor do biblical references to the activities of law courts ever explicitly cite biblical laws.[11] As a result, debates over the purpose and function of ancient law divide contemporary scholarship.

On the one hand, many argue that the Mesopotamian law codes and their near parallels in the Covenant Code (Exod. 21–23) represent a purely academic tradition carried on by scribes completely distinct from actual legal procedures. R. Westbrook observed:

> With one important exception (the Hittite laws...), there is no consciousness of reform in the law codes. The kings who are their supposed authors do not boast of changes made in the system by the codes, nor is there any indication of their rules being valid from a particular point in time. The codes have a timeless quality, as perhaps befits an academic document. External evidence likewise gives no hint of awareness of the code's impact. The often monumental reforms posited by scholars find no echo in inscriptions, letters, or legal and administrative documents.[12]

Unlike law codes, Mesopotamian royal edicts do celebrate change, but according to Westbrook only in the limited spheres of debt cancellation, royal administration and price fixing.[13] Others differ from

10. Boecker, *Law*, p. 56; see F.R. Kraus, 'Ein zentrales Problem des altmesopotamischen Rechts: Was ist der Codex Hammu-Rabi?', *Genava* 8 (1960), pp. 283-96.

11. Ezra does cite a commandment not attested in the Pentateuch to justify the mass divorce of non-Judean women (Ezra 9.11-12). Note the 'teaching' of the law in 2 Chron. 17.9.

12. R. Westbrook, 'What is the Covenant Code?', in Levinson (ed.), *Theory and Method*, p. 24.

13. Categories which he argued also cover the changes emphasized in the more 'reforming' Hittite law codes (Westbrook, 'Covenant Code', pp. 24-27).

Westbrook in finding historical development in cuneiform and biblical law, but still ascribe it to academic reformulation, rather than legal reform. The codes 'represent theoretical reflections on ethical issues', according to Levinson.[14]

On the other hand, Westbrook admitted that aside from the Covenant Code, the bulk of Pentateuchal law reveals a clear penchant for making changes.[15] Others found more widespread reformist tendencies in cuneiform royal edicts and laws, and evidence of legal reforms in the Covenant Code itself.[16] The juxtaposition of three major Hebrew codes in the Pentateuch displays a remarkable tolerance for legal ambiguity and change.[17] And the full range of instructional materials in the Pentateuch calls for comparison not only with law codes but also with the ancient genres of royal grants, treaties and inscriptions commemorating the founding of a cult (see Chapter 2 above), which frequently emphasize the changes being brought about through these documents.

Academic, legal and political intentions clearly lie behind various laws in the Pentateuch. Rhetorical analysis points, however, to the persuasive intent that shapes its large-scale structure and many of its smaller features. The Pentateuch's rhetoric does not try simply to instruct its readers in the academic tradition of law, nor does it intend primarily to reform problematic aspects of Israel's legal practices. Rather, it aims to win adherence to a programmatic ideal of the Torah as the religion's definitive expression (see Chapter 3 above). The

14. Levinson, 'Right Chorale', p. 148; see also *idem*, 'Case for Revision', in Levinson (ed.), *Theory and Method*, pp. 37-59; Sonsino, *Motive Clauses*, p. 33; Hengstl, 'Zur Frage', p. 38.

15. 'The later biblical codes—the Deuteronomic and Priestly codes—share something of the intellectual ferment of contemporary Greek sources and thus some taste also of their new legal conceptions' (Westbrook, 'Covenant Code', p. 28; Friedman, *Exile*, pp. 70-77; for discussion of the Greek use of written law to enhance the public acceptance of change, see Thomas, *Literacy and Orality*, pp. 68-71).

16. Menes, *Die vorexilischen Gesetze*, pp. 25-44; Boecker, *Law*, pp. 55-56; S. Greengus, 'Some Issues Relating to the Comparability of Laws and the Coherence of the Legal Tradition', in Levinson (ed.), *Theory and Method*, pp. 60-87; S. Lafont, 'Ancient Near Eastern Laws: Continuity and Pluralism', in *Theory and Method*, pp. 96-100; E. Otto, 'Aspects of Legal Reforms and Reformulations in Ancient Cuneiform and Israelite Law', in *Theory and Method*, pp. 160-96.

17. Fishbane, *Biblical Interpretation*, pp. 264-66.

rhetorical shaping of the Pentateuch thus employs the products of academic instruction and legal reform for the larger cause of redefining Israel's self-identity.

Imperial Practice and Local Law

The analysis in the preceding three chapters provides indications of the process behind the Pentateuch's formation. First, the pattern of stories followed by lists and then by sanctions governs two blocks of material within the Pentateuch (Exod. 19–24; Deuteronomy) and also the Pentateuch as a whole, suggesting that the latter follows the pattern of older texts which it incorporates. The fact that P's lists and stories are integrated into the story-list-sanction pattern of the whole, rather than reproducing it on a smaller scale as the Book of the Covenant and Deuteronomy do, points to the P writers' role in giving shape to the Pentateuch as a whole.

Second, the separate inclusion of both P's and Deuteronomy's laws indicates that the Pentateuch is a product of a compromise between rival groups but one in which the P writers had the upper hand. Not only do P materials structure the whole, P's laws occupy the climactic position around the inauguration of the sanctuary (Lev. 8–10) and are presented as direct quotations of YHWH. Deuteronomy's laws on the other hand are relegated to the role of prophetic sanctions and scribal instructions, yet they remain privileged as Mosaic and as the authoritative guide for legal interpretation. So P's advocates seem to have controlled the Pentateuch's last major redaction, but still found it necessary to accommodate Deuteronomic concerns.

Third, problems posed by contradictory laws and ritual instructions had less effect on the Pentateuch's shaping than did the need to inspire loyalty to the idea of divine Torah itself. Apparently this is the point on which the tradents of rival law codes found common ground. The Pentateuch unites to claim that the laws of the ideal king, YHWH, as transmitted by Mosaic Torah, define the identity of Israel in partial continuity and partial discontinuity with past Israels. At the time of the Pentateuch's completion, then, the need for community solidarity and identity was more pressing than were controversies over specific legal and religious practices.

The period of Persian domination over Judea (539–322 BCE) is the point in Israel's history in which conditions seem most likely to have produced the concerns that shaped the Pentateuch, as historians have long noted. Judea's lack of centralizing government institutions and the dispersal of its population around the empire provided strong reasons for the Pentateuch's concern for Israel's identity and solidarity with Torah (issues and concerns also expressed emphatically in the Persian-period books of Ezra and Nehemiah).[18] In contrast to the earlier monarchic period, the lack of a Judean king explains the absence of royal concerns in Pentateuchal law codes, whose promulgators in the Persian period had a compelling reason to omit references to royal institutions lest they arouse the suspicion of the imperial overlord.[19] (Deuteronomy 17's requirement that kings read Torah hardly counts as serious constitutional law.) The Jerusalem Temple was the only central institution remaining under Judean control, specifically under the priesthood's control, and this explains the predominance of priestly concerns in P and P's pivotal place in the Pentateuch. And motivation for compromise between Judea's legal factions was provided by the need to ensure legal and fiscal support for the Temple from the Persian Empire, which authorized the laws of local cults in order to facilitate its own taxation system.

The possibility that Persia inspired the formation and acceptance of the Pentateuch as Judea's local law has been hypothesized for a long time,[20] but P. Frei gave the notion much greater prominence through his careful investigation of the Persian-period sources. E. Blum used imperial authorization to explain the composite composition of the Pentateuch itself.[21] Direct evidence for Persian authorization of local law

18. P's stories and even laws may also reflect the interest of diaspora Jews in emphasizing the universality of certain practices (Crüsemann, 'Der Pentateuch als Tora', pp. 263-64; Gerstenberger, *Leviticus*, pp. 12-14).

19. Crüsemann, 'Der Pentateuch als Tora', pp. 265-67.

20. See Alt, 'Origins', pp. 85-86, who noted that the seventh through fifth centuries BCE was a period of national and cultural restoration throughout the ancient Near East. U. Rütersworden noted the anti-Semitic tone which descriptions of Persian authorization took in older critical studies that suggested that the more likely Persian influence is, the less authentic Judaism is ('Die persische Reichsautorisation der Thora: Fact or fiction?' *ZAR* 1 [1995], pp. 47-61 [51]).

21. Frei, 'Zentralgewalt', pp. 5-131; see the summaries and development of the thesis in Blum, *Studien*, pp. 346-56; R. Albertz, *A History of Israelite Religion in the Old Testament Period* (2 vols.; trans. J. Bowden; OTL; Louisville, KY: Westminster/John Knox Press, 1994), pp. 467-68; J.L. Berquist, *Judaism in Persia's*

comes from the trilingual Letoon inscription, in which a Persian satrap authorizes the laws governing a local temple, and the 'Passover letter' from Elephantine which seems to incorporate a Persian imperial decree regulating the celebration of Passover in the Jewish colony there. Ancient historiographic narratives also record Persian interest in local law: the Demotic Chronicle and Diodorus both remark on Darius I's involvement in the collection (so the Chronicle) or the renewal (so Diodorus) of ancient Egyptian law, and Ezra 7 quotes a decree of Artaxerxes (I or II) commissioning Ezra to reinvigorate the Jerusalem Temple according to the 'law of your God which is in your hand' (v. 14). The book of Esther parodies the Persian preoccupation with immutable law (1.21-22; 8.9-14), which at one point includes the promulgation of Jewish religious regulations (9.29, 32).

Considerable debate has arisen over Frei's thesis that the Persian Empire regularly authorized local laws. Major points of contention include the historicity of the idea of imperial authorization, the scope and nature of the laws so authorized, and whether such authorization came at imperial or local initiative. On this last question, the evidence seems mixed and Frei himself was undecided.[22] The historiographical accounts (the Demotic Chronicle, Diodorus, Ezra) give the impression of imperial policy at work in the authorization of Egyptian and Jewish law, but the primary sources (Letoon inscription, Elephantine letter) suggest that requests by local leaders prompted Persian officials to respond with imperial endorsements.[23] The writers of the historiographic accounts had an interest in emphasizing imperial initiative to heighten either the authority of the laws so authorized (Demotic Chronicle, Ezra) or the prestige of the emperor (Diodorus).[24] It seems best, then, to follow the primary sources in concluding that the Persians were well known in antiquity for meeting local requests to provide imperial validation of temple laws.[25]

Shadow: A Social and Historical Approach (Minneapolis: Fortress Press, 1995), pp. 138-39; D.M. Carr, *Reading the Fractures of Genesis: Historical and Literary Approaches* (Louisville, KY: Westminster/John Knox Press, 1996), pp. 324-33.

22. Frei, 'Zentralgewalt', p. 102; similarly Albertz, *History*, pp. 467-68.

23. Rütersworden, 'Die persische Reichsautorisation', p. 59.

24. Diodorus makes Darius the last in a list of six great Egyptian law-givers or preservers (on the distinction, see Rütersworden, 'Die persische Reichsautorisation', p. 54).

25. Contra Blum, who concluded that Persian imperial pressure made Judean

Frei claimed that imperial authorization covered all kinds of laws, but critics have pointed out that the Persians' legal interests seem to have been much more narrowly focused on military, political and financial matters.[26] They also gave considerable attention to the religious laws of local temples.[27] In fact, Persian support for temples served its financial interests. J. Schaper summarized the evidence for Persian use of temples to collect imperial as well as religious taxes and concluded that 'the temple administration therefore acted both as a self-governing religious body and as a branch of the central government's fiscal administration'.[28] Thus Persian influence may well account for the Pentateuch's emphasis on regulations for the maintenance and support of the sanctuary. However, its incorporation of civil laws, other instructions, and stories of national origin is a unique combination in the ancient Near East and must therefore be explained on the basis of specifically Judean traditions.

Similar legal descriptions in the Demotic Chronicle ('law of Pharaoh, the temple')[29] and Ezra 7.26 ('the law of your God and the law of the

consensus obligatory (*Studien*, p. 358); similarly Blenkinsopp: 'it seems the impetus came from outside the Jewish community' (*Pentateuch*, p. 240); and Berquist: the Pentateuch's 'final form represents Persia's imposition of a text upon Yehud' (*Judaism*, p. 138). The pressure to compromise arose rather from self-interest (see below).

26. Frei, 'Zentralgewalt', p. 28; also *idem*, 'Die persische Reichsautorisation: ein Überblick', *ZAR* 1 (1995), pp. 1-35 (5); cf. J. Wiesehöfer, ' "Reichsgesetz" oder "Einzelfallgerechtigkeit"? Bemerkungen zu P. Freis These von der achaimenidischen "Reichsautorisation"', *ZAR* 1 (1995), pp. 36-46 (45). Rendtorff argued for a strict distinction between Persian imperial law and Judean religious law in Ezra and Nehemiah ('Esra und das "Gesetz"', *ZAW* 96 [1984], pp. 165-84; for a critique of this view, see Crüsemann, *The Torah*, p. 338). Schmitt claimed that, to count as imperially authorized law, a text must state explicitly that Persian officials are issuing it ('Suche nach der Identität', p. 264). This requirement seems overly strict, considering the small number of actual texts containing such an authorization which are extant. Note that the Letoon inscription's Greek portion is less explicit about the Satrap's actions than is the Aramaic portion (cf. Metzger, 'L'inscription grecque', pp. 32-33, with Dupont-Sommer, 'L'inscription araméenne', pp. 136-37).

27. Blenkinsopp, 'Mission', p. 413; *idem*, *Pentateuch*, p. 241.

28. J. Schaper, 'The Jerusalem Temple as an Instrument of the Achaemenid Fiscal Administration', *VT* 45 (1995), pp. 528-39 (529); see also Berquist, *Judaism*, p. 135.

29. And perhaps 'the people', but the translation is uncertain (W. Spiegelberg,

king') have provoked a debate on the identification or differentiation between imperial and temple law in the Persian Empire.[30] The argument depends on what is meant by imperial law. No collections of Persian law have survived, though their existence in antiquity seems likely. There is no evidence, however, that Persia incorporated local regulations into a general codification of imperial law.[31] Therefore the phrase in Ezra should not be understood to imply either the parallel existence of two independent law codes or the incorporation of Ezra's written code ('which is in your hand' v. 14) into a written Persian collection. Since the context emphasizes punishing law-breakers, the rhetoric of the phrase points less to documents than to ideology: Persian and Judean law are ideologically equated, so let the disobedient beware!

Finally, U. Rütersworden has challenged the historical accuracy of the accounts of Persian authorization of local laws in the Demotic Chronicle, Diodorus and Ezra. Citing the Letter of Aristeas, a clearly fictional account of the commissioning of a Greek translation of the Pentateuch by Ptolemy II Philadelphus, Rütersworden argued that the idea of Persia authorizing local laws was a back-projection from the later, Hellenistic period.[32] The implication for Ezra is that 'the appearance of holy scripture can be promoted through documents that are historically untrue'.[33] Historical problems bedevil studies in Ezra and Nehemiah, but many scholars defend the historicity of Ezra's imperial commission even if unsure of its exact nature.[34] Though Rütersworden

Die sogenannte demotische Chronik: Des Pap. 215 der Bibliothèque Nationale zu Paris nebst auf der Rückseite des Papyrus stehenden Texten [Demotische Studien, 7; Leipzig: J.C. Hinrichs, 1914], p. 31; Blum, *Studien*, p. 347; Carr, *Fractures*, p. 328).

30. For distinguishing them, see Blenkinsopp, 'Mission', p. 419; for identifying them as the same, see Rendtorff, 'Esra', p. 172 (who, however, understood them to refer only to civil, not religious, laws); Frei, 'Zentralgewalt', pp. 20-21, 53-54; Blum, *Studien*, p. 348 n. 53.

31. Wiesehöfer, '"Reichsgesetz"', pp. 38-39; Rütersworden, 'Die persische Reichsautorisation', p. 60.

32. 'Die persische Reichsautorisation', pp. 47-61. Schmitt also dated the last major redaction of the Pentateuch to the early Hellenistic period ('Suche nach der Identität', pp. 272-73).

33. Rütersworden, 'Die persische Reichsautorisation', p. 48, also 51.

34. E.g. Williamson, *Ezra, Nehemiah*, pp. 98-99; Blum, *Studien*, pp. 347-49; Blenkinsopp, *Pentateuch*, p. 240. For a survey of the historical issues, see L.L. Grabbe, *Judaism from Cyrus to Hadrian*. I. *The Persian and Greek Periods* (Minneapolis: Fortress Press, 1992), pp. 94-98.

thought the clearly Persian-period Letoon inscription and the Elephantine letter describe exceptional rather than typical incidents, other texts
from the period contain at least passing references to Persian involvement in the regulation of local cults, especially in Egypt: the funerary
inscription of Udjahorresnet claims commissions from Cambyses and
Darius I to restore an indigenous cult and revamp the judicial system,
and a demotic letter from the Persian satrap to the Chnum Temple at
Elephantine refers to a command from Darius concerning the choosing
of priests.[35] This accumulation of Persian-period evidence, together
with the absence of Hellenistic-Roman examples of imperial authorization of local cultic laws, authenticates the Persian provenance of the
practice.[36]

The conclusion therefore seems well grounded that Persian officials
frequently provided imperial authorization for written laws governing
the cultic and financial matters of temples. Such authorizations were
usually prompted by local requests and they resulted in the ideological,
but not documentary, identification of cultic and imperial law. This
then is the background for the Persian's support for the Jerusalem
Temple in the reigns of Cyrus, Darius and Artaxerxes as reflected in the
book of Ezra. The Judeans' motivation for seeking imperial authorization of the Temple and its law stemmed from the legal benefits that
accrued to those, both in Judea and in the wider empire, associated with
a legally authorized temple that was integrated into the empire's taxation system. Blenkinsopp described the situation:

> The small province of Judah belonged to the category of temple com-
> munity well attested throughout the Achemenid empire. Political, social,
> and economic status in this type of organization involved participation in
> and support of the cult and its numerous dependants.[37]

The evidence does not go so far as to demonstrate that 'the maintenance
of the cult was seen from the official angle as an essential aspect of
imperial control', as Blenkinsopp goes on to write. Even without imperial pressure, however, official recognition as a 'temple community'
provided great legal and financial motivation for Judah's rival legal

35. Blenkinsopp, 'Mission', pp. 410-13; Frei, 'Die persiche Reichsautorisation',
pp. 16-17.

36. Frei, 'Die persiche Reichsautorisation', p. 15 n. 57.

37. Blenkinsopp, *Pentateuch*, p. 242; cf. Albertz, *History*, p. 467.

factions to compose a unified temple law.[38] (The political importance of
such status was considerable: Tacitus reported that the people of Miles
in the reign of the Roman Emperor Tiberius successfully defended the
asylum rights of their temple on the basis of a 500-year-old grant by the
Persian Emperor Darius.)[39] Imperial authorization required that there be
a written Judean law to authorize, a single financial-cultic code supported not just by priests but also by the lay leaders (who paid the
taxes). The goal of unifying the local and diaspora community around
that law would have been undermined if significant constituencies were
omitted.[40]

Political Hierarchies and Judean Traditions

The theory that Persian authorization motivated the editing of the Pentateuch to serve as Judea's temple law explains well the intentions and
goals behind its large-scale redaction. It does not, however, explain its
literary form. The goal of imperial authorization shows why Judean
editors wished to include both Priestly and Deuteronomic materials, but
it does not account for the Pentateuch's blunt juxtaposition of divergent
and even contradictory traditions.[41] No amount of political/religious
compromise can succeed if it produces a law code that fails to fulfill a

38. Schmitt complained that the theory of Persian authorization depicts the
Pentateuch as simply a political compromise rather than a document concerned
with Israel's theological identity ('Suche nach der Identität', p. 267). Rhetorical
analysis of the implied reader (Chapter 4 above) confirms the Pentateuch's emphasis on Israel's identity. But religious motives are usually a mixture of theology,
politics and much else, as rhetorical theory leads us to expect: ' "Pure persuasion"
in itself is not to be equated with "religious" persuasion. Pure persuasion is disem-
bodied and wraithlike; but the benedictions and anathemata of religious persuasion
are tremendously sanguine, even bloody' (Burke, *Rhetoric of Motives*, p. 291).

39. Tacitus, *Ann.* 3.63; K. Koch, 'Weltordnung und Reichsidee im alten Iran
und ihre Auswirkungen auf die Provinz Jehud', in *Reichsidee und Reichsorganisation im Perserreich* (Freiburg: Universitätsverlag, 2nd edn, 1996 [1984]), p. 284 n.
312.

40. Blum argued that imperial authorization included the following requirements: (1) the law must be written, (2) it must be authoritative, (3) it must be capable of acceptance by consensus (*Studien*, p. 356).

41. Persian authorization of the Pentateuch has been credited for the inclusion
of old laws in a younger framework (Alt, 'Origins', p. 86), for the juxtaposition of
contradictory codes (Blum, *Studien*, pp. 357-60), and for the editors' reticence in
changing written laws (Crüsemann, *Die Tora*, pp. 260-61).

society's minimum legal requirements for consistency and coherence.[42]
Yet the history of Second Temple (and later) Judaism shows that the
Pentateuch 'worked' very well as the law of a religious community, so
well in fact that it became the most famous example of such a law and
created the idea of religious authority based in scripture common to the
major Western religious traditions. Though imperial authorization of
Judean law probably set the conditions for the creation of a Pentateuch
incorporating Deuteronomic and Priestly traditions, other explanations
must be found for its literary form and its religious influence.

This book's analysis of the Pentateuch's rhetoric explains its literary
form on the basis of Israel's tradition of public law readings. Critical
analysis suggests that this tradition derives at least from the monarchic
period, and the Pentateuch claims that it goes back to Moses (Chapter
1). Thus Judean editors possessed within their own rhetorical and literary heritage a set of genre conventions that encouraged the inclusion of
law with narrative in a story-list-sanction pattern (Chapter 2) and
emphasized the rhetorical value of even a self-contradictory document
for community identity and cohesion (Chapters 3). While the overriding need for persuasion allowed contradictory legal details to remain,
the traditional pattern provided a template for making P's regulations
together with the Decalogue and Covenant Code the principal lists of
laws while making Deuteronomy play the role of 'sanctions' to P's lists
(Chapters 2 and 4). Thus the Judean editors did not simply juxtapose P
and D laws but used the story-list-sanction pattern to define their relationship rhetorically. The monumental influence of this Torah on

---

42. See the objections to the imperial authorization theory on this basis by Otto,
'Gesetzesfortschreibung', p. 375 n. 14. One must beware of applying anachronistic
notions of legal consistency to ancient law collections: Hengstl argued that no
ancient culture prior to the Roman showed any concern for the reconciliation of
contradictory traditions of civil law. In Mesopotamian, Greek, Egyptian, as well as
Judean law collections, juxtaposition was the rule rather than the exception, except
of course where imperial concerns were directly at issue ('Zur Frage', pp. 51-54).
Thus P.R. Davies's assumption is unwarranted that contradictions in P law show
that it was not written to govern the Second Temple cult ('Leviticus as a Cultic
System in the Second Temple Period', in J.F.A. Sawyer [ed.], *Reading Leviticus: A
Conversation with Mary Douglas* [JSOTSup, 227; Sheffield: Sheffield Academic
Press, 1996], pp. 230-37). The text's normative intention shapes its rhetoric
throughout. We should rather ask *how* Leviticus's contradictions and utopian provi-
sions functioned as a governing norm.

Judaism and Western religious traditions in general shows the success of their rhetorical strategy.

The question then of *who* was trying to persuade *whom* by creating the Pentateuch, can be answered with some specificity. The intended readers, who are supposed to identify themselves as Israel in partial continuity and partial discontinuity with wilderness (and by implication monarchic) Israel (Chapter 4 above), were the Judeans of the Persian Empire. By accepting the Pentateuch's identification of them as Israel, they became part of the Temple community of Jerusalem and were bound by its laws, regardless of their own location. Becoming YHWH's 'possession ... a priestly kingdom and a holy nation' (Exod. 19.5-6) had social ramifications in the Persian Empire: recognized legal status for Judean communities and distinctive legal, financial and religious obligations for individual Judeans. The urgency of the Pentateuch's rhetoric suggests that at least some Judeans in this period did not find such status and obligations as attractive as some other roles available to them in the pluralistic empire.

The Judeans' religious and legal leaders are the implied authors, as the incorporation of masses of cultic and legal materials in the Pentateuch makes clear, and almost as clear is their association with the Jerusalem Temple. More precise description is afforded by the Pentateuch's unique dual voicing of law by YHWH and Moses. Since they each voice one of the distinctive legal traditions (Priestly and Deuteronomic respectively), each law-speaker rhetorically 'stands for' a particular constituency in postexilic Judea.

Chapter 4 described the Pentateuch's Moses as a prophetic announcer of sanctions and as a scribal recorder and reinterpreter of tradition. The first role matches the content of his law, Deuteronomic legislation, with the characterization of its speaker as the model prophet, which is the Deuteronomistic religious ideal. The larger Pentateuchal context, however, restricts this prophetic role to the task of announcing sanctions just as it places Moses' major speech, Deuteronomy, in the rhetorical role of concluding sanctions. If the Deuteronomic traditions reflected the interests of the Judean elders and the farmers they represented, and if they were transmitted by literary-prophetic circles allied with them, then the characterization of Moses provided on the one hand an honored place for Deuteronomic materials while on the other hand relativizing their authority.[43] Moses' scribal characterization, however, makes up for this loss. For as recorder and teacher, Moses provides a model for the authoritative reinterpretation of written law not just by Temple priests but by any scribe competent to handle the materials. In other words, if the legal traditions of the Judean lay leaders and their allied prophets have been placed in a reduced, secondary role, the publication of authorized Judean Temple law made the role of scribal interpreter available publicly, and the contradictory nature of that law made this role absolutely necessary. Thus the gain in lay scribal influence (including that of Deuteronomistic scribes) offset the loss of authority by Deuteronomistic prophets. The history of Second Temple Judaism shows clearly the religious marginalization of prophets and the increasing religious importance of lay teachers (rabbis) and scribes alongside the continuing power of the Jerusalem priesthood. The Pentateuch foreshadowed and encouraged this development by restricting Moses' prophetic characterization and emphasizing his instructional and scribal activities.

When YHWH speaks the cultic laws of Exodus, Leviticus and Numbers, the priests of God's sanctuary are frequently the subjects and clear beneficiaries of many of these divine regulations. Hence scholarship has with near unanimity considered the Jerusalem priesthood to have been the authors and tradents of this P, for 'Priestly', material. From a rhetorical perspective, however, it is notable that the priests do not transmit the laws in their own voice (such as Aaron's laws to balance Moses') but rather present their traditions as voiced by YHWH. The Pentateuch, then, does not depict priests advancing their own interests; it shows them receiving the rights and responsibilities of their office from a higher, external authority characterized as Israel's royal overlord (see Chapter 4). This theological depiction of the source of P law parallels very closely the political transaction involved in imperial

43. Blum, Crüsemann and Carr argued that the two principle constituencies in postexilic Judea were the priests and the elders representing free farmers, who sponsored P and D traditions respectively (Blum, *Studien*, pp. 343-45, 358-59; Crüsemann, *The Torah*, p. 340; Carr, *Fractures*, pp. 325-26). Others have seen in these two codes the interests of competing priestly groups (Friedman, *Exile*, pp. 70-77; Koch, 'Weltordnung und Reichsidee', p. 305). Gerstenberger has taken the unusual view that the P materials of Leviticus derive from lay scholars in the diaspora (*Leviticus*, pp. 12-14, 26). The P and D legal collections show their competing interests clearly enough, even if the exact identities of their partisans (especially D's) are unclear.

authorization of local temple law. The Persian overlord, at the request of local religious leaders, turns local legislation into imperial law. In both the divine voicing of law and the imperial authorization of law, claims for legal authority are vested in the highest possible source, religious and political respectively. Thus God plays the same rhetorical role within the text as the Persian Empire played in the political world of its compilers and first readers. Religious and political hierarchies frequently become identified in what Burke called a 'mystic participation. The feeling that one is "walking with Destiny" would then be the "celestialized" or idealized counterpart to the quite realistic experience of "walking with hierarchy".'[44] Part of the Pentateuch's persuasive power for Persian-period Judeans derived from its implicit duplication of their political world within its religious rhetoric.

Theology, however, should not be translated simply into an analysis of political and social interests. Reducing religion to politics leads to misunderstanding both, as frequent modern attempts to do so have conclusively demonstrated.[45] The Pentateuch is not simply a religious justification for the distribution of power in the Persian province of Judea. Though imperial concerns may have influenced some of its contents, especially its omission of explicitly Davidic royal claims, the vast bulk of the Pentateuch's narratives and lists cannot be convincingly explained by such a reductionistic political calculus. My point is simply that the Pentateuch's rhetorical congruence with the political situation in which it was published increased its persuasive force and accounts in part for its acceptance by Persian-period Judeans. The Pentateuch's rhetoric was, to use Burke's words, 'grounded in a *form*, the persuasiveness of the hierarchic order itself'.[46]

2. *The Composition of the Pentateuch*

Rhetorical analysis of the Pentateuch's form provides clues to the historical process by which the literature was shaped. Source-critical

---

44. Burke, *Rhetoric of Motives*, p. 307; on the sociological effect of such rhetoric in Judea, see Berquist, *Judaism*, pp. 134-39.

45. Burke himself argued that rhetorical analysis reveals some of the motives behind theology, but that theology itself cannot be equated with rhetoric (*Rhetoric of Motives*, pp. 76, 178, 275-76, 291).

46. *Rhetoric of Motives*, p. 276.

analysis of the Pentateuch in the twentieth century has focused
primarily on narratives. The laws were usually considered secondary
additions to the sources, which were edited together even later to create
the Pentateuch. Therefore many interpreters posited an independent
editor who developed the Pentateuch's overall structure into which P
and the other sources were fitted.[47] Others identified P as the final
redactor of the Pentateuch, who also added considerable amounts of
older, fragmentary P material.[48] Comparative study of Pentateuchal law
has also generated divergent conclusions about composition. Just as the
narrative sources were placed in historical sequence, so also the law
collections have frequently been analyzed as representing different
historical periods, with the earlier being revised by the later.[49] Others
viewed the process as less consistent, producing a variety of relatively
contemporary codes.[50] These complicated arguments over the Pentateuch's composition cannot be reviewed in detail here. I will simply
describe how the rhetorical analysis of the preceding chapters affects
the debate.

The rhetorical structure of the Pentateuch as a whole supports redactional theories of P as its last large-scale editor. This redaction did not

47. As classically described by J. Wellhausen, *Die Composition des Hexateuchs
und der historischen Bücher des Alten Testaments* (Berlin: W. de Gruyter, 4th edn,
1963 [1876–77]), pp. 2-3, 81-83, 135-39. Recent defenders of P as an independent
source include K. Koch, 'P: Kein Redaktor', *VT* 37 (1987), pp. 446-67; J.A. Emerton, 'The Priestly Writer in Genesis', *JTS* 39 (1988), pp. 381-400; Carr, *Fractures*,
pp. 114-40; G.I. Davies, 'The Composition of the Book of Exodus: Reflections on
the Theses of Erhard Blum', in M.V. Fox *et al.* (eds.), *Texts, Temples and Traditions: A Tribute to Menahem Haran* (Winona Lake, IN: Eisenbrauns, 1996), pp. 71-
85.

48. F.M. Cross, *Canaanite Myth and Hebrew Epic* (Cambridge, MA: Harvard
University Press, 1973), pp. 301-23; Friedman, *Exile*, pp. 78-118; Blum, *Studien*,
pp. 222-31, 287; Van Seters, *Life of Moses*, pp. 100-12.

49. The familiar sequence of a pre-monarchic or early monarchic Covenant
Code, late monarchic Deuteronomy, and exilic or postexilic Holiness Code and
priestly laws was established by Wellhausen (*Prolegomena to the History of Israel*
[Gloucester, MA: Peter Smith, 1973 (1878)], p. 383). Otto has recently described
this sequence as stages in an ongoing process of legal interpretation
('Gesetzesfortschreibung', pp. 373-92).

50. S. Amsler proposed a fragmentary hypothesis of the law codes' composition
in which they grew 'in a bushy form around the trunk of the oral tradition' ('Les
documents', pp. 255, also 239-40). Cf. Friedman's description of rival law collections in late monarchic Israel (*Exile*, pp. 70-76).

simply collect older materials together. Rather, the placement of P and non-P materials into the pattern of stories followed by lists concluding with sanctions created a paradigm for interpreting the relationships between texts, as well as for presenting them all together as the divine Torah that defines Israel's identity in relation to God.[51] The evidence that P writers composed this structure includes (1) the voicing of P's laws and instructions (Exod. 25–31; Leviticus and much of Numbers) by YHWH, which identifies them with the older Book of the Covenant (Exod. 21–23) and elevates their status over Moses' re-presentation of the law in Deuteronomy; (2) the placement of P's laws around the climactic inauguration of worship at Sinai (Lev. 8–9) to become the central lists in the Pentateuch's story–list–sanction structure; (3) the use of P's stories (e.g. Gen. 1) to bracket non-P material and to link laws and narratives together.

To be sure, many defenders of the idea that P was originally an independent source argued that the Pentateuch's editor was also working in the P tradition and therefore shared many of P's perspectives and interests.[52] They might then grant these observations and still maintain that the bulk of P came from a single continuous source. That P contains older material is clear; the issue concerns the nature of that material. Did it consist of or contain a narrative running from creation to (at least) Sinai? Did it contain legal material, such as the Holiness Code (Lev. 17–26)?

Israel's tradition of public law-readings, together with the story-list-sanction pattern represented in smaller and larger reproductions of Israel's laws, argues against the prior existence of a P narrative source apart from law and vice versa. The history of source-critical discussion of P has been warped by the *a priori* exclusion of laws from the source analysis, leaving only the narrative rump of P for consideration.[53] However, neither is there much more evidence for a P source that combined narratives with P's laws and sanctions. The vast majority of P material is instructional in nature. If the Holiness Code represents a

---

51. For P as a paradigmatic reconstrual of Israel's traditions, see N. Lohfink, 'Die Priesterschrift und die Geschichte', in J.A. Emerton (ed.), *Congress Volume 1977* (VTSup, 24; Leiden: E.J. Brill, 1978), pp. 189-225; Blum, *Studien*, p. 287.

52. E.g. Wellhausen, *Prolegomena*, p. 385; Noth, *Pentateuchal Traditions*, pp. 8-16; Carr, *Fractures*, pp. 47, 115, 314-17.

53. Noth argued for P being originally narrative only (*Pentateuchal Traditions*, pp. 8-10). See the criticism of Rendtorff, *Problem of the Process*, p. 137.

priestly tradition distinct from P, a point still hotly debated, then it has
sanctions (Lev. 26) but no story, while the P source has stories but no
sanctions.[54] Their combination provided all three elements of the pattern, but with the mass of laws and instructions out of proportion to the
scanty narratives and the single list of sanctions, and the latter not in
final position. The sanctions list in Leviticus 26 does suggest the separate existence and publication of the Holiness Code, presumably introduced by stories now either lost or absorbed into P's narratives.[55] The
bulk of P legislation, however, finds its place as list in the rhetoric of
story-list-sanction only with reference to the Pentateuch as a whole,
including Deuteronomy and the other non-P texts. Its privileged place
within the Pentateuch demonstrates not only that P writers edited the
whole, but also that the P texts were given their present shape for their
role within the composite Pentateuch. Much of P's material may have
existed earlier in fragmentary form, but (with the possible exception of
the Holiness Code) there are no signs that it consisted of a continuous
narrative or narrative-legal source.

Therefore 'P' represents neither a source nor a redaction but rather a
composition that is both and more, as Blum has argued.[56] The P writers
gave decisive shape both to P material and to the Pentateuch by using
Israel's old rhetoric of public law-readings to arrange diverse traditions
into the persuasive story-list-sanction pattern of Torah. Some
modifications seem to have been made to specific texts after the Pentateuch as a whole was in place, but no editor succeeded again in revising
its basic structure.[57] Thus the 'P' tradition of compositional and redac-

54. According to the traditional understanding of H as restricted to Lev. 17-26.
I. Knohl divided P narratives between P and H, thus providing H stories as well
(*The Sanctuary of Silence: The Priestly Torah and the Holiness School* [Minnea-
polis: Fortress Press, 1995]).

55. Knohl argued on the basis of detailed comparisons of especially the legal
texts that the writers of the Holiness Code (including law and narrative) edited P
and non-P to produce the Pentateuch (*Sanctuary*, p. 6). I am instead suggesting on
the basis of the Pentateuch's rhetorical structure that P edited H (which originally
included law and narrative) with non-P to produce the Pentateuch.

56. Blum, *Studien*, pp. 229-32.

57. On the post-P editing of the Pentateuch, see Rendtorff, *Problem of the Process*, p. 194; Blum, *Studien*, p. 287; A.H.J. Gunneweg, 'Das Gesetz und die
Propheten: Eine Auslegung von Ex 33,7-11; Num 11,4–12,8; Dtn 31,14f.; 34,10',
ZAW 102 (1990), pp. 169-80; Blenkinsopp, *Pentateuch*, pp. 240-41. Most such later
changes reflect 'P' interests and concerns, though Blum pointed out that some seem

tional activity seems to have spanned the exilic and postexilic period, and included at one point the overarching redaction of the Pentateuch.

Rhetorical analysis also provides some insights into earlier forms of the Pentateuchal materials, though conclusions become increasingly tenuous the further back one tries to reconstruct the literature. The most obvious result confirms the long-standing conclusion of critical scholarship that Deuteronomy originally existed apart from the rest of the Pentateuch.[58] Its structure presents the clearest use of the story-list-sanction strategy (Chapter 2 above). Its laws conflict frequently with those in earlier books (Chapter 3) and its prophetic characterization of Moses creates thematic claims that the larger Pentateuchal context restricts (Chapter 4). Thus Deuteronomy seems to have been published some time earlier than the Pentateuch as a whole. It provided the literary model for the P writers who appropriated its rhetorical structure to redefine Deuteronomy as the sanctions to P's laws.

The presence of the story-list-sanction pattern in Exodus 19–23 suggests also the independent existence of the sequence of Sinai theophany, the Decalogue and the Book of the Covenant (with perhaps the story of covenant ratification as a conclusion), but here rhetorical analysis conflicts with a host of source- and redaction-critical observations. The Sinai pericope (Exod. 19–24) seems to have had a very complex literary history and evidence of multiple layers marks both the narratives and the laws.[59] We must reckon then with the likelihood that, much like the Pentateuch as a whole, these materials were given their story-list-sanction pattern through later editing. The irregularities in the structure support this possibility: two legal collections, the Decalogue and the Book of the Covenant, with narrative in between; sanctions with little or no threat; concluding narratives. Nevertheless, the prevalence of this rhetorical strategy in Israel's legal traditions should also warn interpreters against using genre to separate sources or redactional layers.[60] Since narratives, laws and sanctions coexist in Israel's extant

Deuteronomistic (*Studien*, pp. 361-78). Cf. the argument for a deuteronomistic final redaction by Schmitt, 'Suche nach der Identität', pp. 277-78.

58. E.g. Blenkinsopp, *Pentateuch*, p. 233.

59. For arguments for the present text's rhetorical structure despite the evidence of multiple sources and redactions, see Chapter 2 above.

60. The same point applies to Mesopotamian law codes, in which separate legal sources have often been posited due to 'the difference in content, style, and language between the laws and the framework surrounding them. Whereas the laws

legal literature, as well as in a variety of ancient inscriptional genres from the cultures of the Near East and eastern Mediterranean, one should not presume merely because of its legal contents that the Book of the Covenant was originally separate from the Sinai narratives.[61] Distinct genres do not demonstrate different sources.

Large-scale rhetorical analysis, however, does not provide any evidence for the form or even the existence of a pre-P Pentateuch. How the non-P narratives of Genesis and Exodus were connected with the Book of the Covenant and with Deuteronomy, as many have maintained, must be left for other methods of analysis to decide.[62] Neither can rhetorical method describe the historical influences between legal codes.[63] It does, however, provide insight into the rhetorical motivations and compositional processes that led to the publication of Israel's laws as normative texts for the Judean community. Rhetorical analysis of the Pentateuch supports Blum's contention that 'Israelite/Judean redactions of law were since Deuteronomy known as nothing other than "Torah", that is as combinations of historical and legal redactions'.[64]

are couched in a highly stereotyped style and written in the contemporary Old Babylonian dialect, the framework narrative is nearly poetic and its language contains so-called hymnic-epic elements' (Hurowitz, *Inu Anum,* p. 90). Despite Hurowitz's defense of the Codes' unity on literary (narrative) grounds, he still argued for the prior existence of the laws as a separate document. That case needs to be evaluated on the basis of internal and external evidence (which Hurowitz supplied) apart from the differences in genre. The combination of genres in many types of ancient Near Eastern literature belies the presumption that each must stem from an originally 'pure' source.

61. This text's complexities may be illustrated by Blum's analysis, which on the one hand found evidence of a pre-Deuteronomistic narrative frame for the Book of the Covenant in Exod. 19.3-8; 20.22 and 24.3-8 (*Studien,* pp. 92-98) and on the other hand considered the sanctions in 23.20-33 to be a post-Deuteronomic and possibly post-P addition (pp. 375-76 and n. 61).

62. See, for example, the arguments for an overarching Deuteronomistic composition of the pre-P Pentateuch by Blum (*Studien,* pp. 7-218), or for J as the exilic writer of the pre-P Pentateuch by Van Seters (*Life of Moses*), or for retaining Wellhausen's Documentary Hypothesis by S. Boorer (*The Promise of the Land as Oath: A Key to the Formation of the Pentateuch* [Berlin: W. de Gruyter, 1992]).

63. As does, e.g., Otto, who argued that Deuteronomy was written in Josiah's reign as a revision of the Covenant Code ('Gesetzesfortschreibung', pp. 380, 391).

64. Blum, *Studien,* p. 355 (my translation).

3. *The Extent and Genre of the Pentateuch*

Rhetorical study of the Pentateuch helps describe not only the process of its composition, but also the nature of the end product. Rhetorical shaping influenced the Pentateuch's extent and genre.

Extent

The story of Israel does not, of course, end with Deuteronomy. Subsequent books of the Hebrew Bible pick up the story without pause to narrate Israel's settlement of the land (Joshua and Judges), the establishment of an Israelite monarchy (1–2 Samuel) and the history of that monarchy until its destruction (1–2 Kings). The perceived need to continue the story has also been manifested in modern critics' unease with the canonical distinction between the five books (Pentateuch, Torah) and the history that follows. The division has been recast to form a 'Hexateuch' of Genesis through Joshua (so Ewald, von Rad), a 'Tetrateuch' of Genesis to Numbers distinct from the 'Deuteronomistic History' in Deuteronomy–2 Kings that follows (Noth), and even an 'Enneateuch' (Schmitt) or 'Primary History' (Freedman) containing all eight books.[65]

The rhetorical strategy of using stories followed by lists concluding in sanctions to persuade hearers and readers is not immutable. Modifications of the pattern, especially to include concluding narratives (e.g. Exod. 24; Deut. 31; 34), appear in Israel's traditions as well as the texts of other cultures. So the possibility that P editors, as well as earlier tradents, continued their compositions into Joshua cannot be ruled out.[66]

Nevertheless, the analysis of this book describes the Pentateuch as a rhetorically complete unit and justifies its separation from the rest of

65. For the proposals of Ewald, von Rad and Noth, see the survey of Blenkinsopp, *Pentateuch*, pp. 7, 16-17; for the Enneateuch ('eight books'), see Schmitt, 'Suche nach der Identität', p. 262; for 'Primary History', see D.N. Freedman, 'The Law and the Prophets', in G.W. Anderson *et al* (eds.), *Congress Volume: Bonn 1962* (VTSup, 9; Leiden: E.J. Brill, 1963), pp. 250-65; *idem*, 'Formation of the Canon', pp. 316-26.

66. Arguments for P in Joshua were evaluated by Blenkinsopp, 'Structure of P', p. 287; *idem*, *Pentateuch*, pp. 237-38. Blum noted evidence of post-P links into Joshua (*Studien*, p. 365).

the canon as Torah.[67] The persuasive strategy that structures the whole
into stories that describe Israel's origins (Genesis to Exod. 29), lists that
specify Israel's obligations (Exod. 20 to Numbers), and sanctions that
spell out Israel's possible futures (Deuteronomy), requires nothing else.
This Pentateuch defines Israel in the past, present and future to
motivate the readers' acceptance of this identity and fulfillment of its
obligations. In contrast to the literary complaint that the narrative plot
has not been concluded, the persuasive rhetoric of the Pentateuch suggests that this story never ends. One may certainly supplement it, as
Jews throughout history have done. But whether one continues to the
climax of Joshua, or to the nadir of the Exile, or further still to the
reform of Ezra, the essential question of Deuteronomy's sanctions
always remains unresolved: will Israel live by this Torah or not? Will
Israel choose life or death (Deut. 11.26; 30.19)? The Pentateuch's
inconclusive plot reinforces its rhetorical strategy of making readers
decide its ending by their own actions.

Genre

The wide variety of materials found within the Pentateuch resist
attempts to categorize it all under a single genre. Yet interpreters
repeatedly attempt to define the Pentateuch's genre because of its theological ramifications. Genre labels define reading strategies, with
important consequences for understanding the Hebrew Bible as a
whole. Knierim observed: 'It may well be that the genre of the Pentateuch constitutes the decisive basis for the authority of the Pentateuch-
Torah over the other parts of the Old Testament.'[68] The multifarious
nature of the material, however, has promoted only disagreement
among scholars.[69]

   Many recent interpreters have argued that the Pentateuch's genre is
biography. The Pentateuch then becomes a biography of Moses with

   67. The separation of Deuteronomy from most or all of the Deuteronomistic
History to serve as the 'sanctions' to P's laws appears to be an intrinsic part of the
Pentateuch's rhetorical strategy. It was therefore part of the Pentateuch's large-
scale redaction, not a later change due to the canon's subsequent growth, as Mullen
argued (*Ethnic Myths*, pp. 67, 83-86, 321-24).
   68. *Task*, p. 369.
   69. For a survey and negative evaluation of the proposals, see Knierim, *Task*,
pp. 370-71.

Genesis as an extended introduction. The story of Moses in the narratives presents a classical biographical description, as Henn noted: 'the pattern of his life corresponds almost exactly with the typical trajectory, the rise and fall, of the tragic heroes of mythology'.[70] Coats found the traditional elements of a heroic saga in the Moses traditions but restricted the heroic portrayal to the J source; P presents a passive Moses.[71] Others maintained that the biographical genre shapes the final overarching form of the Pentateuch. Though older materials probably contained a biographical emphasis as well, Knierim argued that 'the biographical genre is clearly evident precisely in its final and very much expanded form. ...This massive Mosaization is especially clear in the priestly parts of the Sinai pericope and in Deuteronomy.'[72] Sailhamer carried the biographical reading of the Pentateuch to its logical conclusion by presenting Moses as a model: 'the laws in the Pentateuch are not there to tell the reader how to live but rather to tell the reader how Moses was to live under the law'.[73]

Here the arguments for a biographical reading of the Pentateuch show their weakest side. The Pentateuch's explicit model for behavior is YHWH, as the command 'You shall be holy for I am holy' (Lev. 11.45) and many similar statements make clear (see Chapter 4). Even Coats's more nuanced claim that the Sinai stories present 'a construction of tradition about Moses' acts designed to elicit the people's faith and obedience in God' ignores the fact that the motive clauses attached to laws emphasize YHWH's acts, not those of Moses.[74] The difficulty with reading the Pentateuch as a biography of Moses stems from two incontrovertible features of the text: (1) the narratives contain two protagonists, YHWH and Moses, and YHWH is dominant; (2) the majority of the Pentateuch is not narrative,[75] and YHWH and Israel occupy the

70. T.R. Henn, *The Bible as Literature* (New York: Oxford University Press, 1970), pp. 193-94.

71. Coats, *Moses*, pp. 38-41, 195-98.

72. Knierim, *Task*, p. 377 and n. 24. Blenkinsopp noted that it is the late separation of the Pentateuch from the Deuteronomistic History that allows it to be read as a biography of Moses (*Pentateuch*, p. 52). S.A. Nigosian specified the Pentateuch's genre as 'sacred biography' in which the 'mythical ideal, better know as the "biographical image", takes precedence over the chronicling of the life of the subject' ('Moses As They Saw Him', *VT* 43 [1993], pp. 339-50 [345]).

73. *Pentateuch as Narrative*, p. 63.

74. Coats, *Moses*, p. 136.

75. Blenkinsopp, *Pentateuch*, p. 34.

center of attention in the instructional speeches and songs rather than Moses, even when Moses is speaking. 'Biography' might well describe the stories about YHWH, but then there seems no reason to limit the biography only to the Pentateuch.

The non-narrative bulk of Pentateuchal material also presents a stumbling-block to the suggestion that its genre is historiography. Van Seters argued that the biography of Moses was used by the J writer to form part of his larger historiographical project.[76] He cited the ability of ancient Egyptian biographies to incorporate other genres to explain the mixture of material in the Pentateuch.[77] Yet the Pentateuch in its final form seems no more dominated by antiquarian interests than by a concern to present Moses as a model for readers.[78] Thus narrative genres seem unable to account for the intentions and effects of the Pentateuch as a whole. Theological attempts to describe its effect in terms of genre have fared no better. Christian interpretation has always emphasized the Pentateuch's stories over its laws and this tendency still seems to determine some scholars' readings. Thus H-C. Schmitt, for example, emphasized the theological, rather than political, motives at work in the Pentateuch's formation and argued that whereas Deuteronomy is 'a law book with a historical frame, the Pentateuch is a history book with legal parts'.[79] The relative proportion of narrative and non-narrative material belies this claim and undermines the identification of the Pentateuch with any narrative genre. Of course, the presence of so much narrative also presents difficulties for labeling it simply as law or instruction, as translations of Torah, the traditional Jewish name for the Pentateuch, suggest.

I have argued that the intent and effect of the Pentateuch's rhetoric is to persuade readers to accept it as *The Torah* and use its norms to define themselves as Israel. This use of rhetorical analysis raises the issue of genre in a different way, as the classical theorists realized. Aristotle described three uniquely rhetorical genres: 'deliberative' for political speeches intending to motivate decisions about future actions,

76. *Life of Moses*, p. 2-3.

77. J. Van Seters, *In Search of History* (New Haven: Yale University Press, 1983), pp. 181-85, followed by Knierim, *Task*, p. 374 n. 22.

78. Van Seters argues for the antiquarian concerns of the J writer, not of the final Pentateuch as edited by P.

79. Schmitt, 'Suche nach der Identität', p. 266 (my translation); similarly Fretheim, *Pentateuch*, p. 20.

'forensic' for legal speeches in court cases, and 'epideictic' for ceremonial speeches intended for inspiration.[80] In broad terms, the Pentateuch seems to be shaped by deliberative intentions to motivate future
behavior, but again the variety of its material resists reduction to a
single rhetorical genre. The problem is that no genre label, whether narrative, legal or rhetorical, explains the variety and arrangement of
material in the Pentateuch.[81] And such an explanation is precisely the
purpose of genre analysis.

Chapter 2 above discovered a rhetorical strategy in texts of diverse
genres from the ancient Near East and Mediterranean that juxtapose
stories, lists and sanctions for maximum persuasive effect. The variety
of sources suggests that the pattern reflects no single genre, but is rather
a strategy that may be used in a variety of genres to intensify a text's
rhetorical force. Therefore the use of the pattern to shape the Pentateuch reveals not its genre but its persuasive intent. In the context of
ancient literature, the Pentateuch contains many recognizable genres
but in its size and complexity is unique, *sui generis*.[82] However, since
Deuteronomy, the Pentateuch and perhaps the Book of the Covenant all
exhibit the story-list-sanction pattern, there is evidence that this rhetorical strategy became a convention of genre in Israel. The best name for
that genre uses the traditional title of the composition into which all
these other works have been collected, namely Torah.[83]

4. *The Meaning of Torah*

The translation of *torah* has been an issue of ongoing debate. Many
interpreters object to the usual translation, 'law', as too restrictive and
legalistic. They point out that the word also describes instructional and
ethical material well outside the legal sphere. Chapter 4 above noted
that the Pentateuch itself seems to play on the word's ambiguity to
describe simultaneously the 'law of YHWH' and the 'instruction of
Moses'. These observations, however, function at two different levels:

80. Aristotle, *Rhet.* 1.3.1358b.
81. Fishbane criticized the search for 'pure' genres, noting that concern about
mixed genres 'ignores the very anthological nature of ancient biblical and Jewish
literary sources, and the coexistence in them of different "types" of traditional
materials' (*Biblical Interpretation*, p. 276).
82. So Blum, *Studien*, p. 355; Blenkinsopp, *Pentateuch*, p. 41.
83. Blum, *Studien*, p. 288.

torah describes part of the Pentateuch's contents and also describes the religious status of the Pentateuch itself.

Mixing genres seems characteristic not just of the Pentateuch, but of *torah* as well. Purely civil and criminal law codes are hard to find without excising the context and much of the contents of the biblical texts. Even after omitting religious instructions from the Book of the Covenant, ethical teachings remain mixed with the civil laws. The interplay between them seems so integral to the Hebrew tradition that Crüsemann called the combination of religion, ethics and law 'the birthplace of Torah'.[84] He also noted that *torah* soon came to be used of law and narrative together, as in Deut. 1.5 and Psalm 78.[85] Thus the mixture of laws with ethical and religious instructions and their placement within narrative frameworks led to labeling the whole Pentateuch as Torah.

Rhetorical analysis of the Pentateuch suggests, however, that its description as Torah retains 'law' as its primary, though not exclusive, meaning. Chapter 4 described the implicit yet pervasive characterization of YHWH as royal law-giver and enforcer in Exodus, Leviticus and Numbers and Moses' scribal role as interpreter and reformer in Deuteronomy. It also noted the way Pentateuchal laws (civil, religious and ethical) specify the reader's identity relative to the laws. Thus the Pentateuch presents *torah* as legislation issued by a legitimate authority (YHWH) that is binding on all those within its self-described jurisdiction (Israel), in other words as law. This chapter has found that the Pentateuch's rhetoric had specific legal consequences for Judeans in the period when it was first published. Thus in its internal rhetoric and its external effects, the Pentateuch functioned not as stories nor as religious instructions nor as ethical principles but as *law*.

Much of the resistance to this conclusion arises from the concern that it reduces religion and ethics to legalistic exercises. The Christian

84. Crüsemann, *The Torah*, p. 191; similarly Gese, 'The Law', pp. 62-63 on *torah* in Deuteronomy and Hosea, and pp. 75-76 on P; on the latter, cf. Rendtorff, *Die Gesetze*, p. 2. This mixture has not, of course, kept scholars from trying to untangle it: for a recent effort, see E. Otto, *Wandel der Rechtsbegründungen in der Gesellschaftsgeschichte des antiken Israel: Eine Rechtsgeschichte des 'Bundesbuchs' Ex XX 22-XXIII 13* (Studia Biblica, 3; Leiden: E.J. Brill, 1988), and the critique of Crüsemann, *The Torah*, pp. 192-95. For a semiotic analysis of the difference between religious and civil law, see Jackson, 'Ceremonial and Judicial', pp. 125-27.

85. Crüsemann, *The Torah*, pp. 332-33.

interpretive tradition especially has deprecated legal religion and emphasized the moral and theological aspects of the Pentateuch instead. Jewish tradition has, on the whole, found such a distinction between law and ethics foreign to its understanding of Torah. A classic example of these divergent approaches may be noticed in each tradition's use of the Ten Commandments. In separating them from their contexts in Exodus and Deuteronomy and celebrating them as a list of universal moral principles, Christians have frequently regarded the Ten Commandments as the only Pentateuchal laws that are binding (aside from those repeated by the New Testament). Much effort has been expended by interpreters to ground this distinction in the Pentateuchal literature itself.[86] Jewish tradition has, on the other hand, emphasized the equal importance of all the laws to such an extent that rabbinic authorities struggled to explain why the Decalogue, which clearly occupies a prominent place in both Exodus and Deuteronomy, receives no special treatment in the synagogue liturgy.[87] The historical, legal, ethical and theological relationships between the Decalogue and the rest of Pentateuchal law remain an important issue for scholarship. Nevertheless, this book's analysis points out that the traditional Jewish understanding of the laws' equal importance, as well as the traditional Jewish title 'Torah', best summarize the rhetorical force of the Pentateuch as a whole.

The Pentateuch's self-presentation as 'Torah' 'Law', goes a long way towards explaining the origins of the Hebrew canon and the distinctive emphasis in Western religious traditions upon authoritative scriptures. Its rhetoric appeals to readers to accept this Torah as normative for their own identity as Israel, thus welding together political, ethnic and religious loyalties to a greater degree than most ancient texts. Indeed, the difficulties noted above in describing the social effects of Mesopotamian law codes suggest that the description of the Pentateuch as Torah

86. So, e.g., W.J. Dumbrell: 'The Decalogue is primary and permanent, the covenant code derivative and valid only for its age. This important distinction is reinforced, not only by the differences in terminology ("words" v. "judgements") as between Exod. 20 and Exod. 21–23, but also by the fact that the Decalogue came to all Israel directly and personally, while the covenant code came to Israel intermediately (21.1), through the person of Moses' (*Covenant and Creation: An Old Testament Covenantal Theology* [Exeter: Paternoster Press, 1984], p. 93).

87. R. Brooks, *Spirit of the Ten Commandments* (New York: Harper & Row, 1990), pp. 28-36.

meaning 'law' has more in common with modern conceptions of national law and ideology than with the intentions of the Mesopotamian codes.[88] The Pentateuch adopted older legal conventions and rhetorical strategies to achieve a novel objective: the constitution of a people on the basis of religious rather than state institutions. Torah established ideological identification with and submission to the law of the Temple. Its success in doing so was so great that eventually the significance of Torah eclipsed that of the Temple. When the Temple was destroyed, Israel maintained its distinctive identity by means of the Torah alone. At this point, even 'law' becomes too weak a translation for Torah, for the connotations of 'law' evoke its institutional basis in the state or some other governing entity. The English word that best expresses the idea of an independently normative Torah is 'Bible'.

The fact that the book of Deuteronomy employs a similar rhetoric suggests that the normative constitution of Israel had been tried before the Pentateuch reached its present form.[89] Thus the idea of 'canon' may precede the Pentateuch's publication.[90] However, the Judeans' social position in the Persian Empire created the conditions to motivate acceptance of a larger and more inclusive Torah as fundamental to Israel's self-identity. Political circumstances required that Temple law be its central component and the Judean tradition of public law readings provided the literary model for including texts of many other genres as well. The Pentateuch thus became the first canon of Scripture for the Jewish people as a whole. Its political origins as well as its internal rhetoric ensured that the words 'canon', 'Scripture', and 'Bible' have carried connotations of *Torah*, 'law', ever since.

'Without [the law] there would be no Bible', wrote H.M. Orlinsky.[91]

88. P.R. Davies described this shift from academic law to religious norm as occurring after the bulk of the Pentateuch was composed (*In Search*, pp. 149-51). However, the goal of normative law suffuses the Pentateuch's rhetoric and should be credited to the composers themselves.

89. Westbrook observed that around the seventh to sixth centuries in both Israel and Greece, the traditions of academic law and of royal edict were combined, which turned 'the law code into a statute whose text may be cited as authoritative in a court of law' ('Cuneiform Law Codes', p. 222).

90. R.E. Clements, *Old Testament Theology: A Fresh Approach* (Atlanta: John Knox Press, 1978), p. 110; Blenkinsopp, *Pentateuch*, p. 235; cf. Mullen, *Ethnic Myths*, pp. 14, 19-55, who disputed the identification of Torah as Pentateuch or canon until the formalization of the Christian Bible.

91. H.M. Orlinsky, 'The Forensic Character of the Hebrew Bible', in D.A.

Theological interpretation of Scripture should therefore pay attention to legal hermeneutics. This involves not only a theological evaluation of the nature and significance of *torah*.[92] It also suggests that legal interpretation may be an effective aid in understanding the 'scriptural' meaning of the Bible. One benefit offered by legal hermeneutics is a nuanced appreciation of change as well as continuity in interpretation, so that, as Levinson noted, 'The canon itself sanctions—canonizes—the dialectic whereby hermeneuts must simultaneously honor authoritative texts, while yet often needing profoundly to transform them.'[93] The conclusions of Chapter 4 were reached partly by applying such legal reasoning to the literary problem of characterization. The built-in tensions within the Pentateuch rightly provoke historical and literary investigations into their origins and meaning. Literary methods struggle, however, to reconstitute the fragments resulting from historical analysis. It may be that, as Carr maintained, 'the canonical and/or classical status of Genesis lies in its fractures as well as its shape',[94] but it is hard to say what those literary fractures mean. Legal interpretation's focus on reconciling conflicts can provide aid at this final level of interpretation, and the rhetorical demands and shape of the Torah recommend its use. The power of the Pentateuch's canonical authority lies in its self-presentation as 'Torah', 'law', an endlessly reinterpreted norm.

Knight and P.J. Paris (eds.), *Justice and the Holy: Essays in Honor of Walter Harrelson* (Atlanta: Scholars Press, 1989), pp. 89-97 (92).

92. E.g. Clements, *Old Testament Theology*, pp. 104-30; Gese, 'The Law', pp. 60-92.

93. 'Human Voice', p. 38. Blenkinsopp noted that 'a canonical text is also by definition a text to which one must always return in the unavoidable, ongoing dialectic between tradition and situation. In this process, it is safe to say, no text has played a role comparable to that of the Pentateuch' (*Pentateuch*, p. 242).

94. *Fractures*, p. 333.

POSTSCRIPT ON RHETORICAL ETHICS

This book has used rhetorical analysis for purely descriptive purposes in order to understand the literary shape and religious influence of the Pentateuch. Rhetorical theory, however, has always emphasized the need for *prescriptive* analysis, that is for critiques of rhetorical practices and for normative discussions of how persuasion should and should not be achieved. In fact, the origins of Western philosophy in the thought of Socrates and Plato can partly be understood as a critical reaction against the rhetoric of the Sophists. R. Majercik summarized the conflict concisely:

> A critical reaction to the rhetorical art is most evident in the writings of Plato, notably in the *Gorgias* and *Phaedrus*. In these dialogues, Plato specifically attacks that kind of sophistic oratory or extreme relativism (identified with the Sophists in general) which has no fixed moral purpose but only the goal of winning an argument through any persuasive means. Plato equates this type of rhetoric with deceit and flattery and contrasts it with dialectic, which is concerned with knowledge and universal truths. Plato did admit the value of a 'philosophical' rhetoric in the *Phaedrus*, but did not develop this idea in any detail. This task was left to Aristotle... The later Hellenistic period also saw the development of a florid and artificial oratory ('Asianism') reminiscent of Gorgias as well as renewed hostility between teachers of rhetoric and philosophy. The gains would be made among the rhetoricians, and rhetoric would emerge in Rome as the sine qua non of Roman education.[1]

In the modern period, discussion of rhetoric has often been connected to ideological critiques. Burke noted that 'in the use of rhetoric to attack rhetoric, there has been much talk of "unmasking," as rival ideologies are said to compete by "unmasking" one another'.[2] Thus rhetorical

---

1. R. Majercik, 'Rhetoric and Oratory in the Greco-Roman World', *ABD*, V, pp. 710-15 (710-11). For literature on and discussion of 'the constitutive connection between rhetorics and ethics', see Wuellner, 'Rhetorical Criticism', para. 2.4-5.

2. Burke, *Rhetoric of Motives*, p. 99; cf. p. 104. Burke traced this use of rhetoric through the criticism of Bentham, Marx and Carlyle, concluding that 'Marx

theory has from its beginnings to the present day mounted strong arguments for the necessity of normative criticism. This book's rhetorical
analysis would be incomplete without at least an evaluative sketch of
the Pentateuch's persuasive practices in the light of rhetorical ethics.

Previous chapters have already pointed out that classical theorists
resisted many of the methods used in the Pentateuch's rhetoric. They
criticized two of the three parts of the story–list–sanction strategy as
manipulations of the audience's emotions. Aristotle downplayed narrative as either superfluous in a speech or useful only for a 'weak-minded'
audience.[3] Plato equated religious threats with magic and called for
their punishment: let 'there be among us no working on the terrors of
mankind—the most part of whom are as timorous as babes'.[4] In view-
ing both as manipulations of the audiences' feelings, Plato and Aristotle
denounced unethical attempts to win adherents by emotional means
rather than by demonstrating the truth of one's claims through reason.
Other characteristics of Pentateuchal rhetoric also violate the ancient
philosophers' standards of reasoned discourse. Its juxtaposition of rival
law collections tolerates self-contradiction for the sake of rhetorical
effect in order to win the adherence of various Judean factions. In other
words, the Pentateuch sacrifices logical consistency in order to appeal
to its readers' self-interests.[5] Furthermore, it serves the interests of

and Carlyle, taken together, indicate the presence of a "mystifying condition" in
social inequality; and this condition can elicit "God-fearing" attitudes towards
agents and agencies that are not "divine"' (*Rhetoric of Motives*, p. 123).

   3.   *Rhet.* 3.13-14; see Chapter 2 above, and O'Banion, *Reorienting Rhetoric*,
p. 52.

   4.   *Laws* 11.933a; cf. *Rep.* 2.364b-c; see Gager, *Curse Tablets*, pp. 249-50. The
magical, mesmerizing nature of speech is a theme that runs through Sophistic
rhetoric in both the Attic and Hellenistic periods. In reaction, the philosophers subordinated all rhetoric to logic (Romilly, *Magic and Rhetoric*, pp. 4-6, 16, 25-43, 82-
85).

   5.   See Chapter 3. Appeals for a distinctive religious rhetoric which is
'authoritative, oracular, and demanding...[and] contains paradoxes, obscurity, repetitions, and rejection of worldly reasoning', as Lenchak put it (*'Choose Life!'*,
p. 76), received no sympathy from Plato: 'They produce a bushel of books of
Musaeus and Orpheus, the offspring of the Moon and of the Muses, as they affirm,
and these books they use in their ritual, and make not only ordinary men but states
believe that there really are remissions of sins and purifications for deeds of injus-
tice, by means of sacrifice and pleasant sport for the living, and that there are also
special rites for the defunct, which they call functions, that deliver us from evils in

imperial ideology by implicitly identifying the deity with the state, through royal characterizations of YHWH in the laws and by presenting a religious parallel (God–Temple–priests–laity) to the political hierarchy (empire–Temple–priests–laity) of Persian-period Judea.[6] In all these ways, Pentateuchal rhetoric falls far short of the dialectical standards championed by the classical philosophers as necessary not only for rational but also for ethical discourse.

The Pentateuch, of course, is hardly unique in its use of such emotional methods. The above discussion has shown that the philosophers reacted to the rhetoric of both religious and political orators in ancient Greece. Subsequent religious rhetoric has usually employed such methods as well. The various elements (stories, divine sanctions, appeals to the mystery of self-contradiction, reproductions and reinforcements of political hierarchies) can be found in the rhetoric of every period of religious history. Histories of ancient rhetoric usually cite Augustine as its last major theorist because he championed the use of rhetorical forms, not to discover truth as the philosophers had urged, but rather to convince hearers of the truth already revealed in the Christian Gospel.[7]

The Pentateuch's story–list–sanction strategy reappears in various forms as well. Some individual works appropriate the pattern: Joshua moves from stories of conquest to lists of occupied territory to the promises and threats of Joshua's covenant renewal.[8] Collections of religious texts also reproduce the pattern in their lists and manuscripts:

that other world, while terrible things await those who have neglected to sacrifice' (*Rep.* 2.364e-365a).

6. See Chapters 4 and 5. Patrick and Scult explored the interplay of rhetorical and political effect in one part of the Pentateuch and concluded: 'Whether Genesis 1–3 is "sacred" because it captures the logic of human condition or materially determinant because it has been taken as "sacred", it is nonetheless an accurate, "authentic" account of power as it now exists and as it has existed in western cultures. Power *does* rather than *is*. One does not have it by virtue of a "place" within the social-political structure so much as one creates it as a rhetoric that must be performed...' (*Rhetoric*, p. 125).

7. Augustine, *De Doct. Christ.* 4. Following Burke (*Rhetoric of Motives*, p. 76), O'Banion argued that 'The church, convinced of the universality of its story, restricted the arts of invention, narration, and proof to serve the activities of scriptural investigation', and the modern period has simply replaced Christian truth with the presupposed truths of science (*Reorienting Rhetoric*, p. 105).

8. My thanks to Robert O'Connell for this observation (personal communication).

Greek Septuagint manuscripts arrange the Christian Old Testament into histories (Genesis to Maccabees), poetry (Psalms to Psalms of Solomon), and prophecy (Hosea to Jeremiah)[9] while the New Testament presents a sequence of stories (Gospels and Acts), letters (Romans to 3 John), and an apocalypse (Revelation). These collections also show a flair for juxtaposing contradictory material, for example, Proverbs–Ecclesiastes and the four Gospels, usually as distinct books without any attempt to imitate the Pentateuch's literary combination of traditions. These uses of the Torah's rhetorical strategies probably stem less from intentional imitation of the Pentateuch's structure than from the natural tendency to move from past events through present obligations to future possibilities. The Christian collections nevertheless strengthen their claim to being Scripture by reproducing the original Bible's rhetorical pattern. Note that the most variable part of the pattern are the lists, which may be lists in the strict sense (lists of towns in Joshua) or literary anthologies (the collections of poetry in the Septuagint) or letters whose discursive style comes closer to that of the philosophers. But none of these approximates the dialectical logic required by the philosophers' rhetorical ethics. It is rather the emotional methods that they disparage, narrative and sanctions, which appear most dependably and recognizably in the structuring of the two parts of the Christian Bible.

I mention these later examples of Torah-like rhetoric simply to show that the ethical problems raised by rhetorical analysis are not unique to the Pentateuch: it inherited them from common religious and political practices of the ancient Near Eastern and Mediterranean cultures and passed them on to much Western religious rhetoric. (The Jewish rabbinic collections are a notable exception to the tendency to reuse 'Torah' patterns. The Mishna and Talmud do not reproduce the story–list–sanction pattern and restrict themselves primarily to law, thus presenting their contents in a more 'philosophical' fashion.)[10] The Torah's rhetoric and persuasive intentions do, however, become fundamental to the Western idea of Scripture, as Patrick and Scult note: 'The Bible

---

9. Septuagint manuscripts vary in their order, particularly in the prophets. See G.W. Anderson, 'Canonical and Non-Canonical', in P.R. Ackroyd and C.F. Evans (eds.), *The Cambridge History of the Bible*. I. *From the Beginnings to Jerome* (Cambridge: Cambridge University Press, 1970), p. 113-59 (142).

10. In fact, J. Neusner argued that Aristotelian ideas influenced the form and method of the Mishna, though perhaps indirectly (*Studying Classical Judaism: A Primer* [Louisville, KY: Westminster/John Knox Press, 1991], pp. 130-35).

assumes the narrative shape that it does, not because it is most beautiful or most truthful, but rather because this is the form that is most persuasive.'[11] Precisely this opportunistic reasoning prompts a resounding protest from the philosophical tradition of rhetorical criticism beginning with Plato.

The issue of rhetorical ethics is thus almost as old as the Pentateuch itself. Plato's attack on the Sophists protested the moral relativism of rhetoricians who taught their students how to speak persuasively rather than how to find and speak the truth. He also clearly resented the much greater popularity of Sophistic rhetoric over philosophical dialectic (a contrast exemplified by popular rejection and, eventually, execution of Socrates). The conflict between rhetoric and philosophy in the ancient world thus represented in part the friction between an elitist ideal of rational education and a populist strategy for mass persuasion.[12] Later religious rhetoricians rejected the relativism of the Sophists as vehemently as did the Greek philosophers, but embraced in its place not dialectical reason but revealed truth.[13] As a result, the goal of persuasion remained religiously paramount and has frequently been understood to justify any means used for its achievement, including outright coercion. Thus Christian rhetoric, for example, while rejecting moral relativism, still often champions the populist cause and its rhetoric of persuasion at any cost, while rational philosophy still levels against it the old charge of unethical rhetorical practices.[14]

11. *Rhetoric*, p. 104. After my rhetorical analysis of the Pentateuch, I would delete the word 'narrative' from their statement.

12. On the rhetoric of the Sophists and its reception by the philosophers, see J. Poulakos, *Sophistical Rhetoric in Classical Greece* (Columbia: University of South Carolina Press, 1995).

13. For an analysis of Paul's rhetoric as 'sophistic' and as representing a 'sophistic god', see M.D. Given, 'True Rhetoric: Ambiguity, Cunning, and Deception in Pauline Discourse', in *SBL 1997 Seminar Papers* (Atlanta: Scholars Press, 1997), pp. 526-50. Theology has, of course, tried to mediate between philosophy and religious rhetoric and, in the medieval period, actively worked towards a synthesis of the two. O'Banion judged the effort destructive for rhetoric, because it subordinated all narrative to the single Christian narrative (*Reorienting Rhetoric*, pp. 20, 105, 122). His call for balancing the rhetorical functions of narrative and list (pp. 13, 19) nevertheless seems to duplicate theology's attempts to mediate between Scripture and reason.

14. The power of religious claims to reinforce political rhetoric has frequently been demonstrated, and just as frequently denounced: K. Marx has hardly been the

Here then is the rhetorical reason for the separation of philosophy from religion in Western culture. Despite the considerable overlap in their contents, the institutional distinction between them remains entrenched. Its foundations were laid by, on the one hand, the Pentateuch's elevation of persuasion as the overriding goal of Torah-religion and, on the other hand, the Greek philosopher's criticism of rhetorical opportunism. Christianity's rise to dominance in the Mediterranean world juxtaposed the two traditions with theology as mediator. The secularization of the modern world, under the influence of philosophy's most successful offspring, science, has reversed the medieval dominance of religion over learning. Modernity has not, however, significantly altered the rhetorical conflict between philosophy and religion.

Reviewing this history, even in such summary fashion, shows two sides to rhetorical ethics. The Greek philosophers focused on the ethics of form and content, arguing that the search for truth should always be given priority, and in this they have been followed by Western academic tradition. The religious traditions emphasized the ethics of results, arguing that truth should be spread as widely as possible because of the severe consequences at stake in its acceptance or rejection. The urgency of the religious agenda encourages a pragmatic rhetoric for maximal appeal, while the search for knowledge in philosophy and science promotes technical jargon for maximal accuracy. This ethical controversy over rhetorical methods and results remains very much alive in contemporary academic debates over such topics as advocacy vs. neutrality in teaching, and objectivity vs. ideology in research. Western culture inherited this rhetorical conflict from its roots in the Pentateuch and Plato, and has long since institutionalized it in the distinction between philosophy and religion.

only thinker to consider religion an 'opiate of the people'. On religious and political rhetoric, see Burke, *Rhetoric of Motives*, pp. 76, 121 and *passim*.

BIBLIOGRAPHY

Albertz, R., *A History of Israelite Religion in the Old Testament Period* (2 vols.; trans. J. Bowden; OTL; Louisville, KY: Westminster/John Knox Press, 1994).

Alt, A., 'The Origins of Israelite Law', in *Essays on Old Testament History and Religion* (trans. R.A. Wilson; Oxford: Basil Blackwell, 1966 [1934]), pp. 81-132.

Alter, R., *The Art of Biblical Narrative* (New York: Basic Books, 1981).

Amsler, S., 'Les documents de la loi et la formation du Pentateuque', in A. de Pury (ed.), *Le Pentateuque en question* (Geneva: Labor et Fides, 1989), pp. 235-57.

Anderson, G.W., 'Canonical and Non-Canonical', in P.R. Ackroyd and C.F. Evans (eds.), *The Cambridge History of the Bible*. I. *From the Beginings to Jerome* (3 vols.; Cambridge: Cambridge University Press, 1970), pp. 113-59.

Austin, J.L., *How to Do Things with Words* (William James Lectures, 1955; Cambridge, MA: Harvard University Press, 2nd edn, 1975).

Bakhtin, M.M., *The Dialogic Imagination* (ed. M. Holquist; Austin: University of Texas Press, 1981).

Barr, J., 'The Synchronic, the Diachronic and the Historical: A Triangular Relationship', in J.C. de Moor (ed.), *Synchronic or Diachronic? A Debate on Method in Old Testament Exegesis* (OTS, 34; Leiden: E.J. Brill, 1995), pp. 1-14.

Baumgartner, W., 'Ein Kapital vom hebräischen Erzählungsstil', in H. Schmidt (ed.), *ΕΥΧΑΡΙΣΤΗΡΙΟΝ: Studien zur Religion und Literatur des Alten und Neuen Testaments* (Göttingen: Vandenhoeck & Ruprecht, 1923), pp. 145-57.

Beckman, G., *Hittite Diplomatic Texts* (ed. H.A. Hoffner, Jr; WAW, 7; Atlanta: Scholars Press, 1996).

Beer, G., *Exodus* (HAT, 3; Tübingen: J.C.B. Mohr [Paul Siebeck], 1939).

Benoit, W.L., and J.M. D'Agostine, ' "The Case of the Midnight Judges" and Multiple Audience Discourse: Chief Justice Marshall and *Marbury V. Madison*', *Southern Communication Journal* 59 (1994), pp. 89-96.

Ben Zvi, E., 'Twelve Prophetic Books or "The Twelve": Preliminary Considerations', in P.R. House and J.W. Watts (eds.), *Essays on Isaiah and the Twelve in Honor of John D.W. Watts* (JSOTSup, 235; Sheffield: Sheffield Academic Press, 1996), pp. 125-56.

Berquist, J.L., *Judaism in Persia's Shadow: A Social and Historical Approach* (Minneapolis: Fortress Press, 1995).

Blenkinsopp, J., 'The Mission of Udjahorresnet and Those of Ezra and Nehemiah', *JBL* 106 (1987), pp. 409-21.

—*The Pentateuch: An Introduction to the First Five Books of the Bible* (ABRL; New York: Doubleday, 1992).

—'The Structure of P', *CBQ* 38 (1976), pp. 275-92.

—*Wisdom and Law in the Old Testament: The Ordering of Life in Israel and Early Judaism* (Oxford: Oxford University Press, rev. edn, 1995).

Blum, E., *Die Komposition der Vätergeschichte* (WMANT, 57; Neukirchen–Vluyn: Neukirchener Verlag, 1984).

—*Studien zur Komposition des Pentateuch* (BZAW, 189; Berlin: W. de Gruyter, 1990).

Boecker, H.J. *Law and the Administration of Justice in the Old Testament and the Ancient East* (trans. J. Moiser; Minneapolis: Augsburg, 1980).

—*Redeformen des Rechtslebens im Alten Testament* (WMANT, 14; Neukirchen–Vluyn: Neukirchener Verlag, 1964).

Boorer, S., *The Promise of the Land as Oath: A Key to the Formation of the Pentateuch* (Berlin: W. de Gruyter, 1992).

Bracker, H.D., *Das Gesetz Israels* (Hamburg, 1962).

Brooks, R., *Spirit of the Ten Commandments* (New York: Harper & Row, 1990).

Burke, K., *A Rhetoric of Motives* (Berkeley: University of California Press, 1950).

—*The Rhetoric of Religion: Studies in Logology* (Berkeley: University of California Press, 1961).

Butler, T.C., *Joshua* (WBC, 7; Waco, TX: Word Books, 1983).

Cagni, L., *The Poem of Erra* (SANE, 1.3; Malibu, CA: Undena, 1977).

Carmichael, C.M., *The Laws of Deuteronomy* (Ithaca, NY: Cornell University Press, 1974).

Carr, D.M., *Reading the Fractures of Genesis: Historical and Literary Approaches* (Louisville, KY: Westminster/John Knox Press, 1996).

Cassuto, U., *A Commentary on the Book of Exodus* (trans. I. Abrahams; Jerusalem: Magnes Press, 1967).

Charlesworth, J.H. (ed.), *The Dead Sea Scrolls: Hebrew, Aramaic, and Greek Texts with English Translations. I. Rule of the Community and Related Documents* (trans. J.H. Charlesworth and L.T. Stuckenbruck; Tübingen: J.C.B. Mohr [Paul Siebeck], 1994).

Cheney, M., *Dust, Wind and Agony: Character, Speech and Genre in Job* (ConBOT, 36; Lund: Almqvist & Wiksell, 1994).

Childs, B.S., *Biblical Theology of the Old and New Testaments* (Minneapolis: Fortress Press, 1992).

—*Old Testament Theology in a Canonical Context* (Philadelphia: Fortress Press, 1985).

—*The Book of Exodus: A Critical, Theological Commentary* (OTL; Philadelphia: Westminster Press, 1974).

Clements, R.E., *Old Testament Theology: A Fresh Approach* (Atlanta: John Knox Press, 1978).

Clines, D.J.A., 'Beyond Synchronic/Diachronic', in J.C. de Moor (ed.), *Synchronic or Diachronic? A Debate on Method in Old Testament Exegesis* (OTS, 34; Leiden: E.J. Brill, 1995), pp. 52-71.

—*Ezra, Nehemiah, Esther* (NCB; Grand Rapids: Eerdmans, 1984).

—'God in the Pentateuch: Reading Against the Grain', in *idem*, *Interested Parties: The Ideology of Writers and Readers of the Hebrew Bible* (JSOTSup, 205; Sheffield: Sheffield Academic Press, 1995), pp. 187-211.

—*The Theme of the Pentateuch* (JSOTSup, 10; Sheffield: JSOT Press, 1978).

Coats, G.W., *Moses: Heroic Man, Man of God* (JSOTSup, 57; Sheffield: JSOT Press, 1988).

Conrad, E.W., 'Heard but not Seen: The Representation of "Books" in the Old Testament', *JSOT* 54 (1992), pp. 45-59.

Cover, R.M., 'Foreword: *Nomos* and Narrative', *Harvard Law Review* 97.1 (1983), pp. 4-68.

Craigie, Peter C., *The Book of Deuteronomy* (NICOT; Grand Rapids: Eerdmans, 1976).

Crawford, T.G., *Blessing and Curse in Syro-Palestinian Inscriptions of the Iron Age* (New York: Peter Lang, 1992).

Cross, F.M., *Canaanite Myth and Hebrew Epic* (Cambridge, MA: Harvard University Press, 1973).

Crüsemann, Frank, 'Der Pentateuch als Tora: Prolegomena zur Interpretation seiner Endgestalt', *EvT* 49 (1989), pp. 250-67.

—*Die Tora: Theologie und Sozialgeschichte des alttestamentlichen Gesetzes* (Munich: Chr. Kaiser Verlag, 1992; ET, *The Torah: Theology and Social History of Old Testament Law* [trans. by W. Mahnke; Edinburgh: T. & T. Clark/Minneapolis: Fortress Press, 1996]).

Damrosch, D., 'Leviticus', in R. Alter and F. Kermode (eds.), *The Literary Guide to the Bible* (Cambridge, MA: Harvard University Press, 1987), pp. 66-77.

—*The Narrative Covenant: Transformations of Genre in the Growth of Biblical Literature* (San Francisco: Harper & Row, 1987).

Davies, Graham I., 'The Composition of the Book of Exodus: Reflections on the Theses of Erhard Blum', in M.V. Fox *et al.* (eds.), *Texts, Temples and Traditions: A Tribute to Menahem Haran* (Winona Lake, IN: Eisenbrauns, 1996), pp. 71-85.

Davies, P.R., *In Search of Ancient Israel* (JSOTSup, 148; Sheffield: JSOT Press, 1992).

—'Leviticus as a Cultic System in the Second Temple Period', in J.F.A. Sawyer (ed.), *Reading Leviticus: A Conversation with Mary Douglas* (JSOTSup, 227; Sheffield: Sheffield Academic Press, 1996), pp. 230-37.

Dennis, A., P. Foote and R. Perkins (trans.), *Laws of Early Iceland, Grágás* (Winnipeg: University of Manitoba Press, 1980).

Dentan, R.C., 'The Literary Affinities of Exodus XXXIV 6f', *VT* 13 (1963), pp. 34-51.

Dillard, R.B., *2 Chronicles* (WBC, 15; Waco, TX: Word Books, 1987).

Dozeman, T.B., *God on the Mountain: A Study of Redaction, Theology and Canon in Exodus 19–24* (SBLMS, 37; Atlanta: Scholars Press, 1989).

—'Inner-Biblical Interpretation of Yahweh's Gracious and Compassionate Character', *JBL* 108 (1989), pp. 207-23.

—'OT Rhetorical Criticism', *ABD*, V, pp. 712-15.

Dumbrell, W.J., *Covenant and Creation: An Old Testament Covenantal Theology* (Exeter: Paternoster Press, 1984).

Dupont-Sommer, A., 'L'inscription araméenne', in H. Metzger (ed.), *Fouilles de Xanthos. VI. La stèle trilingue du Létôon* (Paris: Librairie C. Klincksieck, 1979), pp. 129-78.

Durham, J.I., *Exodus* (WBC, 3; Waco, TX: Word Books, 1987).

Emerton, J.A., 'The Priestly Writer in Genesis', *JTS* 39 (1988), pp. 381-400.

Engnell, I., 'The Pentateuch', in J.T. Willis (ed. and trans.), *A Rigid Scrutiny* (Nashville: Vanderbilt, 1969), pp. 50-67.

Eslinger, L., 'Freedom or Knowledge? Perspective and Purpose in the Exodus Narrative (Exodus 1–15)', *JSOT* 52 (1991), pp. 43-60; repr. in J.W. Rogerson (ed.), *The Pentateuch: A Sheffield Reader* (Sheffield: Sheffield Academic Press, 1996), pp. 186-202.

Ezkenazi, T.C., *In an Age of Prose: A Literary Approach to Ezra–Nehemiah* (SBLMS, 36; Atlanta: Scholars Press, 1988).

Finkelstein, J.J., 'Ammisaduqa's Edict and the Babylonian "Law Codes" ', *JCS* 15 (1961), pp. 91-104.

Fish, S.E., *Doing What Comes Naturally: Change, Rhetoric, and the Practice of Theory in Literary and Legal Studies* (Durham, NC: Duke University Press, 1989).

Fishbane, M., *Biblical Interpretation in Ancient Israel* (Oxford: Clarendon Press, 1985).

Flusser, D., 'Psalms, Hymns, and Prayers', in M.E. Stone (ed.), *Jewish Writings of the Second Temple Period* (CRINT, 2.2; Assen: Van Gorcum; Philadelphia: Fortress Press, 1984), pp. 551-77.

Fokkelman, J., 'Exodus', in R. Alter and F. Kermode (eds.), *The Literary Guide to the Bible* (Cambridge, MA: Harvard University Press, 1987), pp. 56-65.

Foster, B.R., *Before the Muses: An Anthology of Akkadian Literature* (2 vols.; Bethesda, MD: CDL, 1993).

Freedman, D.N., 'The Formation of the Canon of the Old Testament', in E.B. Firmage, B.G. Weiss and J.W. Welch (eds.), *Religion and Law: Biblical-Judaic and Islamic Perspectives* (Winona Lake, IN: Eisenbrauns, 1990), pp. 315-31.

—'The Law and the Prophets', in G.W. Anderson, *et al* (eds.), *Congress Volume: Bonn 1962* (VTSup, 9; Leiden: E.J. Brill, 1963), pp. 250-65.

Frei, P., 'Die persische Reichsautorisation: Ein Überblick', *ZAR* 1 (1995), pp. 1-35.

—'Zentralgewalt und Lokalautonomie im Achämenidenreich', in *Reichsidee und Reichsorganisation im Perserreich* (OBO, 55; Freiburg: Universitätsverlag, 2nd edn; 1996), pp. 8-131.

Fretheim, T.E., *The Pentateuch* (Nashville: Abingdon Press, 1996).

Friedman, R.E., *The Exile and Biblical Narrative: The Formation of the Deuteronomistic and Priestly Works* (HSM, 22; Chico, CA: Scholars Press, 1981).

Gager, J.G. (ed.), *Curse Tablets and Binding Spells from the Ancient World* (New York: Oxford University Press, 1992).

Gaster, T.H., *The Dead Sea Scriptures* (Garden City, NY: Doubleday, 3rd edn, 1976).

Gemser, B., 'The Importance of the Motive Clause in Old Testament Law', in G.W. Anderson, *et al* (eds.), *Congress Volume: Copenhagen* (VTSup, 1; Leiden: E.J. Brill, 1953), pp. 50-66.

Gerstenberger, E.S., *Leviticus: A Commentary* (trans. D.W. Stott; OTL; Louisville, KY: Westminster Press, 1996).

—*Wesen und Herkunft des apodiktischen Rechts* (WMANT, 20; Neukirchen–Vluyn: Neukirchener Verlag, 1965).

Gese, H., 'The Law', in *idem*, *Essays on Biblical Theology* (trans. K. Crim, Minneapolis: Augsburg, 1981), pp. 60-92.

Gitay, Y., *Prophecy and Persuasion: A Study of Isaiah 40–48* (Bonn: Linguistica Biblica, 1981).

Given, M.D., 'True Rhetoric: Ambiguity, Cunning, and Deception in Pauline Discourse', in *SBL 1997 Seminar Papers* (Atlanta: Scholars Press, 1997), pp. 526-50.

Grabbe, L.L., *Judaism from Cyrus to Hadrian. I. The Persian and Greek Periods* (Minneapolis: Fortress Press, 1992).

Gray, J., *I & II Kings: A Commentary* (OTL; London: SCM Press, 1964).

Grayson, A.K., 'Histories and Historians of the Ancient Near East: Assyria and Babylonia', *Or* 49 (1980), pp. 140-94.

Greenberg, M., 'Some Postulates of Biblical Criminal Law', in *idem*, *Studies in the Bible and Jewish Thought* (Philadelphia: Jewish Publication Society, 1995 [1960]), pp. 25-41.

—'Three Conceptions of the Torah in Hebrew Scriptures', in *Studies in the Bible and Jewish Thought* (Philadelphia: Jewish Publication Society, 1995), pp. 11-24.

Greengus, S., 'Some Issues Relating to the Comparability of Laws and the Coherence of the Legal Tradition', in B.M. Levinson (ed.), *Theory and Method in Biblical and Cuneiform Law: Revision, Interpolation and Development* (JSOTSup, 181; Sheffield: Sheffield Academic Press, 1994), pp. 60-87.

Gressman, H., *Mose und seine Zeit: Ein Kommentar zu den Mose Sagen* (FRLANT, 18; Göttingen: Vandenhoeck & Ruprecht, 1918).

Gunkel, Hermann, *Genesis* (Göttingen: Vandenhoeck & Ruprecht, 5th edn, 1922; ET trans. M. Biddle; Macon, GA: Mercer University Press, 1997).

Gunneweg, A.H.J., 'Das Gesetz und die Propheten: Eine Auslegung von Ex 33,7-11; Num 11,4–12,8; Dtn 31,14f.; 34,10', *ZAW* 102 (1990), pp. 169-80.

Hanson, P.D., 'The Theological Significance of Contradiction within the Book of the Covenant', in G.W. Coats and B.O. Long (eds.), *Canon and Authority: Essays in Old Testament Religion and Theology* (Philadelphia: Fortress Press, 1977), pp. 110-31.

Harris, W.V., *Ancient Literacy* (Cambridge, MA: Harvard University Press, 1989).

Hartley, J.H., *Leviticus* (WBC, 4; Dallas: Word Books, 1992).

Hengstl, J., 'Zur Frage von Rechtsvereinheitlichung im frühaltbabylonischen Mesopotamien und im griechisch-römischen Ägypten: Eine rechtsvergleichende Skizze', *RIDA* 40 (1993), pp. 27-55.

Henn, T.R., *The Bible as Literature* (New York: Oxford University Press, 1970).

Howard, D.M., Jr, 'Rhetorical Criticism in Old Testament Studies', *BBR* 4 (1994), pp. 87-104.

Hurowitz, V.A., *Inu Anum Sirum: Literary Structure in the Non-Juridical Sections of Codex Hammurabi* (Occasional Publications of the Samuel Noah Kramer Fund, 15; Philadelphia, 1994).

Jackson, B.S., 'The Ceremonial and the Judicial: Biblical Law as Sign and Symbol', *JSOT* 30 (1984), pp. 25-50 (repr. in J.W. Rogerson [ed.], *The Pentateuch: A Sheffield Reader* [Sheffield: Sheffield Academic Press, 1996], pp. 102-27).

Johnstone, W., 'Reactivating the Chronicles Analogy in Pentateuchal Studies with Special Reference to the Sinai Pericope in Exodus', *ZAW* 99 (1987), pp. 16-37.

Jones, G.H., *1 and 2 Kings* II (NCB; Grand Rapids: Eerdmans, 1984).

Kaufmann, Y., *The Religion of Israel* (ed. and trans. M. Greenberg; Chicago: University of Chicago Press, 1960).

Kellermann, U., *Nehemia: Quellen, Überlieferung und Geschichte* (BZAW, 102; Berlin: Alfred Töpelmann, 1967).

Kennedy, G.A., *New Testament Interpretation Through Rhetorical Criticism* (Chapel Hill: University of North Carolina Press, 1984).

Kent, C.F., *Israel's Laws and Legal Precedents* (London: Hodder & Stoughton, 1907).

Kessler, M., 'A Methodological Setting for Rhetorical Criticism', in D.J.A. Clines, D.M. Gunn and A.J. Hauser (eds.), *Art and Meaning: Rhetoric in Biblical Literature* (JSOTSup, 19; Sheffield: JSOT Press, 1982), pp. 1-19.

Kirsch, G., and D.H. Roen (eds.), *A Sense of Audience in Written Communication* (Written Communication Annual, 5; Newbury Park, CA: Sage Publications, 1990).

Kline, M.G., *Treaty of the Great King: The Covenant Structure of Deuteronomy* (Grand Rapids, MI: Eerdmans, 1963).

Knierim, R.P., *The Task of Old Testament Theology: Method and Cases* (Grand Rapids, MI: Eerdmans, 1995).

Knight, G.A.F., *Theology As Narration: A Commentary on the Book of Exodus* (Grand Rapids, MI: Eerdmans, 1976).

Knohl, I., *The Sanctuary of Silence: The Priestly Torah and the Holiness School* (Minneapolis: Fortress Press, 1995).

Knoppers, G.N., 'Jehoshaphat's Judiciary and "the Scroll of YHWH's Torah" ', *JBL* 113 (1994), pp. 59-80.

Koch, Klaus, 'P: Kein Redaktor', *VT* 37 (1987), pp. 446-67.

—'Weltordnung und Reichsidee im alten Iran und ihre Auswirlungen auf die Proving Jehud', in *Reichsidee und Reichsorganisation im Perserreich* (Freiburg: Universitätsverlag, 2nd edn, 1996 [1984]), pp. 133-337.

Kraus, F.R., 'Ein zentrales Problem des altmesopotamischen Rechts: Was ist der Codex Hammu-Rabi?', *Genava* 8 (1960), pp. 283-96.

Kreuzer, S., 'Die Verbindung von Gottesherrschaft und Königtum Gottes im Alten Testament', in J.A. Emerton (ed.), *Congress Volume: Paris 1992* (VTSup, 56; Leiden: E.J. Brill, 1995), pp. 145-61.

Lauterbach, J.Z. (ed.), *Mekilta de-Rabbi Ishmael* (Philadelphia: Jewish Publication Society, 1933).

Lenchak, T.A., *'Choose Life!': A Rhetorical-Critical Investigation of Deuteronomy 28, 69–30, 20* (AnBib, 129; Rome: Pontificio Instituto Biblico, 1993).

Levenson, J.D., *The Death and Resurrection of the Beloved Son: The Transformation of Child Sacrifice in Judaism and Christianity* (New Haven: Yale University Press, 1993).

—'The Theologies of Commandment in Biblical Israel', *HTR* 73 (1980), pp. 17-33.

Levinson, B.M., 'The Case for Revision and Interpolation within the Biblical Legal Corpora', in *idem* (ed.), *Theory and Method in Biblical and Cuneiform Law: Revision, Interpolation and Development* (JSOTSup, 181; Sheffield: Sheffield Academic Press, 1994), pp. 37-59.

—'The Human Voice in Divine Revelation: The Problem of Authority in Biblical law', in M.A. Williams, C. Cox and M.S. Jaffee (eds.), *Innovations in Religious Traditions* (RelSoc, 31; Berlin: Mouton de Gruyter, 1992), pp. 35-71.

—'The Right Chorale: From the Poetics to the Hermeneutics of the Hebrew Bible', in J.P. Rosenblatt and J.C. Sitterson, Jr (eds.), *'Not in Heaven': Coherence and Complexity in Biblical Narrative* (Bloomington: Indiana University Press, 1991), pp. 129-53.

Lichtheim, M., *Ancient Egyptian Literature* (3 vols.; Berkeley: University of California Press, 1973, 1976, 1980).

Lightstone, J.N., *The Rhetoric of the Babylonian Talmud: Its Social Meaning and Context* (Waterloo, ON: Wilfrid Laurier University Press, 1994).

Lohfink, N., 'Bund als Vertrag im Deuteronomium', *ZAW* 107 (1995), pp. 215-39.

—'Die Priesterschrift und die Geschichte', in J.A. Emerton (ed.), *Congress Volume 1977* (VTSup, 24; Leiden: E.J. Brill, 1978), pp. 189-225.

—'Die Stimmen in Deuteronomium 2', *BZ* 37 (1993), pp. 209-35.

Majercik, R., 'Rhetoric and Oratory in the Greco-Roman World', *ABD*, V, pp. 710-15.

Mann, T.W., *The Book of the Torah: The Narrative Integrity of the Pentateuch* (Atlanta: John Knox Press, 1988).

Mayes, A.D.H., *Deuteronomy* (NCB; London: Oliphants, 1979).

McCarthy, D.J., *Treaty and Covenant: A Study in Form in the Ancient Oriental Documents and in the Old Testament* (Rome: Biblical Institute Press, 2nd rev. edn, 1981).

McEvenue, S.E., *The Narrative Style of the Priestly Writer* (AnBib, 50; Rome: Biblical Institute Press, 1971).

Meier, S.A., *Speaking of Speaking: Marking Direct Discourse in the Hebrew Bible* (VTSup, 46; Leiden: E.J. Brill, 1992).

Mendenhall, G.E., 'Ancient Oriental and Biblical Law', in E.F. Campbell, Jr, and D.N. Freedman (eds.), *Biblical Archaeologist Review* 3 (Garden City, NY: Doubleday, 1970), pp. 1-24.

—'Covenant Forms in Israelite Tradition', in E.F. Campbell, Jr, and D.N. Freedman (eds.), *Biblical Archaeologist Review* 3 (Garden City, NY: Doubleday, 1970), pp. 25-53.

Menes, A., *Die vorexilischen Gesetze Israels im Zusammenhang seiner kulturgeschichtlichen Entwicklung* (Giessen: Alfred Töpelmann, 1928).

Metzger, H., 'L'inscription grecque', in H. Metzger (ed.), *Fouilles de Xanthos*. VI. *La stèle trilingue du Létôon* (Paris: Librairie C. Klincksieck, 1979), pp. 29-48.

Miles, J., *God: A Biography* (New York: Knopf, 1995).

Milgrom, J., *Leviticus 1–16* (AB, 3; New York: Doubleday, 1991).

—*Numbers* (Philadelphia: Jewish Publication Society, 1990).

—'The Biblical Diet Laws as an Ethical System', *Int* 17 (1963), pp. 288-301.

Miller, P.D., Jr, ' "Moses My Servant": The Deuteronomic Portrait of Moses', *Int* 41 (1987), pp. 245-55 (repr. in D.L. Christensen [ed.], *A Song of Power and the Power of Song: Essays on the Book of Deuteronomy* [Winona Lake, IN: Eisenbrauns, 1993], pp. 301-12).

—'The Place of the Decalogue in the Old Testament and its Law', *Int* 43 (1989), pp. 229-42.

Moberly, R.W.L., *At the Mountain of God: Story and Theology in Exodus 32–34* (JSOTSup, 22; Sheffield: JSOT Press, 1983).

Moore, M.S., *The Balaam Traditions: Their Character and Development* (Atlanta: Scholars Press, 1990).

Moran, W.L., 'The Ancient Near Eastern Background of the Love of God in Deuteronomy', *CBQ* 25 (1963), pp. 77-87.

Morrow, W., 'A Generic Discrepancy in the Covenant Code', in B. Levinson (ed.), *Theory and Method in Biblical and Cuneiform Law: Revision, Interpolation and Development* (JSOTSup, 181; Sheffield: Sheffield Academic Press, 1994), pp. 136-51.

Mowinckel, S., 'Die vorderasiatischen Königs- und Fürsteninschriften, eine stilistische Studie', in H. Schmidt (ed.), *EYXAPIΣTHPION: Studien zur Religion und Literatur des Alten und Neuen Testaments* (Festschrift H. Gunkel; FRLANT, 36/1; Göttingen: Vandenhoeck & Ruprecht, 1923), pp. 278-322.

Muilenburg, J., 'Form Criticism and Beyond', *JBL* 88 (1969), pp. 1-18 (repr. in P.R. House [ed.], *Beyond Form Criticism: Essays in Old Testament Literary Criticism* [Winona Lake, IN: Eisenbrauns, 1992], pp. 49-69).

Mullen, E.T., Jr, *Ethnic Myths and Pentateuchal Foundations: A New Approach to the Formation of the Pentateuch* (SBLSS; Atlanta: Scholars Press, 1997).

Nasuti, H.P., 'Identity, Identification, and Imitation: The Narrative Hermeneutics of Biblical Law', *Journal of Law and Religion* 4.1 (1986), pp. 9-23.

Neusner, J., *Studying Classical Judaism: A Primer* (Louisville, KY: Westminster/John Knox Press, 1991).

Newsom, C.A., 'Kenneth Burke Meets the Teacher of Righteousness: Rhetorical Strategies in the Hodayot and the Serek Ha-Yahad', in H.W. Attridge, J.J. Collins and T.H. Tobin, SJ (eds.), *Of Scribes and Scrolls: Studies on the Hebrew Bible, Intertestamental Judaism, and Christian Origins presented to John Strugnell on the*

Occasion of his Sixtieth Birthday (College Theology Society Resources in Religion, 5; Lanham, MD: University Press of America, 1990), pp. 121-31.

Nicholson, E.W., 'Covenant in a Century of Study since Wellhausen', *OTS* 24 (1986), pp. 54-69.

Nigosian, S.A., 'Moses As They Saw Him', *VT* 43 (1993), pp. 339-50.

Nohrnberg, J., *Like Unto Moses: The Constituting of an Interruption* (Bloomington: Indiana University Press, 1995).

Noth, M., *A History of Pentateuchal Traditions* (trans. B.W. Anderson; Chico, CA: Scholars Press, 1981 [1948]).

—*Exodus: A Commentary* (trans. J.S. Bowden; OTL; London: SCM Press, 1962).

—'The Laws of the Pentateuch', in *idem*, *The Laws in the Pentateuch and Other Studies* (trans. D.R. Ap-Thomas; Philadelphia: Fortress Press, 1967 [1940]).

O'Banion, J.D., *Reorienting Rhetoric: The Dialectic of List and Story* (University Park, PA: Pennsylvania State University Press, 1992).

Olson, D.T., *Deuteronomy and the Death of Moses: A Theological Reading* (OBT; Minneapolis: Fortress Press, 1994).

—*The Death of the Old and the Birth of the New: The Framework of the Book of Numbers and the Pentateuch* (BJS, 71; Chico, CA: Scholars Press, 1985).

Orlinsky, H.M., 'The Forensic Character of the Hebrew Bible', in D.A. Knight and P.J. Paris (eds.), *Justice and the Holy: Essays in Honor of Walter Harrelson* (Atlanta: Scholars Press, 1989), pp. 89-97.

Otto, E., 'Aspects of Legal Reforms and Reformulations in Ancient Cuneiform and Israelite Law', in B.M. Levinson (ed.), *Theory and Method in Biblical and Cuneiform Law: Revision, Interpolation and Development* (JSOTSup, 181; Sheffield: Sheffield Academic Press, 1994), pp. 160-96.

—'Gesetzesfortschreibung und Pentateuchredaktion', *ZAW* 107 (1995), pp. 373-92.

—*Wandel der Rechtsbegründungen in der Gesellschaftsgeschichte des antiken Israel: Eine Rechtsgeschichte des 'Bundesbuchs' Ex XX 22–XXIII 13* (Studia Biblica, 3; Leiden: E.J. Brill, 1988).

Patrick, D., 'Is the Truth of the First Commandment Known by Reason?' *CBQ* 56 (1994), pp. 423-41.

—*Old Testament Law* (Atlanta: John Knox Press, 1985).

—'The First Commandment in the Structure of the Pentateuch', *VT* 45 (1995), pp. 107-18.

—*The Rendering of God in the Old Testament* (OBT; Philadelphia: Fortress Press, 1981).

—'The Rhetoric of Collective Responsibility in Deuteronomic Law', in D.P. Wright, D.N. Freedman and A. Hurvitz (eds.), *Pomegranates and Golden Bells: Studies . . . in Honor of Jacob Milgrom* (Winona Lake, IN: Eisenbrauns, 1995), pp. 421-36.

—'The Rhetoric of Revelation', *HBT* 16 (1994), pp. 20-40.

—*The Rhetoric of Revelation* (OBT; Minneapolis: Fortress Press, forthcoming).

Patrick, D., and A. Scult, *Rhetoric and Biblical Interpretation* (JSOTSup, 82; Sheffield: Almond Press, 1990).

Paul, S.M., *Studies in the Book of the Covenant in the Light of Cuneiform and Biblical Law* (Leiden: E.J. Brill, 1970).

Perlitt, L., *Bundestheologie im Alten Testament* (WMANT, 36; Neukirchen–Vluyn: Neukirchener Verlag, 1969).

Polzin, R., *Moses and the Deuteronomist: A Literary Study of the Deuteronomic History* (New York: Seabury, 1980).

Poulakos, J., *Sophistical Rhetoric in Classical Greece* (Columbia: University of South Carolina Press, 1995).

Powy, J.C., *Enjoyment of Literature* (New York: Simon & Schuster, 1938).

Rad, G. von, ' מלך and מלכות in the OT', *TDNT*, I, pp. 565-71.

—'Die Nehemia-Denkschrift', *ZAW* 76 (1964), pp. 176-87.

—*Old Testament Theology*, I (2 vols.; trans. D.M.G. Stalker; New York: Harper & Row, 1962).

—*Studies in Deuteronomy* (trans. D.M.G. Stalker; SBT, 9; London: SCM Press, 1953).

—'The Form-Critical Problem of the Hexateuch', in *idem*, *The Problem of the Hexateuch and Other Essays* (trans. E.W. Trueman Dicken; Edinburgh: Oliver & Boyd, 1966), pp. 1-78.

Rendtorff, R., *Die Gesetze in der Priesterschrift* (Göttingen: Vandenhoeck & Ruprecht, 1954).

—'Esra und das "Gesetz" ', *ZAW* 96 (1984), pp. 165-84.

—*Leviticus* (BKAT, 3.1; Neukirchen–Vluyn: Neukirchener Verlag, 1985).

—*The Problem of the Process of Transmission in the Pentateuch* (trans. J.J. Scullion; JSOTSup, 89; Sheffield: JSOT Press, 1990 [1977]).

Reventlow, H. Graf, *Das Heiligkeitsgesetz formgeschichtlich untersucht* (WMANT, 6; Neukirchen–Vluyn: Neukirchener Verlag, 1961).

Richards, M.P., 'The Manuscript Contexts of the Old English Laws: Tradition and Innovation', on P.E. Szarmach (ed.), *Studies in Earlier Old English Prose* (Albany, NY: SUNY Press, 1986), pp. 171-92.

Robinson, B.P., 'Moses at the Burning Bush', *JSOT* 75 (1997), pp. 107-22.

Romilly, J. de, *Magic and Rhetoric in Ancient Greece* (Cambridge, MA: Harvard University Press, 1975).

Rosenberg, J., *King and Kin: Political Allegory in the Hebrew Bible* (Bloomington: Indiana University Press, 1986).

Roth, M.T., *Law Collections from Mesopotamia and Asia Minor* (WAW, 6; Atlanta: Scholars Press, 1995).

Rütersworden, U., 'Die persische Reichsautorisation der Thora: Fact or Fiction?', *ZAR* 1 (1995), pp. 47-61.

Sailhamer, J.H., *The Pentateuch as Narrative: a Biblical-Theological Commentary* (Grand Rapids: Zondervan, 1992).

Sandmel, S., 'The Enjoyment of Scripture: an Esthetic Approach', *Judaism* 22 (1973), pp. 455-67.

Savran, G.W., *Telling and Retelling: Quotation in Biblical Narrative* (Bloomington: Indiana University Press, 1988).

Schaper, J., 'The Jerusalem Temple as an Instrument of the Achaemenid Fiscal Administration', *VT* 45 (1995), pp. 528-39.

Scharbert, J., 'Formgeschichte und Exegese von Ex 34,6f und Seiner Parallelen', *Bib* 38 (1957), pp. 130-50.

Schmid, H.H., *Der sogennante Jahwist* (Zürich: Theologischer Verlag, 1976).

Schmidt, H., *Die grossen Propheten* (Die Schriften des Alten Testaments, 2.2; Göttingen: Vandenhoeck & Ruprecht, 1915).

Schmitt, H.-C., 'Die Suche nach der Identität des Jahweglaubens im nachexilischen Israel: Bemerkungen zur theologischen Intention der Endredaktion des Pentateuch', in J. Mehlhausen (ed.), *Pluralismus und Identität* (Gütersloh: Chr. Kaiser Verlag, 1995), pp. 259-78.

Scolnic, B.E. *Theme and Context in Biblical Lists* (Atlanta: Scholars Press, 1995).

Smend, R., *Die Erzählung des Hexateuch auf ihre Quellen untersucht* (Berlin: G. Reimer, 1912).

Smith, C.R., 'Richard Nixon's 1968 Acceptance Speech as a Model of Dual Audience Adaptation', *Today's Speech* 19 (1971), pp. 15-22.

—'The Literary Structure of Leviticus', *JSOT* 70 (1996), pp. 17-32.

—'The Republican Keynote Address of 1968: Adaptive Rhetoric for the Multiple Audience', *Western Speech* 39 (1975), pp. 32-39.

Smith, M.S., 'The Literary Arrangement of the Priestly Redaction of Exodus: A Preliminary Investigation', *CBQ* 58 (1996), pp. 25-50.

Sonsino, R., 'Law: Forms of Biblical Law', *ABD* 4, pp. 252-54.

—*Motive Clauses in Hebrew Law: Biblical Forms and Near Eastern Parallels* (SBLDS, 45; Chico, CA: Scholar's Press, 1980).

Spiegelberg, W., *Die sogenannte demotische Chronik: Des Pap. 215 der Bibliothèque Nationale zu Paris nebst auf der Rückseite des Papyrus stehenden Texten* (Demotische Studien, 7; Leipzig: J.C. Hinrichs, 1914).

Sprinkle, J.M., *'The Book of the Covenant': A Literary Approach* (JSOTSup, 174; Sheffield: JSOT Press, 1994).

Stahl, N., *Law and Liminality in the Bible* (JSOTSup, 202; Sheffield: Sheffield Academic Press, 1995).

Sternberg, M., *The Poetics of Biblical Narrative: Ideological Literature and the Drama of Reading* (Bloomington: Indiana University Press, 1985).

Thomas, R., *Literacy and Orality in Ancient Greece* (Cambridge: Cambridge University Press, 1992).

Thompson, T.L., *The Origin Tradition of Ancient Israel. I. The Literary Formation of Genesis and Exodus 1–23* (JSOTSup, 55; Sheffield: JSOT Press, 1987).

Thompson, W.N., 'Barbara Jordan's Keynote Address: The Juxtaposition of Contradictory Values', *Southern Speech Communication Journal* 44 (1979), pp. 223-32.

Tigay, J.H., 'The Significance of the End of Deuteronomy', in M.V. Fox *et al.* (eds.), *Texts, Temples and Traditions: A Tribute to Menahem Haran* (Winona Lake, IN: Eisenbrauns, 1996), pp. 137-43.

Van Seters, J., *Abraham in History and Tradition* (New Haven: Yale University Press, 1975).

—*In Search of History* (New Haven: Yale University Press, 1983).

—*The Life of Moses: The Yahwist as Historian in Exodus–Numbers* (Louisville, KY: Westminster/John Knox Press, 1994).

Watts, J.W., *Psalm and Story: Inset Hymns in Hebrew Narrative* (JSOTSup, 139; Sheffield: JSOT Press, 1992).

—'Public Readings and Pentateuchal Law', *VT* 45.4 (1995), pp. 540-57.

—'Reader Identification and Alienation in the Legal Rhetoric of the Pentateuch', *BI* 7.1 (1999), pp. 101-12.

—'Rhetorical Strategy in the Composition of the Pentateuch', *JSOT* 68 (1995), pp. 3-22.

—'Text and Redaction in Jeremiah's Oracles Against the Nations', *CBQ* 54 (1992), pp. 432-47.

—'The Legal Characterization of God in the Pentateuch', *HUCA* 67 (1996), pp. 1-14.

—'The Legal Characterization of Moses in the Rhetoric of the Pentateuch', *JBL* 117 (1998), pp. 415-26.

—' "This Song": Conspicuous Poetry in Hebrew Prose', in J.C. de Moor and W.G.E. Watson (eds.), *Verse in Ancient Near Eastern Prose* (AOAT, 42; Neukirchen–Vluyn: Neukirchener Verlag, 1993), pp. 345-58.

Weinfeld, M., *Deuteronomy 1–11* (AB, 5; New York: Doubleday, 1991).

—*Deuteronomy and the Deuteronomic School* (Oxford: Oxford University Press, 1972).

Wellhausen, J., *Die Composition des Hexateuchs und der historischen Bücher des Alten Testaments* (Berlin: W. de Gruyter, 4th edn, 1963 [1876–77]).

—*Prolegomena to the History of Israel* (Gloucester, MA: Peter Smith, 1973 [1878]).

Westbrook, R., 'Biblical and Cuneiform Law Codes', *RB* 92 (1985), pp. 247-64.

—'Cuneiform Law Codes and the Origins of Legislation', *ZA* 79 (1990), pp. 201-20.

—'What is the Covenant Code?', in B. Levinson (ed.), *Theory and Method in Biblical and Cuneiform Law: Revision, Interpolation and Development* (JSOTSup, 181; Sheffield: Sheffield Academic Press, 1994), pp. 15-36.

Whybray, R.N., *The Making of the Pentateuch: A Methodological Study* (JSOTSup, 53; Sheffield: JSOT Press, 1987).

Widengren, G., 'King and Covenant', *JSS* 2 (1957), pp. 1-32.

Wiesehöfer, J., ' "Reichsgesetz" oder "Einzelfallgerechtigkeit"? Bemerkungen zu P. Freis These von der achaimenidischen "Reichsautorisation" ', *ZAR* 1 (1995), pp. 36-46.

Williamson, H.G.M., *1 and 2 Chronicles* (NCB; Grand Rapids: Eerdmans, 1982).

—*Ezra, Nehemiah* (WBC, 16; Waco, TX: Word Books, 1985).

Wilson, R.R., *Prophecy and Society in Ancient Israel* (Philadelphia: Fortress Press, 1980).

Wolterstorff, N., *Divine Discourse: Philosophical Reflections on the Claim that God Speaks* (Cambridge: Cambridge University Press, 1995).

Wright, J.W., 'The Legacy of David in Chronicles: The Narrative Function of 1 Chronicles 23–27', *JBL* 110 (1991), pp. 229-42.

Wuellner, Wilhelm., 'Rhetorical Criticism In Biblical Studies', Published on the World Wide Web at: http://158.182.34.202/ALLIANCE/JD/JD4/2.WUELLNERtxt

INDEXES

INDEX OF REFERENCES

Old Testament

INDEX OF AUTHORS